STREE
WO

Where Peo ls

Tony Gibson

Illustrated by Jonathan Bean

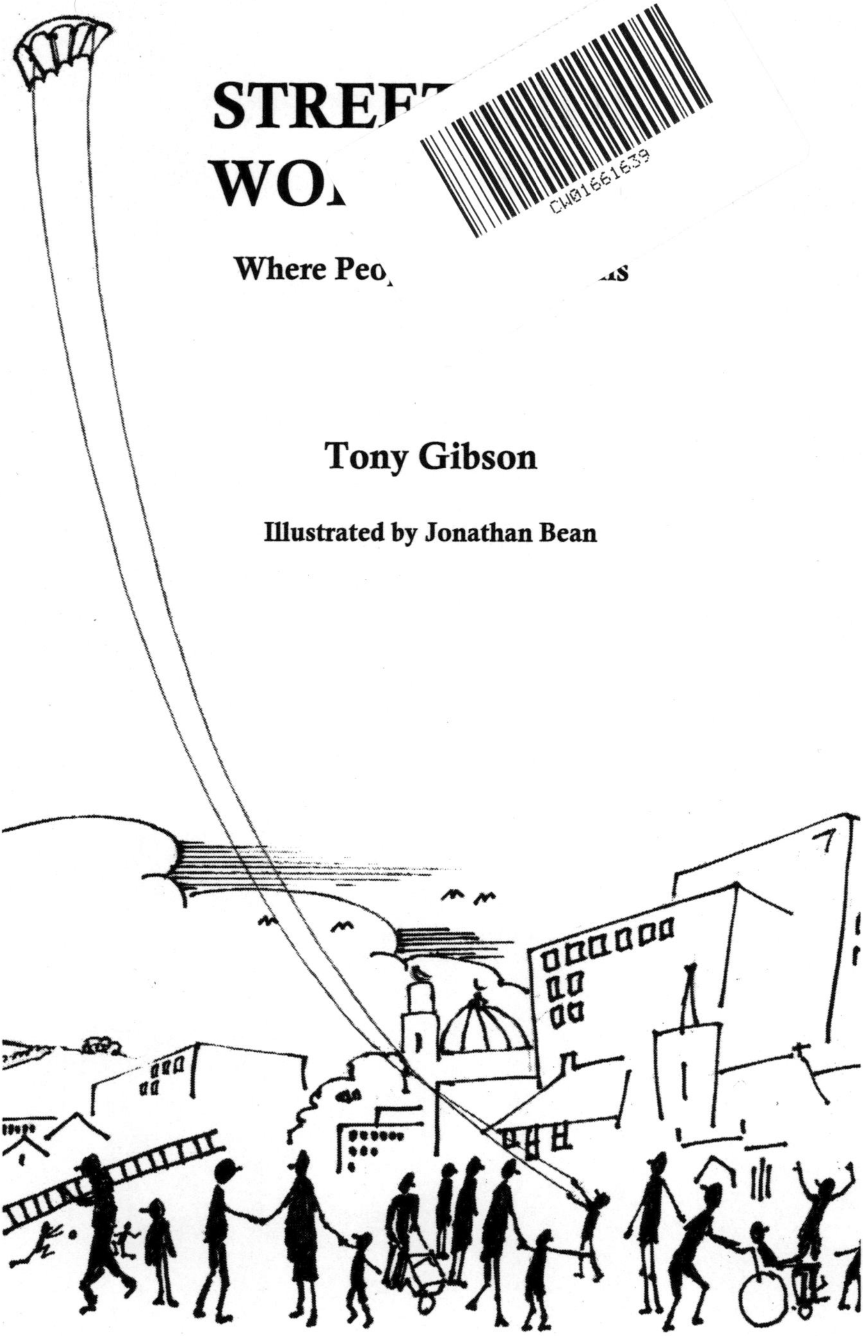

JON CARPENTER PUBLISHING

First published in 2008 by

Jon Carpenter Publishing
Alder House, Market Street, Charlbury OX7 3PH

☎ 01608 811969

jon@joncarpenter.co.uk

ISBN 978 1 906067 03 8

Our books may be ordered from bookshops or (post free) from Jon Carpenter Publishing at the above address

Please send for our free catalogue

Credit card orders should be phoned or faxed to 01689 870437 or 01608 811969

Printed in England by LPPS Ltd, Wellingborough NN8 3PJ

STREETWIDE

WORLDWIDE

Dedication

To teens and twenties everywhere (beginning with my five grandsons and their partners) who have it in themselves to change the world.

Acknowledgements

To Marion Olusoga who has taken down every word that follows and a good many more that we both thought better of. To colleagues in the Neighbourhood Initiatives Foundation, the Scarman Trust and my local Community Association who drew on their field experience to vet the proposals I have made in the final chapters. To Dorothy Noble who reviewed the style and content from the other side of the world. To family members who scanned some sample chapters and came up for more. Thanks all round.

Contents

Foreword

by Lord Richard Best OBE, Former Director, Joseph Rowntree Foundation

I first met Tony Gibson in the early 1990s when he was running the Neighbourhood Initiatives Foundation and putting into practice his innovative "Planning for Real" ideas. The Joseph Rowntree Foundation – I was its Director at the time – supported a number of his projects. I was struck by Tony's energy and directness, and by his unfailing readiness to swing into action with community activists whenever the opportunity arose. This was never more evident than during the period when he worked on the Meadow Well Estate in North Tyneside.

In these pages you can read about Meadow Well and how the death of two young joyriders – after a police chase – sparked off serious riots in which the local Youth Centre (for which Tony was helping youngsters to prepare refurbishment plans) was burned down. The very next day Tony was back at work, helping the whole community to regroup – literally arising from the ashes – and eventually rebuild the Centre and other parts of the estate. JRF was one of the bodies supporting these efforts.

This vignette – and many others recorded in this book – gives a measure of the man and his almost legendary commitment and staying-power. This is not the first book that Tony Gibson has penned. His last book "*The Power In Our Hands*" documented in great detail Tony's beliefs about citizen empowerment and the powerful energies that are released when ordinary people decide – or are allowed – to take control of their communities and what happened there.

This book does more: it provides the historical context for these events. Not just Tony's own personal story – which shows how a non-conformist and radical upbringing shaped his worldview. But also a fascinating and accessible history of London during the 1930s and well as during the Blitz, and of Tony's subsequent work in Italy, China, Africa and the Caribbean.

The later stages of the book provide a lively account of Tony's recent work which coincides of course with a growing interest by both government and non-government bodies from the 1980s onwards, in community involvement and the regeneration of some of the nation's most neglected and rundown neighbourhoods.

As this movement gained momentum, Tony has played a pivotal role. For communities, he provided a practical framework and a method of working which helped them to identify needs, prioritise – and act. For policy-makers and funders, he demonstrates that letting go and handing power to communities leads to dramatic and life-changing results

INTRODUCTION

Things ain't what they used to be. (*Thank God*? or *More's the pity*! That depends on who you are and how you are doing right now.)

What kind of things?

Getting or holding down a job… Family life as a pain or a pleasure … Pictures on the TV of elegant coffee chatter, and starving, war-torn children … Fun and games … Fear in the streets at night …

All things considered most people reckon that life could be a lot better; but might soon be a great deal worse.

This book begins with events and encounters that have shaped my life so far – the cock-ups and the celebrations, first impressions and second thoughts: plus that gut feeling that makes most of us tick, including you perhaps? It's the DIY instinct to get something *right* – the hair-do, the dance step, the skateboard kick-flip, the flowers in the window box, the Yorkshire pudding, the bookshelf that stays up and looks good.

And, deeper down, the love life and laughter, the kids, the neighbourhood, the job worth having, a life worth living; some fellow-feeling for the rest of the human race.

I grew up like many school kids, an odd ball at first, learning the hard way how to fit in; getting to be one of the gang, going once in a while for something funny and a bit far out – to make our mark.

Then World War II and the London Blitz took over. As a student volunteer I was shifting shit from makeshift air raid shelters, fire fighting, first-aiding, coping with nine and ten-year-olds running wild.

All this alongside local people who like me and my mates were doing things they'd never done before, improvising solutions to the breakdown of local government under the impact of the bombing.

Most of my life since then has been spent alongside the same sorts of everyday people, young and old, in the UK, Europe, Africa, China and the Caribbean: people suddenly getting wise to their own ability to take action, against all the odds.

Sounds high-falutin, airy-fairy? That's the problem when you try to describe this self-discovery in words alone.

It's partly to do with the way we've been brought up to think that action stems from the utterances of power-hungry politicians, one-eyed religious fanatics, money-manipulators – whilst the rest of **Us** stay put on the sidelines, making snide remarks and blaming **Them** for all that's gone, or going, wrong.

I can't get used to how old I am; hopefully you won't let it bother you either. The thing is that, looking back over the years, I'm gradually getting a scenic view of the prospect before us, here and now; and what we can do about it.

At the time I couldn't see the wood for the trees, or at best just catch a glimpse. It's been a bit like tackling a jigsaw puzzle. Early on you spot the corner pieces, then maybe the straight edges that you arrange and re-arrange until they connect and make a sort of frame. As for everything else – that's still a jumble, with pieces here and there – a face, a glint of water, a blaze that might be fire or sunset. But that's usually enough to tempt one to go further, and the picture takes shape.

My life so far, from a rumbustious childhood on, has been an eye-opener. (Yours too, I guess.) Not just making sense of who I am and what I'm for; but – much more interesting – beginning to see what wakes all sorts of people up, worldwide; and how once in a while we get a kick out of making things happen; harnessing resources within reach, bridging the gaps between Us and Them – streetwide, worldwide – without the need for interminable talk.

I've called the first chapter COMING SHORTLY. It's a trailer to give you an idea of what most of the book is about: how ideas and actions took shape; where we are all heading; and what we can do about it.

Backward glances are all very well, but what we have to deal with here and now, coming very shortly, are situations and events, good and bad, worldwide and right on our doorstep, that no one in human history has had to face on the same scale before.

Over to you.

PS. Comment by up-and-coming cabinet minister David Miliband:

'To overcome the sense of powerlessness in local communities ... we have to devolve power down to ***street level.*** *'*

Chapter One

COMING SHORTLY

As a babe in arms, so I have been told, my first word – as distinct from a howl or a gurgle – was JOB. Not job, with a short 'o' but JOH – OH – OHB, to rhyme with globe or robe. A regular lip-smacking, jujube response to my father, carrying me around or bouncing me on his knee as he practised his vowel sounds at the bidding of his weekly elocution teacher.

There was a man in the land of Uz, whose name was Job.

(Chorus from me: j-oh-b, j-oh-b, chuckle, chuckle, chuckle)

Not really in keeping with the Bible story of a well-heeled member of the human race laid low and covered with boils by an Old Testament God wanting to see whether he could take whatever hit him and still come up for more.

Father had served as an army chaplain in the disastrous World War One Gallipoli campaign, landing on the exposed beaches of Suvla Bay, evacuated under gun fire from the Turkish batteries on the hills above, returning for the march through Mesopotamia (now Iraq and Syria) to Baghdad.

Back home, married in July 1918 in his major's uniform (bumped up from captain which chaplains usually rated, on the strength of his service on the Gallipoli beaches), he was offered the care of a big London church – one of the plums of Methodism – within easy reach of all sorts of people, including many ex-soldiers who had served with him in 'Mespot'.

Now, a year or two later he wanted to improve his skills in talking to people, not just from the pulpit, but also at the weekends when church services were done, fitting in a regular soapbox stint on Speakers' Corner, Hyde Park, gathering big crowds to promote the idea of a League of Nations and an end to the arms race, with a dash of Christian Socialism thrown in. So being able to project his normally gentle voice, vowel sounds and all, was essential to compete with the traffic round Marble Arch.

Words dominated my childhood. But forget my father's elocution lesson. He helped to bring me up on stories about characters that were the very opposite of Old Testament Job. Uncle Oojah was an elephant with a twinkle in his eye and an engaging family, Mummy Oojah, Sheila and Jimjams. They lived in London and mingled happily with other species including humankind: with frequent friendly encounters with the Prince of Wales who in those days (before he got entangled with Mrs. Simpson) was the subject of all sorts of celeb-worship – Becks, Robbie Williams and Justin Timberlake all rolled into one.

Uncle Oojah was always up to something – a little bit of constructive mischief at the expense of people who took themselves too seriously, usually in and around the places we frequented. Like Olympia and Hyde Park.

The storytelling changed hands in the afternoons when Clarkie, Miss Constance Clark, a family friend in straitened circumstances, helped out whilst my mother was busy attending church meetings, taking me on walks to Kensington Gardens, past the Peter Pan statue, to the Round Pond. The visits were to sail my little boat in amongst much classier craft, with trimmed sails and set rudders, launched by serious-minded grownups. It was the walks to and from the Gardens that stuck in my mind. Clarkie told me stories about True Heart, a magical sparrow who passed on stories about fairies, princes, talkative animals, everything she could resurrect from what she remembered of Hans Andersen and the Brothers Grimm, laced with a few more she invented as we went along.

When I was a little older, on summer holidays with a long walk from the boarding house to the bus for the seaside, there was a new set of storytelling, based on my father's homework each evening, mugging up a chapter from the story of Lorna Doone, brought up in a splendid den of busy West Country robbers, courted by Jan Ridd, a farmer's boy who grew up to wrestle with the chief villain, Carver Doone, and pitch him to his death in Wizard's Slough.

By that time I was reading for myself, on the way from fairytales, via Pooh Bear and then The Wind in the Willows to the fabulous exploits of Buffalo Bill, William Cody, the hard-riding, sharp-shooting frontiersman in the Wild West; spliced with stories about David Livingstone, teenage mill-hand teaching himself Greek from a grammar propped up above the cotton loom, walking from Lanarkshire to London to study as a doctor, trail blazing through darkest Africa, savaged by a lion, confronting slave traders, the first white man to see *the smoke that thunders* which he named, in honour of his Queen, the Victoria Falls. Dying in a remote village, amongst his faithful African friends and followers, who embalmed his body, carried it through uncharted country to the coast, and went with it to the state funeral in Westminster Abbey.

Home from primary school I liked to dress up, with the help of my father's discarded Gallipoli breeches and my own Wellington boots, as a gun-toting cowboy. There was one exception, when I entered the fancy-dress competition at the Church Bazaar – burnt cork moustache and sideburns, peak cap with a cloth at the back to guard against sunstroke – as the great Dr. Livingstone himself. Not that it got me anywhere, the prize went to one of the church leaders getting himself up in Victorian skirts and bloomers, and cart-wheeling before the judges as Charlie's Aunt.

Methodists liked a good sing, and next to that a belly laugh, or at the very least a homely chuckle. They were used to taking part in whatever had to be decided, and that included the choice of their own minister, and the length of his stay.

Methodism inherited John Wesley's habit of moving around. No Methodist minister was expected to stay put forever. The minimum stay was usually three years, with an optional invitation by the local congregation to stay on for one year more; or sometimes, as in the case of my father, for two. So when I was five we moved on to Wimbledon and I found myself attending the services every Sunday; mornings only at first, but as I grew older, evenings as well. Mother and I were expected to set a good example, preferably sitting near the front, under the kindly eyes of the choir (one of whom confided to my mother, on the strength of my occasional fidgets, that they all decided I had caught a flea).

I heard many of my father's sermons since he preached at his local church most of the time, with occasional forays elsewhere when he was invited to do something special on someone else's stamping ground, reinforced with *lantern slides* projected in full colour on a sheet slung across the aisle.

Apart from those sermons to the whole congregation, me included, he never preached to me and most of his sermons were about people who *did* things.

In my teens there was no knowing what would happen next (just like today?). At school we scanned the headlines on the wars in Abyssinia and Spain. Later as sixth-formers we went on an exchange visit to a school in Ilfeld in the Harz Mountains which the Nazis had taken over as a training centre for youngsters on the way to becoming Fuehreren in the service of Hitler himself. But the Germans in our own age group, survivors of the school before the Nazis took it over, joked with us, behind the cycle sheds, in a different language (whether in German or in English) to those, brainwashed from the outset, who followed them up the school hierarchy.

Back home, we looked on as Chamberlain and Daladier met Hitler and Mussolini at Berchesgarten and helped them to dismember Czechoslovakia. A year later we were sitting out the Phoney War, watching from the sidelines the invasion of Poland, Holland, Belgium, France and then suddenly scanning the battles in the sky above us at the onset of the London Blitz.

From then on action spoke louder than words; though people I worked with, inside and outside the makeshift shelters in London's dockland, talked nineteen to the dozen to pass the time waiting for the next attack, using everyday words to tell each other about extraordinary happenings endured at first hand, comparing them with what the radio said about the raids in Coventry, Sheffield and Liverpool.

The first London Blitz ended with a major attack by bomber fleets on 10 May 1941. I moved on to train in hospitals for work with other war victims, first in Sicily, then in South Italy, finally in North China during the last stages of the civil war.

For those seven years, words usually took second place, often after the action, though there were exceptions. Billeted on my own in a requisitioned flat in Ragusa, in the mountainous centre of Sicily, I was besieged by a beautiful Baronessa, President of the local Red Cross who visited, she said, to discuss the plight of the refugees from the Italian mainland; but actually, I suspected, to see how the flat might be de-requisitioned so that she and her husband, the Barone, could re-occupy it. Over several encounters she taught me what true coffee should be:

Nero comm' la notte (black as night),
dolce comm' l'amore (sweet as love),
bruschendo, she purred, *comm' il desiderio* (**burning** as desire).

Later on, in China, hastening back with a donkey laden with supplies for our clinic on the other side of the Yellow River in flood, I found myself suddenly accompanied by two well-armed strangers who seemed likely to be either brigands or communist guerrillas. Hearing the click of a rifle bolt just behind me I remembered the formal Chinese courtesies I was taught in earlier days, struggling to grasp a smattering of the language. I produced the battered Chinese visiting card which each of us had to identify ourselves as relief workers, and presented it with a little bow. I had the right words, too.

Kwei hsing ('your honourable names?') – which got anonymous but friendly replies so that I could follow on, bowing once again, with:

Pi hsing ('my humble name') *Tsai Pe Sen* (the nearest my Chinese tutor got to rendering Gibson in Chinese).

These words did the trick.

Having established a courteous talking relationship, both sides could say '*Pu yao k'erchi*' (no need for politeness) and I could go on to explain that the packs on the donkey were medical supplies destined for our mud hut clinic which people on both sides, and neither side, in the Civil War thought well worth having. As we approached the camp where engineers were trying to replace the railway bridge the River had destroyed, my companions melted away.

For most of those years – improvising street aid in the London Blitz, working alongside destitute refugees from the Italian mainland and their inhospitable Sicilian hosts, seeing Vesuvius suddenly erupt and slowly swallow up whole villages and the vineyards that were people's livelihood; improvising aid for the victims of China's Sorrow, the Yellow River dragon in flood – dikes destroyed to block the Japanese advance; then very slowly tamed by the muscle power of Chinese villagers on both sides in the Civil War – in all this, sights and sounds counted for more than words.

In my thirties and forties, back home at last, I paid my way and helped to raise my young family by writing and broadcasting – some hundreds of BBC programmes, and scores of magazine and newspaper articles about the happenings I had witnessed. Then, as people gradually got used to living at peace, and began to do what interested and pleased them, I got a kick out of making eye-witness *actuality* programmes about the doings of teenagers and twenty-year-olds, scaling mountains, going down potholes, running their own radio, busking across Europe, telling the older generation where they got off.

Alongside these were other BBC programme assignments to cover the birth of new industries and technologies – nuclear propulsion, float glass, automation, pest control, supersonic transport, the electron microscope, plastics research, continental gas pipelines – innovation unlimited! Plus what all sorts of people, doctors, builders, steel workers, bus drivers, even VIPs, were doing for a living and how they adapted to their changing world.

It was all go, and it led over the next fifteen years to trying out ways to break new ground myself: invited to Nigeria (uprooting the family) to help the newly independent Broadcasting Corporation '*to change from white to black and from radio to TV*'; coming back home to recruit and head up a team to develop ways to bring TV making within the reach of teachers, and children, *on their own ground*. That was where some ground-breaking came in: run-of-the-mill teachers trying themselves out with cameras they could handle without fuss in their own way. (At the same time I was also doing a BBC series and making thought-provoking comparisons between what several dozen professionals could do in the studio, with the kind of programme one or two resourceful teachers could contrive entirely on their own.)

What grabbed us all was the response of the children when we broke up the video to allow time between sequences for them to try out their own ideas *hands on*. They used materials we supplied to improvise 3D models – a room, a school, a derelict patch, a neighbourhood – and then to work out for themselves how to explore ways to make improvements – all without the need for formal talk or written work. The video sparked off the action. From then on (like the teachers in the studio) they became self-propelled. Before long we found the video was no longer needed. Once they got their hands on 3D materials, representing their own surroundings – homes, school, public buildings, estate, town, landscape – they took over and began to work out solutions based on their own experience.

Early on in the 1970s these experiments caught on and attracted official support for a four-year collaboration with 200 teachers scattered in eight different local authorities. Object: to find out how other run-of-the-mill children in Junior and Secondary schools could generate their own momentum, using materials they could sort out and put together for their own mini-projects; and (Object number two) what all this might teach the teachers.

The children surprised nearly everyone, their teachers especially, because of their ability to draw on their own experience and work out, realistically, between themselves exactly how to make things much better. What struck the teachers was that in this decision-making process the so-called *low achievers* were often pegging level with the *academically bright*. They used the materials they arranged and re-arranged to **show** what they had in mind, without having to depend, at first, on words. (They talked to each other nineteen to the dozen once they got underway, but seeing and trying out what could be done, exploring alternatives together, reaching a consensus, came first.)

In the years since that thought-provoking four-year revelation I was encouraged by what was then the Department of the Environment, and by some friendly national institutions, to take things much further. So with like-minded colleagues in the UK and abroad, we have adapted those *hands on* materials to get grown-ups equally motivated, sorting out together what needs doing about their own surroundings, and who else besides themselves could help to do it.

In the city of Birkenhead, a year after a successful *Planning for Real* collaboration between residents and professionals, the Chief Executive rang me up to say, '*My officers and local residents are following up ideas in phone calls and conversations on the spot; and they're using each other's first names as they talk.*' So he thought that this improved relationship deserved another, bigger project, the community-led conversion of a set of empty buildings for a range of public uses. A year later the project got the number two Community Enterprise award from the Prince of Wales, the Times and the Royal Institute of British Architects.

The top award went a year or two later to a self-built village on derelict land – Lightmoor – outside Telford. We had started out, long before the establishment of committees and the drafting of Mission Statements, with the prospective self-builders working out on their own homemade landscape model where houses, gardens, roads, sewage pipes and utility lines should go.

Abroad there were the same feelings of surprise and exhilaration. In Kenya hard-pressed local villagers, ignored by an oppressive regime, had launched their own projects two months before the regime toppled, and carried on afterwards with joy. Their spokesman said, '*We have discovered that we are sitting on gold – our own human resources to get things done.*' There was a murmur of general approval and afterwards a local official explained, '*People want action rather than talking. They also want something to be* ***seen***.'

In three crime-ridden, mutually hostile areas of downtown Kingston, Jamaica, the director of the Government-established Regeneration Agency said, '*The community support has been overwhelming.*'

In Stutterheim, South Africa, the area training officer said, '*This comes at the right time. It's what we've been waiting for all these years. Everybody took part ... the less people are talking, the more they are doing.*'

There are hundreds of photos and video sequences that show how people get to grips with the possibilities they reveal to themselves. Two pictures say most to me. One, taken way back in the mid 70s when we were trying out the first schools packs, shows a bunch of children clustering round their homemade landscape model, not just 'attending', but in a frenzy of participation, looking all ways, trying out alternatives, *thinking* as if nothing else mattered.

I took the other photograph during a workshop in Bosnia in the summer of 2005. It shows twenty-year-olds clustering round one of our layouts on which they were enthusiastically sorting out the problems, opportunities, priorities that they had discovered were common to all. What makes it special is that these youngsters are from Macedonia, Croatia, Bosnia, Kosovo, Albania and Serbia and have grown up apart, separated by racist killings and counter-killings and the verbal venom which has constrained their lives.

The thirty years between those two photos have been a toboggan ride for me, hitting occasional bumps but for the most time running free and moving fast. The *hands on* notion, and the range of materials that convey it, have attracted all sorts of people, professionals as well as local residents (often disillusioned about what they see other professionals failing to do). A succession of workshops on the spot, at the locals' invitation, has got things moving in Germany, Italy, the Balkans (see above!), Belgium, Holland, Norway, the Caribbean, Kenya, South Africa and the length and breadth of the UK, with some useful also-rans in Australia, USA, Poland, Belarus, Portugal and France. Meanwhile I have taken on some organisational baggage, setting up the Neighbourhood Initiatives Foundation, joining the Scarman Trust as one of its Trustees. And to keep my toecaps trailing on the ground, there was a four-year stint chairing my local Community Association. Right now I am working on some decision-making packs for youngsters with learning disabilities.

What does all that amount to? Are all these projects no more than coffee breaks between the serious work that is done or undone by the talking shops and their memo-wielding paper-chasers? Can each project be more than a flash in the pan?

I am still attracted to words (and pictures) as well as the possibilities for action. I am also still concerned about words that get in the way of action, that divide, defer and disguise, where we could find things in common and get on with them together. I have a hunch that through the ages the real people who make things matter: a footloose, well-connected young Indian from the Himalayas, a Nazareth carpenter's son, a bunch of Galilee fishermen, an Arab businessman based in Mecca, and more recently an Essex stay-maker's apprentice, a bunch of young ex-weavers, jobless in Rochdale, a black woman on a bus in Alabama, an Israeli nuclear refusnik, a fledging London lawyer concerned about people imprisoned without trial, a Bangladeshi professor inventing ways for villagers to borrow money for their own enterprises and cut out the middlemen, 6.5 million borrowers, scarcely any defaulters – all these carry conviction because what they say about people's needs and opportunities is second to what they do about them.

On the whole, seeing is believing. Showing what can be done is halfway to 'getting involved', first as a curious spectator; then, if you're clustered together, rubbing shoulders with everyone else (not sitting in rows in a public meeting), gradually joining in.

Joining in to do what? '*Well*', you might say, '*something practical, something to show for what we've been up to … as long as it doesn't commit me too long.*'

After I came back from China and began writing and broadcasting for a living, I collaborated with a BBC colleague and wrote *The Spare Time Book* about the things the younger generation was getting up to. Later I came across a statistic for average life-expectation in the Western world. A teenager or twenty-year-old could expect to live until 70. So, I thought, *Fifty More Years to Live* would make a good title for book number two about what could be done by the rest of us within that lifespan.

I have lived those fifty years since then, and in between times I have written another nine books (which paid their way). But not that one. What follows, in this book, fills in the pictures I have hinted at in this chapter.

Coming Shortly is a kind of trailer to give you an idea of what you're letting yourself in for if you read on. It is an account of what I have been doing (sometimes unwittingly at others' expense) – and also what I have seen others do together, sometimes joining with them, in projects that were overcoming the barriers of race and caste and religious doctrine.

It's also a pointer to what lies ahead of us. If H.G. Wells hadn't got there first, I might have called it *The Shape of Things to Come*. The word I picked up in China, it's my favourite, is *wei-chi. Wei* is what you shout if you are speeding on a bicycle and you want someone to get out of the way – *Danger!* But if you are feeling polite you say *wei-chi* which means *danger/opportunity* – the opportunity being to meet danger by taking action to outflank it and go one better.

The upshot is my belief that we can get further and fare better by doing things in a way that differs from the usual approaches to politics and society. That means leaving a lot less to the fluent talkers and working a lot more from the ground up.

'*Never doubt that a small group of thoughtful, committed citizens can change the world. Indeed it is the only thing that ever has.*'

Margaret Mead, anthropologist

Between us all we have that DIY capacity – and deep down, the yen – to make things happen, little by little at first – and (which is crucial) to make the process not just worthy and rewarding but, for most of the time, actually enjoyable, even fun.

So what will you make of what follows? Being a book of words it has its limitations. But words can sometimes be a cue for action.

Here and there you'll find boxes like this for you to brush past, or think over as indications of what we're up against, and (later in the book) what can be done about it.

Chapter Two

GETTING GOING

Father was christened John Clark Gibson to celebrate an ancestor, a tenant farmer who got into trouble because he allowed John Wesley to preach in his barn. Wesley was an ordained member of the Church of England but his enthusiasm (a dirty word to church officialdom) had got him debarred from preaching inside any church he visited.

What he had to say, and the heart-warming way in which he spoke, attracted all sorts and conditions of people, high and low, whom the rituals of the established church had failed to touch. So he went on horseback up and down the country, 8,000 miles a year, preaching wherever there were people wanting to listen. When he came to where John Clark lived there was John Clark's empty barn on offer. So Wesley preached in it to a capacity congregation, and went on his way.

For this, John Clark's landlord turned him out of his home and off the land from which he made his living.

Sixty years later, his granddaughter, Miss Jane Clark, married Henry Gibson, a Chatham shipwright, recently widowed, with a large family, and provided him with another bunch of children. She made sure their eldest son maintained the John Clark tradition (and he passed those two names on, via my father, to me, and via me to his great-grandson).

Her husband was all the more agreeable because he too had an independent mind. He had been a spare time preacher for Wesley's 'Methodists' whilst he was still earning good pay in Chatham docks. Now, soon after his second marriage, he chucked his good job, spent a year learning to read the New Testament in Greek (noting the dates he worked through it on the flyleaf of his copy) in order to become a fully-fledged minister.

Like John Wesley he had a gift for words which reached out to all sorts of people without the need for fire and brimstone added. He moved with his growing family from place to place in Kent, Norfolk and then on to South London, building or reinforcing the local church membership and then moving on to fresh fields as was the Methodist custom.

The family could not afford to keep their sons at school after sixteen. My father got a job in a papermaking factory. Out of hours he and other teenagers made music together and pottered with a decrepit car, tuning it up to the point where it might actually venture on the Brooklands racing track.

They played jokes on each other, once in an extra special way. There was a patriotic bonfire celebration of the relief of Mafeking, a turning point in the Boer War. Young John Clark Gibson had opposed the war from the start. So as a *pro-Boer* his friends frogmarched him, in a friendly manner, to attend the proceedings in the front row round the blaze.

He became a spare time preacher like his father before him, and then like him 'opted for the ministry'. This meant living on next to nothing whilst he became a student at the Methodists' Theological College in Didsbury, Manchester. Here the flower of Methodism was brought to bloom for the benefit of the raw students, the visitors speaking as near as possible with the tongues of men and angels to inspire these youngsters to a life commitment.

In fact the students were already quite well committed. No one *went for the ministry* expecting the live the life of Riley. And being young they still had what you might call an undergraduate sense of humour. One earnest lecturer dwelt on the value of living '*a healthy life, with each day's work ushered in by a brisk cold shower, leaving you feeling rosy all over*'.

'*Nice for Rosie*', whispers a voice at the back.

Completing the course, making the big commitment, ordained as a fledgling Methodist minister, my father followed in his father's footsteps, out on the Norfolk coast. But this time, technologically with it, going the rounds on a motorised tricycle which everyone made jokes about. A local cartoonist sent him homemade picture postcards addressed only by the registration number of the tricycle.

Older members of his congregation told him how when Henry Gibson, his ex-shipwright father preached and appealed for people to come forward to recommit themselves, seasoned sailor men clambered over the pews in their haste to get to the front (just like the audience for striptease at the Windmill, I thought).

Later, in the years just before the outbreak of the World War I, he was based at a big church on Brixton Hill in London. He had shown his father's knack of *speaking to people's hearts and minds* without the need for *eloquence* or *rhetoric*, making it person to person, sharing what he had seen and learned about the way ahead.

Before long, he and a few supporters were squeezing time after the Sunday service to make for Speakers Corner, Hyde Park. Here anyone with the gift of the gab could get up on a soapbox or similar, and say what he felt about whatever he thought mattered. Father's feelings about war and peace, and about the way people should treat each other and make common cause, got crowds of passers-by stopping short to listen, and afterwards to respond in a free-for-all Question Time.

Back in Brixton his congregation grew for the same reason.

It was already a thriving church and like others in Methodism celebrated its strength and fuelled it, with an annual Bazaar in which many different groups had stalls where they sold, for the church's benefit, whatever they could make themselves – cakes, pastries, non-alcoholic drink, knick-knacks, knitted jumpers, embroidery – with the proceedings enlivened by bursts of song from the choir in full throat.

There was always a formal opening by someone of note in Methodism. On this, for my father, extra special occasion, the VIP was to be Mrs. Davey, wife to a staunch Liberal, William J. Davey, J.P. who had done well in the Party hinterland in Cornwall and Devon. He had recently emigrated to London as the parliamentary representative of Hawksleys, a big engineering firm who built reservoirs in the West Country and elsewhere. His office was a stone's throw from the House of Commons and the Lobby where he was on friendly greeting terms with the likes of Lloyd George and the young Winston Churchill.

Getting Mrs. Davey to open the Brixton Hill Bazaar was quite a coup, but at the last moment she caught a cold and sent her daughter Winifred in her stead.

My father fell head over heels in love with her from the moment she stepped down from the platform. At the time, Miss Davey thought him quite an interesting young man, but nothing more.

Her childhood had been comfortable, and stimulating. She grew up in a corner house overlooking Wandsworth Common. It was big enough to contain her parents, her four brothers and Ellen, the rather deaf cook-housemaid; with Sarah, the part-time char, and a part-time gardener as day workers.

Mr. Davey had hosts of friends, didn't make a fuss of himself, but loved a bit of fun. Especially at Christmas. When Winifred was barely six she was with her brothers and her mother on Christmas Day, waiting in the big attic bedroom for the arrival of Father Christmas downstairs. The understanding was that everyone stayed clear to allow him to come in by the front door (helpfully left ajar) and dump everyone's presents in the hall. Then he would go out, banging the door as he left. That was the signal for everyone to tear down the stairs and claim their presents. This particular Christmas little Winifred chose to run with the others down the big staircase, leaving her brothers and the presents behind, whilst she reopened the front door and rushed out. She just caught a glimpse, as she told everyone, of the tail end of Father Christmas' red robe as he vanished round the corner. Then she went back for her presents and to convince everyone that she had really, really, seen him – or at least a bit of what he was wearing.

Her father, who it so happened was never among the party in the upstairs bedroom, joined in the present-opening party and encouraged his daughter ever after in her claim. He loved a practical joke – so long as everyone took it seriously and played up.

Growing up with four brothers made his daughter a bit of a tomboy in order to compete. She held her own in the Junior school, and made her name when she bet the rest of the class that during a rather boring lesson she could submerge herself in the back row, crawl past everyone's feet and out of the door, nip down to the village shop and return, with goodies, by the same route, back into her place before the end of the lesson. All without the teacher noticing. She won her bet and never looked back.

Her agility paid off at the boarding school where she became Captain of Games, and Head Girl with an affectionate respect between her and her Headmistress, keeping in touch for many years after.

Emerging from school like a butterfly from the chrysalis she found herself invited to enter Society. A cousin who was a West Country Conservative MP needed a partner to show off to other up-and-coming people, including the young Winston Churchill. The balls and soirées she attended were mostly in the great houses overlooking the Park and Marble Arch. It's unlikely that she took any interest in what went on at Speakers Corner.

Her father, the Liberal stalwart, introduced her to other rising politicians frequenting the National Liberal Club. But so far as she was concerned, politics and most politicians, were in the background. The main thing was to meet all those up-and-coming young men; and occasionally get engaged to one or other of them.

All this changed with the outbreak of World War I. She left her home where everything was discreetly organised for the family's comfort, to live in a shack in Coventry as a voluntary worker serving rough-spoken munitions workers. She learnt how to use her *joie de vivre* and her sense of humour to get on with the sort of people she had not dealt with before. Then, as the war neared its end, two of her brothers died in France. The oldest was killed in action. The youngest who was her very best friend, went absent without leave in the last month of the war, having become what the family would call *entangled* with, and it may be infected by an *unsuitable* local girl. For three days he wandered about the barren countryside and then he shot himself.

In such ways my mother learnt about the real world. My father had returned from Gallipoli and they got in touch. They talked things out together. Eventually he asked her to marry him and she accepted. After the wedding they were photographed at the reception garden party at her parents' home with the best man (my father's brother) and the bridegroom in military uniform, inoffensively displaying their medals.

My mother was able to supplement my father's modest salary with a small *allowance* paid by Mr. Davey, still doing well as the parliamentary representative for his engineering firm. The extra money paid for my early schooling until the time when I got a place in the boarding school subsidised by the Methodist Church for the benefit of its ministers' sons.

The dame school I first went to was reached up and down the hill from where we lived and along the edge of Wimbledon Common. It took some time even in the early days when I went on the pillion of my father's bicycle, each day urging him to pedal further up the hill *to break the record* before dismounting. Later on I walked the distance with a school friend, Peter Boyce, who lived even further away. We established a good working relationship each time we joined forces, by swapping headgear. I had a gor blimey cap which kept my ears warm. He had a schoolboy's cap with a badge on the front. I was eager to risk chilblains in order to impress any passer-by that I was at a real, proper school.

We both graduated to bicycles and found that there were lorries, especially steam lorries, that went up the hill slowly enough for us, pedalling like mad, to grab on to the back and cadge a free lift.

Apart from Peter there was no one from the school within easy reach, and out of school hours, in the evenings and the weekends, his family tended to keep themselves to themselves. But for a month or two, thanks to my father, we had a Sunday afternoon get-together with several children from the other side of town whose parents were church members. They were picked up by a car-owning parent and delivered to our front room for a desert journey two and a half thousand years ago, in six weekly instalments, setting out from Ur of the Chaldees on the banks of the River Euphrates, south of modern Baghdad.

The desert was a homemade sand tray spanning the bay window recess. Ur of the Chaldees was a temple made of plasticine surrounded by cardboard cut-out houses in 3D. The rest of the tray was desert sand with here and there a sprig of garden foliage and a scrap of mirror to represent an oasis. Exactly how the journey ended is more than I can remember, but the going, thanks to my father's memories of Mesopotamia, was always good and we identified with the cut-out figures of Abraham and his family, all the way.

With the journey completed we dispersed and the nearest we got to seeing each other afterwards was in the throng of church attenders moving purposefully out of Sunday morning church in the direction of each family's Sunday lunch.

The road where we lived was just up from the local Council school and needing company I tried hard to gain acceptance with some of the children who attended it. To impress I dressed up in my father's Gallipoli breeches, the extra length stuffed into my Wellington boots, and told everyone what I had read about the exploits of Buffalo Bill.

To show our prowess as marksmen, we played ducks and drakes across the road, skimming stones beneath passing cars. This practice ended when one rather lush car stopped and the driver chased us, in my case, back home, where there was a show down.

From then on *playing in the road* was off limits; and so were contacts with the children from the Council school.

That left me even more aware of being *an only child*, rather self-centred, not well used to mixing it outside school hours. I read a lot and played on my own with my tin soldiers and my model building set. Then, one summer there were two of us self-centred seven-year-olds. My parents took me and another small boy – a total stranger, rather withdrawn (from what I can see now was *a broken home*) for a seaside holiday on the Isle of Wight. The seaside would give each of us room to be on our own, but as it turned out the seaside did not figure much.

We lodged in a hamlet three miles inland where it was cheaper, with a pillar of the local Methodist chapel called Mrs. Butt. She seemed to us, breadth-wise, enormous. She worked in her kitchen beside an equally capacious cauldron, called a copper. It had a little fire below to warm up the water for the washing which she 'took in' to make ends meet.

On the other side of the lane there was a brickfield. It was dominated by another barrel-like structure into which the raw clay was dumped, mixed with gravel and chopped straw. In the middle was a wooden paddle attached to a horizontal bar extending a dozen feet from the top to connect with an old carthorse, pensioned off to pace round and round *half asleep in a slow silent walk*. Slowly but surely the paddle turned and churned the clay.

We were allowed to ride on his back, surveying the workbenches ranged round. As soon as the mixture was good and ready it was excreted through a little doorway at the bottom, loaded on to wheelbarrows and delivered in great dollops to the brick-makers, shaping the bricks one by one in wooden moulds, sprinkling a little sand like sugar on the Christmas pudding, ready to be wheelbarrowed to the ovens.

Horseback was good, though slow. What we most delighted in were the old clay workings, a field away. We found them much more attractive than the distant seaside.

Sandcastles are all very well, but rich red mud with quiet pools and stagnant trenches where the good clay had been excavated – that was something else. Day after day we tunnelled into the old clay banks, making shallow caves with outer walls laced with rushes to hold them firm. Occasionally we were watched by a little girl, Joyce, whose parents ran the corner shop at the end of the lane. None of us had much to say to each other but plenty to do. Our combined operation, me and him with an occasional contribution from her – created a bond where there hadn't been much to go on before.

When the two of us returned home, clay-covered from head to foot, Mrs. Butt was unconcerned. '*Pop them in the copper, Mrs. Gibson*' and that's where, one at a time, still in our clothes, we climbed into the lukewarm soapy water and gloried in it.

In 1929 we moved to Bristol and I went to a *preparatory school*. Mentally I was still in the Buffalo Bill mode but my uniform had now to be grey shorts, standard issue jersey, and shirt with a stripey School Tie.

This was partly an alternative to the fashion for Eton collars set by the boarders at the school.

These boarders had richer parents who could afford to be rid of them during term time, and compensated them for this with lavish pocket money. The Headmaster made his money mainly out of the boarders, and so his staff indulged them. The rest of us, day boys, were second class citizens – a cut above the Council school kids, resenting the privileges of the better off, but determined to make ourselves felt in all departments.

Three of us in particular, backed by the rest of the class, managed to make life a misery for a new inexperienced teacher. Each time he took us for a lesson we had a ball. When the headmaster heard his story the whole class was mobilised for a beating. He sat us all in a large anteroom to his study. The door was left open so that each individual summoned was seen by all of us going along the passage and then heard by all of us getting six of the best, finally seen again, howling and clasping his behind as he went past. We three were kept till last.

This did not entirely deter us so a few weeks later the three of us were summoned for special treatment. Later, when I was having my bath my mother looked in to remark on the precision and colouring of the stripes received.

There was a tendency to assert ourselves, not just at a fledgling teacher's expense, but also by making fun of one or two others who looked funny because they were fat, or skinny. The parents of one boy who I had singled out complained to my father. We bicycled fifteen miles across country to the boy's home, so that I could apologise. I cannot remember repeating that kind of offence.

There were compensations. Some lessons brought us all together, when the good, long-experienced teachers took us over. Mr. Knapman turned algebra into a detective quest for the identity of X. The two Wells brothers, gentle but well experienced, guided us geographically and historically around the commercial resources of the British Empire; plus the victories and defeats of would-be monarchs from William the Conqueror on.

The best for me was Miss Rust, our English teacher, who gave us all a taste for reading. Admittedly it was a bit frustrating when the selected book – Robert Louis Stevenson's *Black Arrow* and its stories of derring-do in the War of the Roses was read 'round the class'. Each boy had to read a couple of pages aloud and then pass on the baton. I was usually caught out when it came to my turn, reading to myself half a dozen pages ahead; but Miss Rust's rebuke was always gentle and friendly.

She put other books in our way, for our private enjoyment. The book that caught my fancy was Stevenson's *Kidnapped.* I liked the idea of this Scottish orphan lad, taken over by what gradually proved to be a Wicked Uncle designing to appropriate his inheritance. So David Balfour found himself kidnapped. But the vessel on which he was spirited away hit rocks and went down in a storm. He managed to cling to a floating spar, and landed up, the sole survivor, exhausted on a sandy beach. He got up next morning to set off to walk back home to Edinburgh to confront his uncle – only to find that he was on an uninhabited island; and he couldn't swim. So he spends three days of desperation, because being a townee he doesn't know the first thing about what to pick and eat without ill effects.

Then – salvation at last! He sees a small fishing boat approaching and shouts for help. But the two aboard laugh at him and pass by. When he is in despair they return, having lifted their lobster pots and take him across to the mainland of Mull, and civilisation. On the way they tell him that he could have walked off the back end of the little island at low tide.

Reading such books on my own was a private passion. In public my mates and I were into comics. I had this Great Idea to form a Schoolboys' Union. What it boiled down to was that we comics addicts began to club together to share and circulate the Wizard, the Beano, and, to keep up intellectual appearances, the Modern Boy. We kept them all in an empty log box at home, and lent them out, a bit worse for wear as time went on.

We felt the need for some form of insignia and found a slot machine in Temple Meads railway station. Here for a penny a time you could pull a lever and emboss up to 22 letters on a strip of aluminium that was slowly disgorged when the penny dropped. So we made ourselves badges: S.U. for *Schoolboys' Union.* Allowing for the full stops between you got seven sets for a penny and we stuck them on card to pin on our caps or jerseys.

Next step, I felt, should be a Meeting – to consider Next Steps. We met one evening at my home round the dining room table (also used by my father for church committee meetings) in the room tactfully vacated by parents. The meeting was packed out, with me presiding. But as I rose to speak someone turned off the light and when I got it switched on everyone had disappeared under the table.

That put me off public meetings for keeps.

The comics library system survived intermittently, as long as the log box remained accessible. The badges didn't last, but the idea of having them was in keeping with the principle on which the school itself was based. We had to have badges, proper badges, on our school caps and blazers, and our own School Tie to show the world that we were special. Not like those kids down town wearing floppy caps and clothes to match.

We resolutely became a sort of middle class. Our feelings of superiority over the kids who attended the Council school were matched by our determination not to be put down by those of our fellow students who were boarders, and got, we thought, favourable treatment from both the teaching and the domestic staff.

As day boys, determined to show the upper class boarders where they got off, the big opportunity arose when it was decided there should be a Model Car Competition. We all had bits of Meccano (Lego's forerunner) but the boarders were more lavishly supplied with everything – including model car kits.

Three of us formed a syndicate to outsmart everyone else by building a rocket car. We reckoned to win on originality where we might otherwise lose on the limited range of the materials we had available. All that was necessary was four good wheels and a chassis on which sixpenny rockets could be mounted. Sixpence was a week's pocket money so we could not afford more than one preliminary trial, in my back garden. A solitary rocket propelled our vehicle at least fifteen yards. So between us we bought six more, mounted them and placed them on display on the day of destiny; only to find that the Headmaster and his staff had decided the competition should be by appearance – a *concours d'elegance*, and all the well-to-do boarders with their opulent sets of Meccano left us standing.

But not for long.

We decided to meet on the following Sunday afternoon in order to test out our six-rocket car. We found a quiet street where there was no traffic likely to disturb the trial, and lit the fuses. In our innocence we had used wax tapers of varying length in order to get a succession of boosts. But the first taper enflamed the others, and as a result there was an almighty explosion and the rocket car disintegrated. One wheel actually reached the gutter of the nearest roof. The big bang attracted an irate householder, wakened from his Sabbath rest and he stood beside the smoking ruins of what was left of our car threatening all sorts of action. But in the smoking ruins one rocket still remained, and it blew up at his feet.

At this point we decided to abandon our research and legged it home.

Like other eleven-year-olds I was encouraged, inspired, by the exploits of William Brown, chronicled in a series of books, *Just William, More William, William and the Outlaws,* by Richmal Crompton; doing for us what J.K. Rowling's *Harry Potter* does for everyone, worldwide, today. William and his mates – the Outlaws – Henry, Douglas and Ginger were happy innovators, critical of normal society, especially females such as the lisping Violet Elizabeth (who dealt with opposition by threatening to '*thscream and thscream until I'm thick*').

Brought up in single sex schools my limited experience of the real thing was challenged when my parents began to drop hints about a forthcoming addition to the family, perhaps a little girl. On a routine trip my mother happened to point out the local orphanage. I became convinced that the newcomer would be coming from there. So it was a revelation, after a week away with cousins, to find the real thing, a baby sister called Jennifer.

Away at boarding school, then university, we admired each other's progress mostly at a distance as she qualified as a physician, trained briefly as a medical missionary, and then got to work where it was needed most – in desperately under-staffed hospitals in Mysore, India, Ibadan, Nigeria, and war-torn Sierra Leone qualifying as an FRCP, picking up an MBE '*for service to medicine and the community*' as she went along. Like our father (and me) retirement hasn't figured so far. Home leaves have been enlivened by field-work for CND and she's still going strong. Perhaps this is because all three of us have had the luck – and the job satisfaction – to land ourselves in situations where you can't help wanting to break new ground, or recover what's become derelict, and hopefully join in to make it flourish.

At about this time my father had been made the Christian Organisation's Secretary of the League of Nations Union. This was the national body formed to back up the international League of Nations and put pressure on British delegates to make things work.

My father's job as a Methodist minister, (now moved to Bristol with the usual run of meetings, services, pastoral visits, Sunday School sessions, baptisms, marriages, funerals, hospital attendance, and church Bazaars to cope with) filled most of his working days in what seemed to be a seven-day working week.

Somehow he managed to find time to go back and forth for meetings at the League of Nations Union offices, just below Hyde Park Corner. Once in a while his trip to central London included an outing for me, perhaps to Madame Tussauds and its patriotic glories. It usually ended with a visit to the League of Nations Union canteen for cups of tea, buns and lots of spoiling by canteen ladies and LNU supporters dropping in.

In 1931, at long last the world's leaders were meeting to confer about *Disarmament*. Would they get anywhere? Actually start to scale down their arms spending by mutual agreement? Or would it all end in talk?

Father's big idea was to mobilise church people of all denominations – and not only them but parents everywhere; facing up to the hard fact that their children would be at the receiving end of the arms that everyone was paying for.

Beginning with the church leaders and rank and file in Bristol he set out to involve them in mass meetings with a difference.

Working his way round all the religious denominations he got agreement for children in each of the Sunday Schools (which in those days were well attended) to give everyone else the lead. There were to be not one but six *Disarmament Demonstrations* in different parts of the city, with processions of Sunday School children, each a thousand or so strong, leading to open air meetings, each attracting (at the very least) all their parents and relations.

So there was twelve-year-old me in my Sunday best on Durdham Downs, on the back of an open truck, straining up to the stand microphone, confronting the biggest crowd of children and adults I had ever seen: bigger even than the cricket crowd for Don Bradman. All I had to do, just as five other children were doing in the other Demonstrations, was, from the heart, to read out Isaiah's prophecy of a time (already overdue) when,

They shall turn their swords into ploughshares, and their spears into pruning hooks, and nation shall not war on nation any more.

Behind me on the back of the truck were two VIPs waiting their turn to voice support. One was the Sheriff of Bristol, flanked by his wife in a very ugly black hat. The other was a man my father had got to know because they had each been in the Gallipoli campaign. Mr. Sackett had fared worse than my father under the Turkish bombardment. He lost a leg.

He was now, I discovered shortly after, my future Headmaster.

Chapter Three

FINDING OUT

Kingswood, founded long ago by John Wesley, was a school, the Headmaster told us, *for the sons of intelligent paupers*. It was subsidised by the Methodist Church for the sons of Methodist ministers. None of our fathers earned much, and all of them managed to clear one room as a study, lined with books. (We all rushed off to look up what 'HM' meant by paupers, and whether this was an insult or just a jokey statement of fact.)

I began life at Kingswood in the third form, two years after all the others who had joined aged ten. They were well away with customs, cliques and slang which I lacked. Besides that I had strong opinions about everything, including my own worth (having been top of the class most terms in my prep school). It shook me when I came 23rd out of 24.

What was much more unnerving was the attitude of all the old hands to this initially, (but not for long) bumptious new boy.

Some of these were the sons of Methodist missionaries with both parents abroad. Perhaps this deprivation made them more inclined to take it out of anyone available. After the PT classes in the gym there was a tendency to organise impromptu courts-martial followed by what was called a *scragging*. The victim had to run the gauntlet between two lines formed by everyone else, punching you as you passed from one to the other. I was usually the target, for something that I had said, or worn.

My first term was a baptism of fire. Later on the scraggings were fewer. The last one featured another oddball, rather small in stature, not good at socialising, wanting to make his mark by using a *swear word*. Was it *blast* or *damn* or *bloody*? I can't remember. Certainly no one was into *fuck* or *cunt*.

We did however learn to substitute one word in the song we had about the Wesleys:

There was a man who had two sons
And these two sons were brothers
John Wesley was the name of one

And Charlie was the other's.
Now in this school they had a game
They called it KS rugger
John Wesley tackled Charlie low
And Charlie said 'how ***hugger****'.*

Hugger being the slang word for anything supposedly good, though that was not what Charlie probably said.

Whatever the swear word that our 12-year-old classmate chose to impress – it misfired and gave everyone an excuse to subject him to a scragging. I found myself so angered that I ignored the lines and went across to the far end and stood beside him facing the others with contempt as he crouched sobbing on the floor. I felt, for once, glad not to belong to the mob.

That was the last of the scraggings, but for the rest of the year there were periodic fights which gathered everyone round the two who had been set up as the attraction. Afterwards they might cheer the winner – not usually me, because I had been brought up on what I thought to be boxing rules, such as not hitting anyone when you had got him flat on his back on the floor.

The fights were staged after school hours, out of sight of the authorities, usually in an empty classroom. But once the Headmaster happened to pass by and saw us through the window. Being the man he was, he chose not to intervene, but sent a prefect to disperse us, without making the whole thing unnecessarily important.

He was probably aware of a lot that was going on; but at the time the only direct encounter I had with him was when he came clumping on his artificial leg along the corridor behind me, and put his arm across my shoulders, saying, '*Well! One of these days perhaps you will be reading the lesson in the chapel*' as he went on his way. Reading the lesson was a height I never attained; it was only the topmost of the school prefects who got that far. But I felt his words were a sign that he thought I would survive.

'HM' had been appointed by the Methodist Board quite recently, to succeed a man notorious for beating everyone eligible for the slightest punishment. Sackett was capable of doing the same, but it only happened once during my six years stay; and then for two boys who bunked off, not for home, but for adventure wherever they might hope to find it, meanwhile driving their parents and everyone else up the wall. In the gym the next day, they hitched up their gym shorts to show us their wounds.

The school began to change from the beginning of Sackett's reign. He instituted the Whole Holiday – an unscheduled day off for everyone, entirely at HM's choice, when the weather looked good. The kitchen staff would be set to making up three hundred packs of sandwiches. Just as we were on the way across the school playground to our classrooms, the bell would ring and we'd all reassemble to hear briefly from HM (filling in a few minutes to give the kitchen staff time), that we were to be off the premises, and as far away as possible, for the rest of the day.

One of my form mates composed a triolet (at the stage when we were all busily versifying)

HM's looking at the sky
Whole Hol today you chaps
Perhaps that is the reason why
HM is looking at the sky
Oh let us to the kitchen fly
They're cutting sandwiches perhaps
HM's looking at the sky
Whole Hol today you chaps.

Once issued with sandwiches, with our destinations noted by our respective housemasters, we had to stay clear of the school and could go wherever we chose. Sometimes in gangs, sometimes alone. I remember walking the Mendips Hills, blissfully on my own, shouting at the top of my voice:

I've been a sinner and a scamp
But now I'm ready to trim my lamp
So blow – Gabriel – blow.

– all Cole Porter's umpteen verses from *Anything Goes*, to make the valley ring.

On one Whole Holiday two of us decided to bike 30 or 40 miles to visit a place my father had told me about where there was a 'Bruderhof' of pacifistic people, one of whom he had come across, who could be our introduction. When we got there everyone looked very busy and rather boring, and the chap who was to have been our introduction had disagreed with the commune's regimen and moved out. At the end of the afternoon we got on our bikes and set off back to school. By this time it was snowing and we got a bit lost. We arrived three hours late to find a message that we should immediately go to see the Headmaster.

This turned out contrary to our fears. We were given beans on toast, served up by Mrs. Sackett in front of the gas fire in their sitting room, while they plied us with questions about our visit, and sent us off to bed long after Lights Out, feeling heroes not villains.

It used to be said that '*Methodism was born in song*'. We sang a rousing hymn in chapel every morning and at two full-blown church services on Sundays. We were used to letting rip to drown the organ. The Sunday sermons were mostly by leading Methodist ministers, my father three times included. They were *eloquent* in all sorts of ways; some, like John Wesley himself, able to get through to us in a still small voice. Others were notable not just for a turn of phrase, but for a tone of voice, from the very loud to the very soft, sometimes in the same sentence.

We found these more interesting for their manner than for their message. In our mid years we occasionally took part, inconspicuously, in a secret competition. You had to make a little clearing of the throat, a small cough even, when the man in the pulpit first used a word beginning with A – then B, then C. And so on, with some rather better at spotting the word needed to keep up the sequence. So the coughing was dispersed over time. Until, that is, a preacher with the splendid name of Bardsley Brash kept us all waiting at the letter J. J was all right of course, Jesus kept on coming into the picture. But nothing further until Reverend Brash declaimed the words '*Kings of Kings and Lord of Lords*!' – at which there was a cascade of coughing throughout the middle section of the congregation, for which, later that day, we were all summoned to account.

HM usually gave the end of term address, and no one felt like coughing at his words. No rhetoric, no playing to the gallery, just words that made you think, said not from the pulpit but from behind the lectern, as a layman not a cleric.

What he said was pithy, sometimes amusing, short, sharp and provocative.

For a Nonconformist endowed school we were pretty conformist so far as timetables and lesson schemes were concerned. HM abided by the system – *on the whole.* Those three words, said in his sermons and at Assemblies, became the catchphrase that everyone used when we imitated his gait and looked for the slogan that seemed to sum him up: *'One the whole this .... on the whole that ...'* Looking back you could see this was a man who took a lot of things into consideration, could see other sides besides his own, reviewed all the facts available, and then, on the strength of the evidence, came thumping down to a firm conclusion.

His reign was full of surprises. He enjoyed the funny side of things and introduced us to Earnest Bramah's delicious send-ups of literature, commerce, government and society in the storyteller Kai Lung's *Golden Hours*. There were eye-catching pictures in the passages by modern artists, not Old Masters. Half a dozen times a term we were freed of *prep*, (the evening work set by our teachers, one hour for juniors, two for seniors), in order to assemble in the big hall for an Event. Sometimes this was a concert by a full-scale orchestra brought up from Bath, sometimes a play by a travelling repertory company, sometimes a solo recital – Myra Hess was a friend of the music master – sometimes a talk, not as bad as that might sound, because it could be T.S. Eliot who did the talking, or a forthright Quaker called John Hoyland who challenged us to think, and maybe act, about what were then known then as *the distressed areas.* And there was an evening of films produced by the recently formed GPO Film Unit (the birthplace, almost, of the documentary film movement). Breathless we watched *Night Mail*, with W.H. Auden's words and Benjamin Britten's music, matching the rhythms of the train.

Later on we got hold of Grierson's *Drifters*, deep-sea fishermen going about their everyday life. Such films took real people in their everyday surroundings, showed them as near as dammit as they actually were, *documenting* them, not dry as dust in a filing cabinet, but brimming with life. All the time you were wondering what it would be like to be in their shoes, or fishing boots; and if you were, whether you would have a hand in making things happen, not just reacting to what others do.

There were word pictures too.

Form Three had Mr. Redfern taking us for English, reading aloud with lip smacking relish Charles Lamb's *Dissertation on Roast Pig*. This was the spoof legend of the Chinese villager long ago whose house caught fire with the family pig in it: ushering in the revolutionary discovery that you could transform raw food by a process, later known as cookery, and make it unforgettably delicious.

Next year we had Mr. Innes who walked into the classroom one day and the first words he said were those that Robert Browning put into the mouth of an Italian Duke – talking casually to a go-between from a neighbouring Count, as they strolled towards a life-sized picture in the Duke's collection:

That's my last Duchess, there upon the wall ...
Looking ... as if she were alive.

Fra Pandolf's hands worked busily aday –
And there she stands.

He explains that she was always beautiful, and no one could forget her smiles.

But she smiled just the same to everyone – not just to me, her lord, the Duke.

I gave commands and all smiles ceased together.

Nothing more needs saying about her. The purpose of the visitor is to arrange the deal for *the Count's fair daughter* to become the *next* Duchess.

What did they look like, the Duke, the go-between, the portrait on the wall, the palace that contained them? Not a word to get in the way of our own imaginations.

We heard and read a lot of words, which at the time seemed to be what education was about. Two of the three Rs – Reading and Writing took precedence over 'Rithmetic and the Sciences. As for Art – that was a lovely excuse for sneaking off to the art room out of hours, unlocking it with a key loaned to us by Mr. King, the slightly off-beat art master, listening with 40 million others to Henry Hall's *Guest Night* on a crystal radio, concocting whatever was uppermost in our heads during the time outside lessons and the paperwork we had to do each evening in answer to the questions set us for our *prep*.

Words were something to roll around one's tongue, but the fewer they were the better they seemed to work. Like the jewel described in Marlowe's *Faustus*, they were *infinite riches in a little room*.

The poem that then impressed me most was G.K. Chesterton's *The Secret People* ordinary, everyday people without much affectation and maybe precious little schooling, people who had what it takes but whose time was still to come.

In fame and foam at Trafalgar,
On Albuera's plains,
We fought and died like lions –
To keep ourselves in chains.

Smile at us, pay us, pass us;
But do not quite forget.
For we are the people of England,
That never have spoken yet.

come naturally, not farfetched
most part about what they were

nted society but looking back that
remember one encounter with a
old daughter of an influential offi-
d impulse I gave her a hug just as
ay, looking askance.
n that rather tougher, tomboyish,
nine-year-old, Joyce. the ramparts of the clay fortifications the two of us were building in the brickfield. At one point she even lent a hand, but nothing else.

Then there was Monica Sumatra, adopted by a retired local couple who had found her homeless in what were then called the East Indies. We met once in a while on a derelict patch at the end of our road. Being into legends of knighthood and chivalry I built her a *bower* in the one tree that remained. But she never ventured into it.

So in my teens I emerged from the home-based chrysalis knowing, and feeling, very little about girls in general, and without anyone in particular in mind. The breakpoint was when we started going for our summer holiday to West Runton, a village on the Norfolk coast where everyone staked out, picnic-fashion on the beach with a row of canvass huts to take refuge in when we stripped down to our one-piece bathing costumes. There were other families alongside us, full of children so that very quickly we became part of a much larger bunch. Occasionally we all went off on picnics inland, contriving treasure hunts with clues planted up and down the countryside. Mainly we stayed on the beach, chatting each other up.

We made great fun of two black-clad males, still wearing their clerical collars, seated near us. They were affronted by an attractive young woman strolling past them, and wearing - what was an innovation on English seasides at the time – beach pyjamas. They got up from their deckchairs and denounced her as '*an abomination in the eyes of the Lord*'. She took refuge with us, and we had a daily giggle together about the Lesser and the Greater Abomination, related to their respective thinness and fatness.

My father, a different kind of cleric, in holiday slacks and an open neck shirt, did his best not to laugh.

At home, when my father had more than enough of visits, funerals, meetings with church trustees and work on his weekly sermons; and had caught up on his reading of *The Manchester Guardian* and of the books he borrowed or bought second-hand – he would retreat upstairs to the attic if we had one, downstairs to the cellar if we had moved to somewhere where we had not. Over the years he used his hands on an improvised carpenter's bench; cupboards for the kitchen, a bureau (which I still have) for the sitting room. Nearly all out of bits of discarded timber which he picked up on his rounds, visiting the old, the sick and the disgruntled.

Getting to grips with pieces of wood was an inheritance from his father, and grandfather, the former Chatham shipwright. Now that we were holidaying on the coast he turned his hand to elementary seamanship, putting together three discarded inner tubes, acquired from a friendly garage, wedged between a latticework of wooden strips making upper and lower decks in the form of a floating sandwich. The decks were strapped to the top of our old Morris Minor, and everything reassembled on the beach soon after we arrived. Two of us, boys of course, launched the raft on a calm sea, boarded it gingerly, and paddled a very short distance to universal applause. (A few years later rafts were all the go but at the time no one on the beach had ever seen anything quite like it.) Before long we were venturing further, but not, we were told, to be out of our depth. Still, honour was satisfied as we voyaged safely on a gentle swell, with grown-ups, bathing-costumed, on the watch to rescue us in case of shipwreck.

Next year father went one better. The sandwich was now six inner tubes strong, two layers of three with each pair of tyres encircling a drop keel – an inch thick wooden plate, as wide as the tubes would allow, with a cord attached that allowed the crew to let it down once we were properly afloat. And more – a mast, slotted in the wooden decks, with a sail that could be hoisted as soon as the drop keels made us stable.

We were now old hands, and, at fourteen plus, old enough in years to venture further. My mate was Harry, one of a large family happily surnamed Sparrow who flocked around us as we celebrated the official launch (with a bottle of juice broken vaingloriously over it – the fragments instantly retrieved by my father before they could injure barefoot bathers).

We found navigation easier because there was another plate of wood, with a tiller fastened to it, held at one end of the deck, as our rudder. So after demonstrating the navigability of the craft to admiring families and other beachcombers enjoying the event, Harry and I ventured further and decided, since the going was so easy, to round the point from West Runton to East Runton.

We were out of sight of our families before they or we quite realised. They were beginning to think coastguards and rescue parties whilst we sailed peacefully on; only to discover that we were making our way through the East Runton sewage outlet. At this point we turned tail and paddling furiously returned with honour to the West Runton beach.

After that we stuck to navigation within the West Runton bay, with occasional changes in the crew. The most significant new partner was Rosemary, Harry's sister. She and I were in close touch once aboard, but never got into what might be called a clinch, once ashore. We bunched together with Rosemary's brothers and sisters and the girls and boys of two other families, with a bit of rough and tumble but absolutely no rumpy-pumpy. Rosemary and I went around together inland, prospecting dropping points for the clues we invented for an inter-family treasure hunt, contriving rather elaborate phrasing based on the fact that we each had Chaucer's Prologue to the Canterbury Tales as our set book. Some of the others on the treasure hunt who hadn't been doing Chaucer themselves, made wild guesses, got stranded, and told us furiously off at the picnic rendezvous.

Next year we were into Shakespeare, and by this time I had survived the worst of the fights and scraggings at boarding school. With another addict I spent the summer term contriving a send-up which we called *The Tragedy of MacBamlet*.

Back on the beach for the summer holiday, the younger members of the friendly families were dragooned into back garden rehearsals for an end of holiday Show. Fortunately *MacBamlet* was only a small part of it. The hit which brought the house down was a mime to the tune of *Greensleeves* played on a gramophone record, with words spoken off-stage, like one of the Sitwells, that went:

There was a blooming sparrow
Went up a blooming spout

Cue for little Barton, the youngest Sparrow, on a folding ladder climbing up within an enormous cylinder of brown paper.

Down came the blooming raindrops
And washed the bloomer out.

Rosemary, on another ladder emptying a watering can from the top.

Then came the blooming sunshine
Dried up the blooming rain

Rosemary brandishing a gleaming brass tray.

And then the blooming sparrow
Went up the spout again.

Barton ascends, and emerges at the top to thunderous applause.

Rosemary and I kept up our working partnership for the rest of the holiday, and arranged, back home, to meet together and go to a real, West End show. Our trains converged on the suburban section of Kings Cross where I waited for her on platform 9 (later celebrated as next door to 9¾, the entry to the Hogwarts Express), but there was no magical event. Rosemary stepped down from the carriage all dressed up and wearing a pillbox hat. This transformed her from a seaside tomboy to a young lady with whom I could offer no conversation to speak of. So we went to the show, almost silent, came back from it and went our ways.

Chapter Four

UP AND DOING

Back at school I had reached the Lower Fifth. We had grown out of fights and scraggings and I began to feel I belonged to a fairly civilised society, enjoying all sorts of interests and opinions. And of course fluent in swear words in which those sons of overseas missionary parents tended now to be particularly adept.

Acting, in one way or another, was our way of life – putting ourselves across on the sports field, in our dealings with our teachers, and especially in the amateur concerts at the end of term, that took place in each of the Houses into which we were divided. These were opportunities to send up everything else that went on in the school especially the contributions made by the more self-important VIPs who came to enlighten us. So on one show I became a female lecturer recently returned from Vulgaria and introducing the Vulgarian National Orchestra. This included instrumentalists on a bicycle pump (blowing across the top and varying the thrust of the plunger), a brass curtain rod with a mouthpiece, a violin-stringed tennis racquet, a xylophone of bottles, and an array of pots and pans. We played the Vulgarian National Anthem – *Pop Goes the Weasel* in slow time. I had to contribute the final 'pop' with a starter pistol; but standing to one side of the stage, just beside the curtain, this inadvertently set fire to it. Once extinguished there was only a very small hole. But we felt we had made our mark.

Seven of us filled in most Sunday afternoons by moving up to the wood just behind the school to do some *active play-reading*, in the spirit of Bottom and his team in *Midsummer Night's Dream*. Our Seven Society borrowed sets of plays from the English Department and acted them out, books in hand, as we read. In *Macbeth*, as First Murderer I had to fall on Banquo, a rather short lad, 'Babs' Beaty, with whom in earlier days I had lost a couple of fights, and who later became a Battle of Britain DFC. I fell on him so enthusiastically that we both hit the rugged, rooty ground; but without ill-feelings.

For me, acting began to take second place to contriving what the acting was about. If you couldn't be the author of the play (William Shakespeare had got there first), the next best thing was contriving the action; being a *producer*. In turn this took second place to directing the filmmaking which had captivated us all. We had seen what the GPO Film Unit and all the other documentary filmmakers were up to. Making films around real people, real places, real life stories, was excitingly new, and of course newness, because it was different, was just what we went for.

My father had bought a secondhand 9.5 mm Pathé film camera which I borrowed in order to set up our own film unit. Eight investors each contributed the equivalent of 25p for the purchase of film stock in order to make OUR independent, free-ranging documentary of Kingswood itself.

Suddenly our capital was more than doubled by an unsought contribution of £5 from the Headmaster. He made no demands on content, though when he looked at the final version he thought it had too many feet in it. This was because of my determination to show the pace at which things happened through the day – close-ups of running feet as people rushed from point to point, down stairs, across playgrounds, into classes – *cinema verité*, just like the compelling obsessions of the documentary pioneers.

The highlight of the film, it was generally agreed, was the shots we included of my bald housemaster, universally known as The Egg. We had discovered his habit of a pre-breakfast jog all the way round the borders of the school grounds. We placed ourselves out of sight behind a convenient wall where we could command his passage along the distant, hedge-lined road. So there, in one long panning shot, was, not his feet, but his gleaming head, gliding above the hedgerow, making our day.

Having secured these shots and fitted them into the rest of the film (with all those feet), we felt our mission achieved. The film as a whole showed what usually occurred during the school day. *On the whole* it recognised that most of what happened was worthwhile, and, as it seemed to us at the time, a bit ahead of the rest of the world. But not so far ahead that we were *eccentric*. So the film succeeded with everyone, even The Egg, and was replayed year on year, long after I left, until, I was told, the one and only copy fell apart.

Next year was to be the anniversary of John Wesley, the school's founder, reluctantly attending an evening meeting in Aldersgate Street. He listened to a passage in which Martin Luther described '*the change which God works in the heart through faith in Christ*' and he '*felt my heart strangely warmed*'. That re-conversion was the beginning of fifty years conducting almost a one-man campaign to reach people who might be church-goers, but whom the routines of the established church had failed to touch. He became a 'field preacher', attracting huge crowds of people in the markets and the fields, responding to a message shorn of the usual pulpit rhetoric. The establishment more or less outlawed him, denying him the right, as an ordained minister, to preach within any church. So on one occasion his congregation came together in my great-great-great-grandfather's barn. On another, he went back to Epworth where he had been born, rescued as a child from a raging fire, brought up by his father the rector, and when he was refused entry to the church, he mounted his father's tombstone, saying that this was what he had paid for, – so there!

1938 was the two-hundredth anniversary of that Aldersgate re-conversion and my own father scraped enough money to cover the cost of a celebration film which he and I would put together, with the help of various Methodist groups; in particular a Yorkshire drama group which had recently put on *The School for Scandal* and still had the costumes. Father found a young Methodist pastor, with a face similar to John Wesley's, apart from the fact that he had a rather receding chin. I put this right with some make-up putty which occasionally fell off when we were getting him in close-up. The Methodists in and around Epworth were very interested and laid on a couple of horses so that we could introduce the sequence with John Wesley and his lay colleague, John Taylor, ambling along a country road, with John Wesley, as usual, discoursing from one of the books he carried, as they rode. I was cast as John Taylor, being fairly tall and that helped to cut the John Wesley character down to size. We had some difficulty even in ambling together because the two horses didn't really get on, so there were fervent mutterings, not recorded, addressed to the horses rather than to each other, to try to keep them side by side. Then there was an entry to the market square, with characters dressed up from *The School for Scandal* conveniently masking up-to-date traffic signs.

The churchyard tombstone pulpit worked very well, given the re-takes for reconstitution of Wesley's chin. My Uncle Frank, roped in as an extra, and getting himself up in the right kind of peasant costume, took part initially as a jeering onlooker, and later on clasping his three-cornered hat against his chest, as a convert. All done over the weekend, with some retakes, Uncle Frank included, done afterwards against the church wall of father's base in Stoke Newington.

I got down with relish to editing, but there were interruptions as the threat of war grew closer to all of us. May 1938 was dominated by the prospects of war with Germany and Italy, and the double-dealings of Prime Ministers Neville Chamberlain and Edouard Daladier, culminating in the September

Crisis. I put the rough-cut version on one side, – where it has stayed ever since.

Back at school, alongside the filmmaking, there had been rumbustious upper-school debates, alternating with stage productions by the Senior Literary Society. I got the lead, type-cast, in Ibsen's *Enemy of the People* – the well-intentioned old doctor who got across the authorities and in the long run the media, for challenging the *compact majority* who wouldn't face up to the pollution of the local water supply.

Later on I had to lead a debate and we won the motion that '*this house believes there is no God*'. Not quite what was to be expected in a school endowed by the Methodist Church. But walking down the passage next day, HM came clumping after, put his arm across my shoulder, said, '*Of course, we should be putting you in the dungeon for all that*', laughed and went on his way.

He made one other comment, off the record as it were, when later on I had responded to my housemaster, The Egg, who had just launched an elaborate scheme to create a *House Parliament*. His idea was to encourage all of us to have our say – on acceptable topics and pre-arranged innovations.

This seemed to me a splendid excuse to activate my pet subject in history.

I was deep in the study of 17th century Oliver Cromwell and his fellow MPs, responding to King Charles I. I figured that it would be in keeping to organise His Majesty's (the Egg's) Opposition. In the same role-playing manner, we got together to advance some alternatives. This did not go down well with my housemaster and he deputed the senior prefect, his Head of the House, to tear a strip off me in a one-to-one interview in the corridor outside our common room.

This came at the time, our second year in the sixth form, when some of us were to be chosen as House Prefects. Not, however, me (though I got there in my third year). HM chose this moment, shortly before the announcement of the new appointments for the second year, to mention to me, rather casually, that '*Your Housemaster doesn't want to make you a prefect*'. The implication being, I thought, that HM in his place would think differently, but had no intention of interfering.

What people did to make 'history' had grabbed me ever since I was about seven. My teacher at the dame school told us all about the Battle of Bannockburn and I did a picture which showed how the losing side, at the top of the hill, had lined up all their 'camp followers' silhouetted on the distant horizon, waving flags and clashing pots and pans so that the English, winning side below, thought they were a reinforcement and decided to call it a day.

So the losing side (the Scots) won.

At my prep school one teacher liked telling us about his childhood in Ireland during the Troubles, being driven to school in an armoured car. But we couldn't make much of it, or of the Troubles he talked about.

We heard vaguely about the Crusades – a form of folklore reinforced when on holiday by a visit to a village church where there was a stone effigy of a sleeping Crusader. There he was, great sword clasped at his breast, above the tomb where the man himself had been laid by admiring tenants. Along the sides a bas-relief showed him fighting with a misguided people called the Saracens, who had occupied what should have been *Our* Holy Places in old Abraham's land.

Outside school there were first person reminiscences – my father's occasional mention of what it was like on the Dardanelles beaches in the Gallipoli campaign. My mother's account of the munitions workers in Coventry. Primitive newsreels giving glimpses of life on the Western Front. More recent events tended to be shrouded in party political controversy. There was one exception: the 1926 General Strike and even that only registered when the strike ended with the miners' defeat and the months of jobless privation they had to endure after the support funds ran out. I remembered, as a seven-year-old, my normally happy-go-lucky mother – distraught. She had gone out on the streets of Wimbledon to sell flags (miniature miners' lamps) in aid of the miners and came home in shock because a passer-by had stopped, attracted a little crowd, and denounced her for a Red.

Learning about history at Kingswood was another matter. For a start we found out that the school itself had a bit of history – being founded by John Wesley (who set some stiff routines for later generations to follow). We also heard about those who were called The People –not kings and courtiers and battle commanders – people who lived by tilling the soil, trading their goods in the market; and sometimes how they died – by the Plague, or famine, or in battles between rival dukes and would-be kings, at home and abroad.

The Peasants' Revolt I had taken in my stride. There was a young king involved, and when the peasants' leader was assassinated by one of his nobles, he seized the initiative and turned the rebels' heads by proclaiming '*I will be your leader*'. There were fascinating glimpses much later on of the relations between royalty and subjects, now beginning to be called *citizens.* At the height of the 17th century Civil War when the king's forces seemed to be triumphing, and the parliamentary opposition was almost at its last gasp, there was *the self-denying ordinance* whereby everyone on the parliamentary side surrendered their ranks and official positions, so that the command could be re-organised from scratch; and from that moment, it seemed, the tide turned.

There was even a hymn occasionally sung in the more radical of the Methodist churches I sometimes attended:

God save the people
Not kings or thrones but men.

At school we heard, briefly, about 1848 and the various popular movements that took shape about that time, some of them later reflecting the ideas of a middle-aged, middle-class gentleman called Marx and his friend Engels. (The less said about them, we gathered, the better.)

Abroad, did not feature much – until when I was around fifteen HM took us on for history projects. The mere idea of a *project*, an opportunity to find things out, and reach conclusions about them on one's own, was an eye-opener. We could choose more or less whatever we fancied. My father had Japanese friends and he had relayed their stories about the Japanese tradition of *bushido*. With the booklets he passed on to me I put together my project on Japanese chivalry, lavishly illustrated with pictures of Japanese knights and the ceremonies they went through to acquire merit.

Currently the Japanese were invading China and slaughtering 350,000 citizens of Nanking. But I didn't get round to that.

History came closer with Mussolini's invasion of Abyssinia. In our common room at school we got a daily paper – the News Chronicle – and could mark on it the bits we wanted to cut out each evening for our own collections. Sports tips maybe, more often battle maps, and occasional pictures of the aftermaths. The Emperor Haile Selassie escaped and took refuge for a while just outside Bath, downhill from our school. (I bumped into him, literally, on the platform of Bath railway station as he and his entourage emerged unexpectedly from the luggage lift.)

Up to that point warfare was still remote. Then came the Spanish War, with more and more people actually going from our country as volunteers to fight for the Republicans (and occasionally for the Fascists), and sending back firsthand accounts of what war was really like from the inside.

We were into volunteering, on the strength of that talk by John Hoyland about *depressed areas*. He told us about *work camps* where schoolboys went in their holidays to work in Welsh mining valleys where nearly all the livelihoods had gone.

RECENT INVASIONS*

		In	Out
Abyssinia	Italy	1935	1941
China	Japan	1937	1945
Poland	Germany	1939	1945
Czechoslovakia	Germany	1939	1945
Indo China	France	1946	1954
Suez	Britain and France	5/11/56	22/12/56
Vietnam	America	1965	1973
Lebanon	Israel	March 1978	June 1978?
		June 1982	May 1983?
Kuwait	Iraq	August 1990	January 1991
Iraq	US-led coalition	January 1991	February 1991
Iraq	America and Britain	March 2003	?????

*Not counting, Romans, Crusaders, Saracens, Huns, Mongols, and the land campaigns of Napoleon, the Kaiser, Hitler, Stalin and the Allies.

Eight of us signed on for three weeks billeted in jobless miners' homes in Cefn Fforest, near Bargoed in the Rhymney Valley. We were treated with kindly interest and allowed to show our goodwill by cleaning up a bit of derelict land. In between times we picked up a little of what it was like for people of our own age and above to be without prospects and yet entirely self-assured.

We learnt about the tradition of *miners' solidarity* going back for generations. People could still sing marvellously together on their way to work when it was available. In their spare time they cultivated superb allotments, organised homemade operettas, trained for football. At the weekends they continued to dress very *sharp*, knowing without having to say it, '*Who's better*!'

By the time I was into amateur filmmaking and going on the Welsh work camp scheme, the issues glimpsed long ago during the Disarmament Conference were coming closer to hand. So a few of us started a magazine *For Peace* with quotes from leaders in the anti-war lobby, and a pirated version of an Arthur Wragg cartoon – a soldier spread-eagled on a cross made by the capital T for the Aldershot Tattoo. (Aldershot was the venue for the army's crowd-pulling annual pageant, attracting everyone to admire military marching, brass bands, gymnastics and sham fights.) The cartoon didn't reproduce properly on the ancient duplicator we operated in the school basement. But our first, and to a lesser extent our subsequent issues, sold very well when we hawked them in the dormitories just after prayers and before Lights Out.

We were waking up to all sorts of contrasts. The girls' school down the hill from us had been strictly segregated, until the snow came one year and we had a snowball fight. But even this did not bring us to close quarters. The nearest we got, in our final sixth form year, was a visit by five of their sixth formers to take part (in chairs set on the opposite side of our tutor's study), in a cautious seminar.

Then it was 1938 and we began to see things *for real*. We went to Ilfeld in the Harz Mountains on an exchange visit with a German school which had once been run by the Lutheran church. Every year our sixth form had exchanged with theirs. But five years ago the school had been taken over by the Nazis to become a Leader Training school. There, we met, among our contemporaries, the son of Von Ribbentrop and two of Goering's nephews.

It was a mind-boggling regime, with everyone else dressed in a military sort of school uniform, even to the sheath knives held in people's knee-length stockings. Engraved on each knife blade were the words *Blut und Ehre*, Blood and Honour. But this revealed to us something special about the Germans who were of our age, and had been for their first year in the Lutheran-run school. They were the survivors of the purge of students when it was taken over. They were rather more like us, we felt, than those handpicked future Leaders in successive years. They had an offbeat attitude, apparent when we chatted over cigarettes behind the cycle sheds and they explained that the main function of those sheath knives was not for Blood and Honour, but for *Brot und Käse* – Bread and Cheese.

The younger intake were different. One 15-year-old out on the day's military manoeuvres broke his ankle early on, but continued for the rest of the day rather than let the side down. Two others in the same year group took me to the local cinema to see a war flick. It had the usual battlefield scenes, although in this case the people who came out of their trenches with their hands up to surrender were British Tommies, not German Krauts. On the way home I thought to bridge the communication gap by talking about the British film based on the splendid novel *All Quiet on the Western Front* by the German ex-soldier Erich Maria Remarque. I was cut short as soon as I got to his name. '*He is a Jew.*' We went on back home in silence.

Whenever time and pocket money allowed, we used to nip down the hill to the village shop where we could buy delicious *Kuchen* for not very much, perhaps try out our pidgin German, and maybe venture peaceable comments about the rumours of imminent war. If the lady behind the counter was middle-aged or elderly and no one else was present, this could go well, but the chat stopped abruptly if anyone else came in. We took all this in our stride, being aware that the country was in the hands of what the media back home would call a *totalitarian regime*. What that really meant emerged later on, and what it meant in Ilfeld came out in 1945 when one of our party returned as a Major attached to the Allied Military Commission investigating the concentration camp at Nordhausen. It was just up the road from us. Everyone in the village knew its existence. Many helped to supply it with food and other support services.

We got up rather earlier in the mornings that we were used, to go on a controlled run. In our case it became freer-range. We spurted ahead in order to be first in the queue for a very basic breakfast. In the field manoeuvres which took the place of other sports, we were supposed to lie in ambush or to infiltrate enemy lines, in order to make kills by breaking the thread of coloured wool encircling the enemy's upper arm. Our tendency was to gang up in a sort of rugger scrum, and go for whoever happened to be nearest without much reference to military strategy.

Meanwhile, back home, everyone was worried sick about the prospect of war. This was the *September Crisis* with Prime Minister Chamberlain meeting Hitler and Mussolini at Munich to sign a pact which let them get away with the dismemberment of Czechoslovakia.

The master in charge of us had Quaker leanings and was anxious to keep up our friendly relations with the Germans, and demonstrate our belief in a peaceful settlement. So at first he ignored the telegrams sent by HM, ordering us all home.

When eventually we got back, I went around inner London with my father's newly acquired second-hand 16 mm camera, borrowed to take shots of preparations for war – filling sandbags in Whitehall, posting a policeman outside the adjoining offices of the Czech and German Tourist Boards.

At school, the previous year, I had become a pupil of HM himself. Along with other sixth formers, as the intelligent son of a pauper, I depended entirely on winning a scholarship to get to university. At that time Kingswood had the scholarship record, for our size, for the rest of the UK. My subject, and HM's, was modern history and his tutorials largely consisted in argument. He told me at the outset, '*Anything you say, I shall go like a cannonball in the opposite direction.*' So I had either to unsay it or to challenge his response. I think it was this that got me, and a dozen of my contemporaries, our places (free of charge with supplementary grants from local councils) at Oxford or Cambridge. In some cases, including mine, we got offers from both. Cambridge offered £10 a year more, so clearly, Cambridge was for me.

We all heard our scholarship results during the summer term and that left a little gap – not a Gap Year – with the pressures off, time to enjoy our prospects and wonder what university life would really be like.

Meanwhile I was keeping contact with another kind of University.

Jimmy Butterworth was a pint-sized Methodist convert who had served in the ranks in World War I as one of the *Lancashire Bantams*. He reckoned himself, always, as working class, but studied to become a Methodist minister and was sent to a down-at-heels church on the Walworth Road in South London. It had a few mainly elderly adherents, and occasional additions, not lasting very long, from younger ones who had grown up through the Depression and were now footloose, mostly jobless, not thinking much of anybody else.

Jimmy often talked afterwards of the way things began. The church premises had never been up to much, and were beginning to fall apart. One day, he said, he was beside the washroom sinks in the basement where people cleaned up, sometimes, after knockabout football in the street. There was cracked mirror above the sink, and Jimmy found a chunk of soap and scrawled on it:

This shall be the Cathedral and University of the working boy.

Everything else took second place to the needs and potential of adolescent boys and early twenty-year-olds. The church services were simplified, with lessons read by youngsters more often than the elderly, and the choir at first shouting, soon singing the hymns as if they were the chants of a football crowd.

Some of the older members dropped out; others caught on to Jimmy's vision. The place became not just a youth church but a centre for all the interests and capacities youngsters shared. It got its name and fame as Clubland. Mr. Sackett, my Headmaster, heard about it, got in touch, negotiated a link between *Us* in school on the hillside above Bath, and our opposite numbers, *Them*, in Walworth. We swapped places, much in the way that we were exchanging with the young Germans in Ilfeld. But the swaps were not short-term. Clubland welcomed any of us who wanted to join in, necessarily during holidays, and take a share in what was going on.

The share I took was centred on a mutual addiction to all sorts of dramatics. Funny sketches, more ambitious productions once in while, all taken as part of the everyday life of the place.

My home was up on the northern edge of Islington, where my father had his latest church job. Every so often I walked across middle London to Walworth and back, down through The Angel, past Kings Cross, skirting the West End highlights, on to the Elephant and Castle and then the final stretch, very ready for a cup of tea and a bun at the Clubland bar. (On the way back, trudging uphill from Kings Cross towards The Angel, treating myself to a lingering look at female flesh displayed on the magazines in a sleazy newsagent's window.)

The dramatics we went in for were none of them up to very much, but they justified my existence as a visiting Clubland member, alongside one or two other Kingswood visitors with parallel interests in football and athletics.

We were there to join in, not to be *public school types* passing on their superior skills. So the permanent Clublanders tended to adopt us, make allowances for us, be friendly. They had an annual excursion to Guernsey, saved up for, with a bit of outside support from people and organisations that thought well of Clubland. We visitors were allowed in on what turned out to be the last of those summer trips before World War II intervened.

We camped out near Herne Bay, and made the most of a lovely summer. By this time Clubland had as many girls as boys. One couple tended to adopt me, instead of wandering off on their own, trying in a kindly way to see what made me tick. I was doing very much the same for them, and puzzling to myself about the differences, as well as the interests and attitudes we had in common. We could all three see some differences, and laugh at them sometimes; we could also spot what we had in common beneath the skin of our schooling and our upbringing.

Returning on the boat from Guernsey stayed, I suspect, in nearly everyone's mind. We knew that war was imminent, and we all sang our heads off, leaning over the ship's rail as we neared home. Not a patriotic song, or a hymn, nothing particularly relevant to war clouds looming over Europe, just an excuse to belt out, as one:

South of the border,
Down Mexico way,

the song hit made famous by Gene Autry, the Singing Cowboy.

Back home in North London, I was invited by one of the stalwarts of my father's church to a celebration party. This was northwards to Boreham Wood where people lived in style. The family lived in a big house with room for a small professional band, and a spacious dance floor with gossips round the edge.

When the invitation arrived, a fortnight beforehand, my parents took me on one side and said that as this was to be an extra special celebration they had decided to spare £10 sterling so that I could go to the dance in a tailor-made dinner suit.

£10 then was good going, even better because the tailor, as a fellow Methodist, was friendly disposed. He fitted me out in a tailcoat and trousers of what he called *midnight blue.*

I already had a nodding acquaintance with the daughter of the house we were to visit and I felt like a novice would-be champion entering the medieval lists.

Everyone who mattered in local Methodism was there. The elderly on the outskirts sipping teetotal wine, the younger ones showing their prowess on the floor. Several of them to my dismay were in turns partnering Moira, my target. All I could do was to strike a reflective pose on the sidelines.

Then someone announced the Supper Invitation Dance. This seemed to me the last chance to get to Moira before one of her partners took her off.

On the other side of the floor there she was beside what seemed to me an elderly person (actually, it turned out, a rather boring 30-year-old).

So I crossed the Rubicon and invited her. As she left him behind she said, '*Thank goodness you came over, at last.*'

I found that whoever you invited to the dance could be claimed not just for supper but for – thereafter. So our thereafters on the dance floor, were very cosy.

Later on there were more thereafters, going for a walk, visiting friends, a bit more advanced ice-skating. Other people began to notice us and we were included, as a pair, in other excursions.

On one of these we clung together in the back of someone's car when it ran over a rabbit and the driver and partner went out to deal with the corpse.

But at this time, when the world around us seemed about to change, it was just about as far as we thought we could go. My father moved on to his next job, in South Wales. I went *up* to Cambridge. We corresponded a little and then we faded. And Cambridge took over.

Chapter Five

SHOWING OFF

I began to put this chapter together on a Sunday morning lie-in in the last week of January 2004. The winter sun is shining intermittently on a beech hedge, as if cast in bronze; tall bamboos bright green last summer, now ivory, shifting gently in the wind, the colours fading up and down as if a stage electrician was in the wings trying out the dimmer to make the scenery glow. I am considering getting to London and back next week in what's forecast as *arctic weather*. Looking forward to all sorts of enjoyable encounters for the work still in progress; and tucked away at the back of my mind is a nagging concern about the future: the beginnings of the *Jihad* prompted, or maybe reinforced by the invasion of Iraq, famines, local civil wars, pestilence, global warming – reported daily in the news bulletins, getting second mention in the tabloids.

This mixture, zest for the present, and future forebodings, is a reflection of the feelings I can remember back in September 1938. Coming home from

Ilfeld and the Nazi Fuhrer school, filming war preparations, sandbags being filled in Whitehall, news reports from Czechoslovakia; the Munich Agreement to pass by on the other side negotiated by Prime Minister Neville Chamberlain (guided by Foreign Minister Lord Halifax), Daladier, Hitler and Mussolini. *'It's peace in our time'* says our Prime Minister, waving the piece of paper celebrating the agreement to let the Germans plunder the Czechs. And now I am *up* in Cambridge, with my scholarship from Queens' College (former residents: Erasmus, a few centuries back, and more recently my unpopular house master, The Egg). As a Scholar I get rooms (plural) in college in my first year. (Everyone else has to go into digs outside college until their second year.) My bedroom window overlooks an escape and re-entry route for those deciding to stay out of college after hours so I sometimes hear them clambering by. My living room looks out on boring college offices, but Guy Somerset, a second year Scholar who becomes a friend, lives two storeys up and we have conversations shouting up and down through our respective windows.

All the hundred first year students assemble for a group photograph and there I am, six foot two in the back row wearing my well-to-do Uncle Charles' double-breasted suit, handed down and altered at the waist because I am a bit thinner than him. I throw out my chest, square my shoulders and feel that I am looking good, a shade better than the average, because, I think I have inherited from my mother what my father used to call her *bony beauty*. This had brought her that series of on-and-off engagements with eligible members of London society before she finally took him on.

The gas ring in my room brews tea and mid-day soup, but I can't afford much else. However we are all happily obliged to attend at least five dinners in Hall each week. They are, compared to what I had been used to, sumptuous. Each of the half dozen Scholars in our year takes a turn to say Latin grace. Or rather gabble it. We are timing each other to see who can beat the record. Always subject to a warning glance from the high table, where the President of the College eats with his fellow dons.

The only other assembly of our whole year takes place when we queue to sign the Register of National Service. For me it's a turning point. After not a great deal of thought, I am staying a pacifist, *a conscientious objector* to military service. I am not the only one in my year and in the next few months there are some who change their minds, in either direction. There has been no confrontation so far. All any of us had to do was to sign on, one way or the other. Later there is a Tribunal at which each objector has to put forward his case. The Board of the Tribunal tends to assume that objection will be on religious grounds. I think there is a perfectly good religious case for rejecting swords in favour of ploughshares, but I make a political argument – using the enemy's weapons against him is in the long run mistaken because it affirms what Hitler preaches – that might is right, and the only way to defeat it is to go one worse. The magistrate in charge of the Tribunal decides that like most other student pacifists I should be exempted from military service *on condition that the applicant continues and completes his studies.*

In the Easter vacation Guy Somerset and I nip off to Paris to attend an international student conference where *socialism* and *militarism* overlap on the agenda.

We crossed on the channel ferry and stopped over in the Youth Hostel in Dieppe under the steely eye of a female Hostel Warden. Hitchhiking to Paris was a doddle. But the conference proceedings began to be a turn-off. So meeting a couple of other students with the same resistance to interminable talk, we all bunk off to see the sights. Especially, and where entry was cheap – the cabarets which were really strip joints. Here I had my first encounter with the unclothed female body in 3D (pink and resilient, unlike conventional stoney-grey sculptures). One encounter was closer than most. It was at a stage quiz: everyone in the audience shouting what they hoped would be the winning number on the giant roulette wheel spun by members of the chorus. I guessed right and the number I shouted brought me a three-quarters naked young lady skipping down the aisle. She kissed me firmly on the cheek. My fellow students, also-rans, had to give me the next best thing to artificial respiration as we moved outside. I was still in shock.

Guy and I set off home rather late on our final day, relying on the success of our hitchhiking on the outward journey. The first hitch landed us in a village where there was a *kermesse*, a general jollification where everyone danced in the street, including us. When we decided to move on we had to wait for a long time for a hitch. The lorry traffic by now was over. But then a beautiful car approached us and stopped. Looking us over, the daughter from the back seat was carefully transferred to the front between her parents. We sat in the back for the journey, being questioned about ourselves in rather basic English. We managed all right, and even ventured a little French. Time passed easily until they reached their destination and dropped us off.

We then found we were far off the beaten track and for the next hour and a half sought lifts in vain. Finally Guy sat down by the roadside and hugged his leg as if it was broken, and as a lorry approached I went out into the middle of the road arms outstretched to halt it. Yes, they were going to

Dieppe. The driver and his mate took us aboard, one on either side. Then there was more conversation, in French, mainly about what they did and what they carried. We couldn't understand this until they switched on the light in the back of the truck, which showed a heaving mass of heifers.

When they dumped us near the Youth Hostel in Dieppe it was well past midnight. We remembered the steely-eyed Warden and decided not to wake her up. We got into the hostel common room through an open window and lay down on the floor, determined to wake up early and get out by the same way. But we slept too well and woke to find everyone breakfasting all around us. The Warden was saying affably that though we hadn't arrived in time to register we were nevertheless liable for the normal overnight fee. So we paid up and left on good terms, feeling that the *entente cordiale* was intact.

Back in Cambridge everything seemed to be opening up at once like a flowerbed in spring. I joined the Mummers, the dramatic society with a rather cheaper membership fee than the Cambridge Amateur Dramatic Club. It had been founded a few years back by Alistair Cooke, and consisted of lots of *interesting* people (like myself, I thought) all intensely interested in each other as well. There were *nursery* productions of one-act plays in which newcomers got the chance to show what they were made of; and weekly play-readings in the café overlooking Kings College Chapel. With the war looming I was half afraid that my pacifism would put people off. But that did not seem to happen and I reckoned I was at least as good as everyone else when it came to putting myself across on stage; and afterwards over coffee.

I joined the Union Society, went to its debates, and signed on with a few others for a short course in public speaking run by the Union President. This was really a quick entry ticket to getting the President to give you the nod when you rose from your seat on the benches to contribute to the debate. I was determined to see what it was like. Just once. I said my piece, put in a joke, sat down after the traditional five minutes – and got a mention in the student newspaper as '*a promising maiden speaker*'.

That was enough to be going on with of talking for talking's sake. I much preferred acting, and getting *an audience response*. Besides I also had essay writing and attendance at tutorials to justify my existence. I found my college history tutor rather off-putting. I learned he was a Roman Catholic, and at that time I thought all Catholics were to blame for the victory of Franco and his Catholic supporters over the Republican government in Spain. If I hadn't been a pacifist, I thought, I might have got round to volunteering for the International Brigade; though probably not just then. At that moment it was important to show the world, my parents, my old school, and my fellow undergraduates that I was making the grade.

So I beavered away at the weekly essay, usually finishing it off near midnight at the Union, which happened to be close to the home of my external tutor. He was a much more congenial character. I once delivered my essay around 11 pm when he was hosting a small drinks party. Everyone held their breath whilst this earnest student protégé delivered the goods which would have been quite acceptable handed in next morning. Embarrassed by the silence of suppressed laughter, as everyone watched the handover, I withdrew.

I went to all the right lectures, did my weekly assignments, attended tutorials, socialised with fellow Mummers. I was drinking coffee rather than carousing in pubs. I had promised my father to stay on the wagon and anyhow I couldn't afford the drinks.

Autumn 1939. My second year took everything in the previous year for granted and added new excitements.

Second year students had the chance to move base. There was, thanks to the war just beginning, an accommodation shortage. So I shared with a friend. Our ground floor billet was in the Old Court, immediately next to the main entrance to the College. We found ourselves lumbered with many friends and acquaintances using us as a staging post on the way in to the compulsory Hall dinner; and afterwards lingering longer, on the way out. So there was more conversation, growing more intense as the *phoney war* developed.

We all knew that Hitler and co were having their way with the rest of Europe, but apart from the accommodation shortage and a little bit of food rationing, it wasn't really affecting us physically, though our minds were in turmoil at the prospect some politicians favoured: making a deal with the enemy and getting out.

Hitler, and later Mussolini, were still *the enemy* for everyone. As pacifists we couldn't put ourselves down for the RAF, or the Navy or as a last resort the PBI – the *Poor Bloody Infantry*. So what was the alternative? Some decided to stay as they were, without compromise. Others had found there was a Quaker organisation revived from World War One, called the Friends' Ambulance Unit; and they decided to put themselves down for that. I wasn't too sure about enlisting in what I thought would be an offshoot of the Army, but I tracked down another organisation, still in embryo, called the Pacifist Service Units. It seemed to be more independent, with a wider-ranging agenda, though it hadn't much in the way of equipment such as ambulances. As yet it wasn't recruiting volunteers. I put myself down on the waiting list, with some misgivings.

The Mummers had chosen me as Stage Director, so in my first week I had to entertain prospective members. So there was I, standing before the fireplace, confronting a galaxy of eager freshmen, in particular freshwomen, some sitting on the floor, literally at my feet as I outlined the obligations and the glories of membership. On the floor in particular were Anne and Christine, who became close friends with me and with Philip, the current President of the Mummers.

We began to go together after the weekly play-readings, to drink more coffee, and occasionally, when we had the cash, a very little alcohol. In my case, still on the wagon, ginger beer. Afterwards, we paired off for the walk back to Newnham College and it was here, under the trees outside, that I ventured to kiss Anne on the cheek. I got no resistance apart from a gentle question, '*Why did you do that?*' for which I could find no satisfactory answer.

As the year went on each pair tended to go their own way, talking nineteen to the dozen, about everything under the moon. So I found myself sitting on a park bench with Anne, talking my head off as usual about the world and how to change it, until Anne, head on my shoulder, said, *'You're so good!'* and burst into tears. At this point I realised it was all over, because clearly she had got quite the wrong impression.

We kept up a modest friendship, mainly through our weekly play-readings, but Philip and Christine seemed to be coming apart; so we swapped. It was then Christine and I who went off for the follow-up conversations and the meanderings back to Newnham.

For better or worse I was preoccupied with a myriad of activities: rehearsals for the lead in the Mummers' annual production; helping to form branches of the Peace Pledge Union, and of the Independent Labour Party, selling copies of their respective weeklies outside the Conscientious Objectors Tribunal; and having intense political arguments with others in and outside the university.

I suddenly discovered that the crucial examinations were approaching and I was way behind. My tutor had the same impression and arranged for me to move out of college into local digs. Freed from most of the socialising I could begin to catch up.

It was here, just by the hat stand in the modest entry of my digs that I had my third kiss, this time on the lips, from Christine. It was not of course further indoors where the lightest kind of cohabitation was *verboten*.

At the end of term with exams over, we were all wanting to celebrate. In May Week many of us Mummers and our friends went down to the riverbank to charter punts. Christine and some of the others went ahead. I saw them from the riverbank, already afloat in midstream and summoned her back across the water. She got the others to steer her across to land. Quite soon afterwards she was in my arms, lying together, fairly circumspectly on the grass with my uncle's double-breasted jacket off, to make a kind of pillow.

This gentle juxtaposition, hugging each other and not talking very much, seemed to me to clinch matters. The term ended and we all dispersed. Two of us, short of cash as usual, had struck lucky with the Independent Labour Party. They gave us free accommodation as caretakers in a four-storey building in Clapham North. The four assembly rooms took up nearly all the space available. We had room to cook for ourselves, and we dossed down in a small storeroom. In between sweeping the floors, and letting people in and out, we attended all sorts of meetings – by local union branches and *action committees* on this and that.

I seemed to be adopted by the London headquarters of the Independent Labour Party as prospective talent, made my first entry into journalism with a bombastic article on the front page of the Party's *New Leader*, and was taken out for tea and a snack at one of the cheaper cafés nearby. In parallel I frequented meetings of the Peace Pledge Union, with some slight reservations at the back of my mind because they seemed what I called to myself a bit fuddy-duddy. There was one exception, a bunch brought together by David Spreckley who was able to draw on some of his brewing family's finances to fund *The Forward Movement of the PPU.* We met in his attic digs with one wall emblazoned with a slogan distilled from William Blake:

RELIGION IS POLITICS, POLITICS IS BROTHERHOOD

In between such encounters we dropped in on a down-at-heels café off the Tottenham Court Road called the Coffee An (being short for Coffee And ... whatever cheap food we could afford). We talked a lot, about the events unfolding across the Channel, but mainly about ourselves and each other. We were not on the march making history as we would like to be, but on the side-lines, busily marking time.

Meanwhile I got on with what I saw as a cunning plan to enlist various interesting, and sometimes important, people, pacifist and nearly pacifist in an association which would act as an long-term alternative to the war effort.

We called ourselves CORDS, a co-ordinating group to pool our rather vague ideas. Non-violent resistance to a German invasion? What we would actually do was still uncertain, because the war was as yet still *phoney*, at least here in the UK. All the soldiering was happening, mainly by other nationalities, across the Channel.

Then like summer lightning everything suddenly changed. The first bombing flights from the Luftwaffe appeared in the skies above us, en route for RAF airbases. There was news of military defeats abroad.

The Battle of Britain was just beginning. I decided that life and living conditions, even life expectations, were all about to change. So it was time to establish a sort of landmark. I took a week's leave from joint care-taking and hitchhiked to the southern tip of Wales where Christine had found herself a vacation job in the Land Army on a local farm. I made my way under summer skies punctuated by vapour trails and bursts of anti-aircraft fire, as the first German reconnaissance planes met our Spitfires in what were then called dogfights. I got as far as Haverfordwest on the first day, late at night, ten miles short of my destination, and dossed down in an empty barn.

Next morning I told the friendly farmer where I was heading and who I was after, and he lent me his bicycle. By midday I was there. The first thing I saw was my friend Philip driving a tractor. As if he belonged. Christine and her sisters were also there, together with their mother who had come down to make sure everything was above board.

That evening, already aware that circumstances had changed I popped the question and got No for an answer.

Next day I returned the bike and hitchhiked back to Clapham North. Both of us caretakers were still short of cash, and a friend told us that you could earn not less than 50 shillings a week, cutting logs outside York. So we arranged a temporary stand-in for the care-taking, and hitchhiked north. On one of the first lifts the lorry driver mentioned he had come from the London docks, and '*there'd been a bit of activity*' as he was leaving.

It was a good road for lifts and we were in York by early evening. We made contact with the student friend who was going to put us up and found out that we would have to board a bus at 5.30 in the morning in order to get us to the logging camp when work was due to start.

It took no time to learn the essentials of the job in hand. Tree trunks, freshly axed, were brought in and dumped for us to lift and place on trestles. We were paired off with more experienced workers and learned the formula. Two trestles stood side by side and the trunk lay on the ground between them. We had to lift the log up and rest it on a plank laid across the trestles. The formula was '*lift the bugger up and push the fucker in*' or sometimes '*lift the fucker up and push the bugger in'*. Afterwards you sawed off the first chunk, and then repeated the formula to leave one chunk after another clear for the double-ended saw to get to grips.

A long day of this, and an hour's bus journey home left us with just enough energy to eat and then sleep it all off in time for a rude awakening in the early hours of the next morning.

It wasn't until Wednesday night that we stayed awake long enough to catch up on the news. The London Blitzkrieg, beginning with that *bit of activity around the dock*s, was in full swing.

Chapter Six

UNDER FIRE

We decided to wait until Friday, so that we could collect our 50 shillings pay. In mid afternoon we hitched south, reaching our base in Clapham North as the night's bombing was getting underway. Our four-storey ILP building had an attractive parapet around the roof, so we were able to get out through an attic window and sit there as spectators. There was a low pink cloud – of smoke not moisture – lit by distant and mid-distant fires. Occasional incendiaries dropped within eyeshot. A Dornier bomber slid out of the clouds just above us and disappeared again under machine gun fire from an invisible pursuer. Later, far off, we saw a parachutist descending from a plane that had crashed somewhere near Kennington.

We sat it out until the small hours, transfixed like spectators at an intoxicating ballet performance. As twenty-year-olds we were exhilarated, not cast down, scarcely thinking of the victims of the bombing. After all we were right bang in the middle of everything, ourselves.

When we got up next morning we learned that student friends of ours had moved in as volunteer workers somewhere in Poplar. So we took the Tube from Clapham North as far east as it would go. This proved to be Aldgate. Beyond that, we learned, Tube travel was out, and bus services cancelled. We tried to charter a passing taxi, but the driver said taxis weren't going any further than Aldgate East either. So we walked down Commercial Road past streets empty of the usual traffic – a landscape of rubble, here and there silhouettes of office buildings stripped of their façades like the backstage view of scenery flats, a sagging upper floor with a desk on the edge, telephone receiver dangling. Air Raid Precautions workers searching and sifting, a stretcher party feeding an ambulance. Everywhere dust.

We were already becoming used to the devastation, and in an odd way we were on a high. Awed, but aware that we were part of something everyone had been expecting, dreading. Now we were in the middle of it and in a strange way no longer afraid. We were concerned about the destruction, the dangers, the uncertainty. We knew that people were suffering injury, loss, and that death might be just around the corner. But we were no longer spectators. We were in the middle of events and could soon be up and doing.

We got to Poplar Town Hall where our fellow students were based. They told us they had plenty of help already, but further west (almost on the path we had followed) in Stepney, there was a lot to do, particularly in a patch beside the docks, called Shadwell. We made our way back from Poplar past the Limehouse Basin and along Cable Street. The street down which, back in 1936, Oswald Mosley's Blackshirts, imitation Fascists, thousands strong, had tried to march, headed by mounted police. And local people, Jews, Catholics, communists, and all sorts, had barricaded the entry, and stopped them in their tracks; with children rolling marbles under the police horses' hooves.

Parallel with Cable Street was the old Ratcliffe Highway (one-time haunt of Jack the Ripper), at one end the Bernard Baron Jewish Settlement, halfway down a cluster of the 'Highway Clubs', which their organisers and patrons had turned into a *Rest Centre* for all comers, especially people suddenly homeless.

In charge was Vera Grenfell, a tall, very able member of the Conservative élite. She had done the spadework in getting sponsors to fund the clubs and she used to drop in regularly to lend a hand with the clubs' activities. Now she had moved in, full-time, dossing down in the ladies' loos in the basement when the sirens sounded and the nightly bombing started. Alongside Vera was the Baroness Ravensdale, a relation of Lord Curzon. She was clad for all comers in green *beach pyjamas* (just like that young beach lady who was so Abominated), dishing out the mugs of tea with the patience of a Lyons Nippy, hour after hour after hour.

Vera and the Baroness, and Denis, the long-suffering male youth leader, welcomed us without fuss. So we went back to Clapham whilst it was still light, notified the ILP that our care-taking jobs were no longer needed (nobody was likely to come to nightly meetings in the premises), packed our belongings, locked up, and got back to Shadwell in time for the night's performance. This was September 16th, generally regarded as a sort of red-letter night-and-day, with some bombing by daylight as well as by firelight at dark.

The Rest Centre premises had once been a pub called The Swan, its signboard wrongly identified, it was alleged, by a visiting Irishman and known ever after as *Paddy's Goose*. Being an ex-pub, the basement was well served with toilets, mainly male. So whilst Vera and the Baroness and one or two of their socialite friends bedded down in the Ladies, we slept beside the urinals in the Gents.

Thanks partly to their affluent and influential contacts Vera and co had managed to get hold of tea, milk, bread and a variety of fillings and were catering day in day out for upwards of 1200 people, taking refuge during daylight hours after the sirens sounded the All Clear, dodging back to makeshift shelters when the sirens sounded the Alarm and the bombers came.

For the next week we worked flat out, boiling up water, filling great canisters with tea, making cheese sandwiches, dishing it all out, and once in a while joining in the choruses of anything that people felt like singing, to compete with the drone of the passing bombers, and the ack-ack gun fire.

My old man said, 'Follow the van,
Don't dilly-dally on the way!'
Off went the van with the home packed in it,
I walked behind with my old cock linnet.
But I dillied and dallied, dallied and dillied
Lost the van and don't know where to roam,
You can't trust the 'specials' like the old time 'coppers'
When you can't find your way home.

SOME BOMBERS' KILLING SCORES

Guernica , 27th April, 1937	1645
Shanghai, 3rd December, 1937	1740
Warsaw September, 1939	50,000
London 7-8 September 1940	842
Coventry 14-15 November 1940	380
Liverpool 20-22 December 1940	365
Berlin (22nd November 1943)	2,000
Hamburg 27th July 1943	40,000
Dresden (est.) 13-14 February 1945	35,000-500,000
Hiroshima (est.) 6th August 1945	66,000-237,062
Nagasaki (est.) 9th August 1945	39,000-108,000
Jerusalem (King David Hotel) 22nd July 1946	91
Omagh 15th August 1998	29
New York (Twin Towers) 11th September 2001	2,750
Madrid, Spain, 11th March 2004	191
Faluja, Iraq, April 2004	470
Beslan School, Russia, 3rd September 2004	344
Central London 7th July 2005	56
Sharm el-Sheikh, Egypt 23rd July 2005	90

Effected by German, Italian, American, British, Russian and Japanese Air Forces and at ground level by Irgun Tsvai Leumi (Israeli), IRA, Hamas, Chechens and Al-Qaeda.

Aerial bomb suppliers include Krupp; Lockheed Martin, Boeing, Northrop Grumman (US); BAE Systems (UK); EADS (Europe).

Ground level bombs often homemade.

Towards the end of this week I began to think of the Pacifist Service Units. Finding a telephone that worked, I rang them up, and suggested there were some useful services right here, waiting to be delivered. So they said they would send a team. By the end of the week, in dribs and drabs, by no means a team, a mixed bag. There were ten of us in all. When I asked who was in charge, the lady at the other end of the line explained that it was to be me.

THE TIMES leader, November 26th 1940.

> The complaints are not vague: on the contrary they are specific. Named shelters, notably in the East End of London, suffered from named defects and are the scenes of named scandals. They are consistently and vilely overcrowded. They lack in some cases all sanitary provision, and, where such provision exists in primitive form, it lacks all privacy. They lack any reasonable degree of lighting. They leak. They have mud floors. Some of the people using them are ill or disabled and some of them are physically offensive. In these conditions of stench, filth, vermin and darkness hundreds of people pass the greater part of their lives. The effects on the minds, as well as the bodies of children and young people need no elaboration. And these conditions in these particular shelters have continued practically without improvement, sometimes even with gradual deterioration – for ten weeks.

Early on in those ten weeks I set out on a scheme partly inspired by Vera Grenfell and the Baroness.

At nighttime and often during the day people were huddled in whatever shelter they could find. During lulls from the raids, they went back to their homes if these were intact, or to the ruins of their homes where there might be some sticks of furniture to be salvaged. In between times, they sat, gossiped, sang and swallowed sweet tea at Paddy's Goose.

The shelters, so-called, provided by the government, were mostly flimsy brick boxes set up on the roadside which, after the first night or two, were no longer tenanted, and in most cases no longer tenable.

The alternatives, mainly thought up by local people, included the basements of nearby warehouses invaded by the dockers who served them, bringing their families. Shadwell had grown up over a couple of centuries to serve the dock; its people were in turn served by the churches. They were built partly with the money subscribed by residents who turned up in modest numbers for the Sunday services, and en masse for christenings, weddings and funerals. The church buildings included burial places, the basement crypts, and now people slept alongside the stone coffins and the memorial tablets.

There were also the Arches supporting a railway line running at roof level right across Stepney. Each arch had been hurriedly bricked in, leaving a doorway for people to come in, doss down and perform all the usual functions of people getting ready for bed. The beds were mattresses that people brought in if they still had anything left, otherwise it was cardboard or the macadam surface of the roads that ran through the arches. As for functions like washing or urinating or having a panic shit – there were sometimes buckets, clustered near the entrance, and sometimes just the original gutters bordering the road beneath each arch.

Everywhere, people found themselves thrust back on their own resources. In the improvised shelters, impromptu committees sorted out the bedding space, so that each family knew where to put its mattress. In the entrances, younger men lingered to keep a lookout for incendiaries and go after them with whatever lay to hand, buckets, flails, before long – stirrup pumps. There were disputes, just as in everyday life, but people in this part of the world knew enough about each other to sort out the awkward cusses, and get them to behave – or else.

Improvising, making do, was the key to everything. So our Big Idea, hatched out with the help of Vera and the Baroness, was to organise a daily round to Get Rid of the Shit.

Along with our first *PSU* volunteers had come an ancient Morris van which would now gain a much more varied life – subject of course to our getting petrol, and a few other items we would need from the Council.

Stepney Borough Council – being in trouble with allegations of corruption – the government had decided to substitute rule by the Town Clerk. The situation was complicated by two direct hits by German bombs – one destroyed the local telephone exchange, the other the Council's filing system, together with most of the Council offices. So the centre of local government was now the People's Palace, a lovely big theatre on Commercial Road erected to encourage the performing arts throughout the borough. It now housed a different set of performers. The auditorium, cleared of the theatre seats, was divided by many temporary screens into little offices. Each contained an official surrounded by box files, In and Out trays and occasionally a salvaged filing cabinet. Officers dealt patiently or despairingly with queues of applicants for every kind of emergency support. Some queues were so long that they dispersed when the sirens sounded and reassembled day after day. Up on the stage sat the Town Clerk, looking, I thought, bewildered.

I had heard about these goings-on and arrived with my shirt buttoned up and a tie. Under my arm I carried the leather briefcase presented many years back to my father embellished with a little metal clasp '*In Appreciation from Officers and Members of the Onward Youth Club*'. Now it was newly shined up with boot-blacking and stuffed with newspaper to give it an important look. I made my way past the office screens in the auditorium, and up the steps on to the stage, to speak unannounced and unappointed with the Town Clerk. He seemed almost relieved to have someone to talk to and gave me chits to obtain regular supplies of petrol, disinfectant, bug powder and stiff brooms; plus huge metal keys with which to open the manhole covers above the sewers (wherever they still functioned).

Thus armed, we were really and truly a Service Unit and people at first overlooked the fact that we were pacifists, and later on reproved soldiers returning from the Dunkirk evacuation for referring to us as *bloody conchies*.

Our order of battle for the day started in the van, visiting one *shelter* after another. We took the shit buckets on board, or carried them by hand, to the nearest manhole, unlocked it, tipped out the buckets, returned with the empties, added a dash of disinfectant, and did a brisk sweep up and a general bug powdering to follow. Then on to the next.

When we really got going we scored about 200 buckets a day. But that was just the morning's work. In the afternoon we went around to homes where people had been bombed out. Their homes were no longer habitable, but there were still articles they could salvage. Quite often these included a piano because East-enders were very hot on singsongs. The householders identified the items they wanted most (piano included); we loaded up the van and took them to wherever they had managed to find a temporary base, taking care not to dilly-dally on the way.

At the end of the afternoon we cleaned out the interior of the van and loaded up with 3-foot high canisters of hot, sweet tea. Then we toured the shelters; not just the big ones, but little hideouts in the half-basements and coal holes of terraced houses bordering Commercial Road. Soon we equipped ourselves with shoulder-bags containing useful first aid dressings. We tended to linger at each point rather longer than was strictly necessary, when bombs were dropping nearby. That was when we really touched people as persons, little families crouched together, hoping for the best, fearing the worst, making little jokes to cheer up the old and frail.

Then out into the smokey, dust-laden air. We had one helmet between us, and nobody liked to be the one who monopolised it. So most of the time we were all bareheaded, but easily recognisable by the brown dungarees we had as our uniform, and by our armlets marked PSU.

There was a diphtheria epidemic. I too fell sick, and delirious; half-conscious as the van sped me through the Rotherhythe Tunnel to the South East Fever Hospital. Here each patient had a little bed table on wheels, sliding over your bed to hold your meal tray. This also served as cover when the raids were on; you slid down the bed with your head, at least, somewhat protected beneath. We only had one bomb dropped near enough to break the windows and send the little nurse on duty diving beneath the nearest bed in case the next bomb in the *stick* should come closer.

Meanwhile, being too many for the small doss-down in the Rest Centre urinals, the Unit moved into a half-basement further along the Highway. Then that too was bombed out. So by the time I came out of a fortnight in hospital, we had moved a few hundred yards further on to our top flat in a tenement called Ring House. We managed to stay there, even after the flat below got a direct hit, for the rest of the Blitz.

December 29th was another Red Letter Night, the biggest London blaze, it was said, of all time (perhaps rivalled in Pepys' day by the Great Fire). It was centred on the square mile around Fleet Street and St. Paul's Cathedral. Incendiaries lit everything up as if it were high noon. We reckoned that was in readiness for the bombers who would follow.

There was a lull while we waited for the bombers to return with the high explosives to extend the firestorm and give the *coup de grace*. But the Channel weather turned nasty, and this time the bombers did not come back. For a little while the activities we were all used to ceased. There was nothing that anyone outside the shelters could do except to marvel at these new Illuminations, with St. Paul's, saved by its amateur firewatchers, resplendent on the summit of Ludgate Hill. Colin, joining the Unit from life as an *Observer* journalist strayed up to Fleet Street, and came back like a pyromaniac, shouting his wonderment.

Night after night the top flat in Ring House was a vantage point from which those of us not on duty in and around the shelters could spot where the opportunities might be to take useful action.

Our services were more and more in demand. Later, we got a couple of bicycles and loaded them with the tea cans, the first aid bags, and, hanging over the back wheel, a canvass bucket and a stirrup pump. All told, we looked and felt much like the White Knight confronting Alice in her kind of Wonderland. From our balcony we could spot where the incendiaries were dropping, and nip down to see where we might have a go at putting them out, as a kind of extra to the routine work in hand.

We learnt mainly on the job, with a crash course in elementary fire fighting at the local fire station during a lull in the bombing. Our initial amateurishness was tolerated. Once in a while we went for incendiaries with our stirrup pumps on foot or on bicycle. For the bigger fires we took refreshments to the real fire fighters as they worked. Two of us, venturing deep between the fires blazing in a bombed warehouse, thought we were bringing refreshment to the fireman hosing down what still remained. He was very grateful until he found that all the hose-work had rendered the tea stone cold.

Extract from my progress report to PSU supporters:

> New conditions of devastation, of disrupted families and patched-up homes have challenged us … We found children running wild in shelters and bomb-craters, adolescents walking the streets, more *juvenile delinquency* than anyone knew how to cope with. We found families so debased by poverty and bombing that they did not dare to approach the authorities to make their War Damage claims, did not know enough to use their own food ration coupons … The streets around us teem with youngsters gradually reverting to gangsterism; in one street near the Unit there are thirteen concurrent probation cases. The only things that seem to touch the problem are constant and unfailing friendship and service.

We were a mixed bunch ourselves and had to get used to each other on the job. Day by day, night after night, it was all go. We were among all sorts of friendly acquaintance, giving us a nod in the streets by day, sharing a scrap of gossip in the shelters by night. We had no time to negotiate our way with the professionals who had been coming to live and work in Shadwell for most of their adult lives. They were a fascinating array of what nowadays would be called *support workers*. They took us as they found us, without fuss. Mostly they belonged to local churches and synagogues which in turn had spawned youth clubs and drop-in canteens, set up in pre-war days when most able-bodied residents were out of work and on the dole. Now, in wartime, with everyone busy, clubs and canteens like Paddy's Goose turned themselves into the Rest Centres where people took refuge when their homes were no longer habitable, if they existed at all.

So we found ourselves in *working relationships* from the start. Lending a hand in the youth clubs and canteens in spare moments, we learnt about each other – the locals and the incomers – coming up for air and a cuppa without the need to introduce ourselves formally and be polite. The first of what later became three Stepney Pacifist Service Units included an architect, a fledgling Scottish don, a van driver, a wildly enthusiastic vegetarian, that journalist from *The Observer*, Michael (much later Lord) Young who dropped in from time to time, and a feisty ex-football coach who took the piss out of anyone who got too academic by wrestling him down to the floor and biting him, gently, on the ear – to general applause.

Stepney in general, and Shadwell in particular, had its history enshrined on the tablets of its churches, and in the late thirties the headlining local initiative of the STEPNEY TENANTS' RENT STRIKE. This was the hard-held decision to stop paying the exorbitant rents levied by the commercial owners of much of the housing in the Borough. It hit the headlines enough to get some success in cutting the rent increases. It held together and succeeded partly because its leader, Father John Groser, already had a down-to-earth reputation, along with his colleagues – *Anglo-Catholic Reds* as they were sometimes called, based in the parish of St. George's in the East. Father John, lanky, striding about in a worn cassock, was out and about on the move, finding out who was in need, doing something about it himself, getting others to join in, within and outside his church congregation. There were others like him, though less easily recognised. 'Lex', short for Alexander, Miller was the minister of the local Scots Presbyterian church, and, I discovered, sharing our pacifist views on peace and war, but without pushing them down the throats of the church people he worked with. He said little, did much, and found a lot of life funny without laughing out loud.

There were also people like Ethel Upton who outsiders might label *the diocesan worker*. She lived further down the Highway, enjoyed a bit of pub life nearby, knew everyone and their friends and relations within walking distance of her little flat. She catered for whatever people needed, including a chiropody service for the elderly. She had, for a small person, a chuckle descending to a belly laugh at off-colour jokes; such as someone mentioning *a propos* official shelter-building, '*the number of erections in the park*'. She liked the look of us, taught us from her repertoire of moderately rude songs and anecdotes, fuelling us with a great deal of coffee and an occasional glass of something stronger. She still got up early to go to Mass, kneeling at the altar rail, Father John striding round his church beforehand swinging incense, and then dispensing the consecrated Bread and Wine.

We had a nodding acquaintance with the Jews who ran the Bernard Baron Settlement further down the road towards Aldgate. The Blitz had brought them together with most of the other faiths in the area, seeing needs and opportunities wherever they occurred, joining forces whenever the job in hand was too big to cope with on their own.

We had rather closer links (not primarily theological) with a lively couple of Quakers who had come in as volunteers, billeted in a small flat overlooking the anti-aircraft battery in King Edward VII Memorial Park at the end of the Highway. We kindled to them not least because one of them was adept at producing an apple turnover, which was heavenly to us otherwise dependent on ham-fisted cookery with everybody taking turns, coping for a dozen or more at a sitting, in our tower block eyrie. (Later on Colin the journalist proved himself a brilliant amateur.) Once a week or so we got invitations, for two or three at a time, to try out the apple turnovers. My turn, with two others was on an evening with a lot of *activity*, including the operation of the ack-ack based in the little Memorial Park. In the midst of the barrage, we scooted along the pavement, with our recently acquired steel helmet shared between us; but still not feeling justified in anyone of us actually putting it on to ward off the bits of ack-ack shrapnel which tinkled down on the pavements as we scurried on.

Our hostess and her partner were young like most of us, enjoying the life we led, but not quite so rumbustious. They had some of the *quietness* that imbued the weekly Friends' Meeting where people seldom spoke during the proceedings unless they really had something brief and relevant to say.

In one sense, temporary or permanent we were all of us immigrants, settling in Shadwell to live and work at what lay nearest to hand. Alongside us, quite often ahead of us, were people whose families dated back to the beginnings of dockland, the Baynards, the Williamses and the Coxes and others who found us a little bit odd to start with, and then welcomed us in. The welcome extended once in a while, when for a night or two the raids slackened, to getting round one of the upright pianos which many people possessed, for a singsong. On one splendid New Year lull someone's piano was trundled out on a coster's barrow and we serenaded street after street together.

We still had links with Paddy's Goose, which supplied the cans of hot tea for the shelters. In daylight there were occasional visits by VIPs from Vera's and the Baroness's socialite past. One day we were invited with the other Rest Centre workers to greet Lord Halifax. He had been Foreign Minister and helped Chamberlain to negotiate the Munich Pact with Hitler and Mussolini. Now he was here to show his appreciation of the team in the Rest Centre which included Alf Williams, a docker's son. We were all invited to welcome the visitors, but most of us skulked in the background. Alf stood forward, so that the visitors could all hear him make his own announcement '*I am not going to shake hands with that bastard!*' The rest of us, on the sidelines, felt it helped to make our day.

Government people, Winston Churchill included, made occasional daytime walkabouts and sound bites which looked and sounded good and showed the outside world that government *really cared.*

This was not quite the same as *really caring for the people*, night and day, at the receiving end of the bombing.

There was a yawning gulf between Us and Them. 'Them' being the civil servants and the politicians they served. In between were the likes of Anglican Father John Groser, the Presbyterian, Lex Miller, and the Rabbi at the Bernard Baron Settlement – each trying to make common sense to the people in Whitehall. – Nice people with nice manners but almost clueless about what to do (apart from keeping the files up to date.) Lex summed it up in a report to his fellow pacifists.

> The traditional form of life in East London was finally shattered in ninety minutes of bombing on 'Black Saturday'... the Saturday afternoon which battered and fired the river areas precipitated a major social change for London and for England... Before September was half over the river areas of East London were made definitely uninhabitable. In scores of streets surrounding my own church there is scarcely one usable house: and there are areas further east which are worse, much worse, the effects of the bombing being exactly comparable to those of a major earthquake.... The experience of those of us who have had to haunt Whitehall these last weeks is that there is a very great deal of real compassion among permanent officials. If goodwill would do it the thing would be done. You go to a government office your mind afire with the horror of the human situation. ... You are welcomed by men of good will equally concerned with yourself, who are on duty night and day, smoking their homely pipes and plotting how to do good to all men. ... They know as you know that the spokesmen for the administration are soft-pedalling on the real tragedy, and they are prepared to work endlessly, to the limit of their powers and beyond to see that plain human needs are met. You come away satisfied, wait day after day, and nothing happens beyond more government assurances that the thing is in hand.... The

leaders continue to put the best face possible on a rotten situation, the officials make promises in all sincerity, but slip up constantly on performance.

In the lifetime since those days I can't remember anyone asking me how it **felt**, as distinct from how it was, in the Blitz. Come to that I can only remember one answer I got, as a teenager, when I asked a World War I survivor what it was like to be in the trenches – *bloody boring* was all the reply I got. The Blitz was different in that respect. Always something new happening. Never a dull moment. Our bicycle patrols were the excuse for showing our capacities, as fire fighters and first aiders, without necessarily putting them daily into effect. We spent more of our time with the shit buckets and the furniture removals, by day, and, before long, by night, with the amateur first aid posts we established in some of the shelters. This kept us busy into the small hours with anything from burns to belly aches; and occasional forays outside when incendiary bombs dropped nearby.

There wasn't much you could do about high explosive, but a batch of thermos-sized incendiaries might be countered in an amateurish way by putting them out before their surroundings caught fire. One evening I was on duty in the crypt shelter of St. George's when we heard the rustle of a cluster of incendiaries coming down uncomfortably close. I put on my asbestos fabric gauntlets (special issue for handling burning debris) and rushed out. There, like a November 5th display, was a *Molotov breadbasket* of incendiaries in full flame. On the way to them I heard more coming and hit the ground fast, biting the edge of one of my asbestos gauntlets on the principle that bomb explosions tend to make you bite your tongue. Tongue stayed intact, but I still remember the taste.

Beyond there was a terrace flat and I could see that an incendiary had landed through an upper window. The room was burning bright. So I rushed over, banged open the door, tore up the stairs and found a (very attractive) young mum, with baby, in the stone-floored kitchen where the bomb had landed.

The thing to do was to stop fiery fragments that the bomb was spreading from catching the rest of the room (including the nappies on the drying rack) on fire. So with what I thought at the time was notable initiative I seized the baby's metal chamber pot and put it over the little bomb. Rather to my surprise, this proved effective. Between us we dowsed the smouldering nappies. I bid a heroic farewell to the beautiful mum and rushed downstairs in search of more derring-do. Incidentally noticing at the foot of the stairs a perfectly good bucket of sand which might have done the job rather better.

At first the incendiaries simply sprayed burning fragments wherever they landed. Later on there was an added ingredient, an explosive charge which burst on one of us just as he was trying to put one out. He landed for a while in hospital while the rest of us carried on, and then came back to work. The bigger (high explosive) bombs arrived with a rushing sound and a whine and blasted holes in buildings (including our tenement block) or brought them lurching down. At first it was only the terraced houses that were entirely wrecked. Then came the *landmines*, parachuted, silent, exploding at ground level, not penetrating deep. We got up one morning to discover the whole of Exmouth Street, nearby, laid flat.

We were being reinforced by all sorts of part-timers, mainly from amongst the British Federation of Young Co-operators, coming to work at weekends or occasional weeknights.

I put together a pocket-sized booklet, '*The Complete Conchie and Blitzgoer's Guide*' with all the information we could muster from our own experience, and from the advice we got from the Save the Children Fund, a Ministry of Health Welfare Inspector, a medical post nurse, and an architect. We included addresses and phone numbers of every kind of support agency describing exactly what help there might be on offer.

Here are some specimens of what we had to offer.

STREET WORK

Your dungarees protect you from jagged glass, flying splinters and spray; they stand up well to dives for cover. Your gumboots are invaluable in clambering over debris, they keep your legs dry, they insulate you against electric shock from bombed mains and they protects your second most vulnerable part from liquid gas. Your eye shield enables you get close to the centre of a fire without your eyes becoming too hot. ... Your gloves are essential in entering bombed houses through broken windows as you can grasp the jagged edges with impunity; they will also stand up to burning wood or paint for some time and are very useful in beating out flames on clothing.

Emergency canteening for night blitzes. The following will provide us at once with supplies of hot drinks and usually food, in their own containers, for emergency cases in the area from Christian Street to Free Trade Wharf and from the river to Commercial Road: Paddy's Goose, St. Georges 1941 Club, the Watney Arch canteen, the Old Mahogany Bar mission, the Bernard Baron settlement. The Mahogany Bar will provide raw materials for making up hot drinks and sandwiches if we have to make the stuff up ourselves nearer to the incident.

Firefighting. Don't waste time helping at a fire if there are already a few Auxiliary Firemen there unless they are very shorthanded or there is additional danger of which they are unaware. The best thing for incendiaries is sand, if you can get any, in preference to water unless the fire caused by the incendiary is a greater danger than the incendiary itself. Carry a sandbag or a tub of sand in front of your face, double up as you approach the incendiary and get away as quickly as you can after you have smothered it. Every basket of incendiaries may have one or more explosive charges in it. These usually take up to two minutes to explode. Wounds caused are very dangerous as thermite and magnesium quickly cause blood poisoning. If an incendiary drops in the street, you would be wise to wait those two minutes unless you think the danger to yourself is counterbalanced by the aircraft above picking out a light and bombing it. If there are no other fires in the vicinity and an aircraft appears to be approaching or circling, the light of bomb is dangerous; otherwise not. In dealing with an incendiary indoors use an overturned table or a mattress or a wardrobe as a shield. Endeavour to put the incendiary out with sand first, or with the spray from the stirrup pump (the ribbed end of the trigger) and risk the possibility of the incendiary exploding. If the fire is already underway, use your jet (the smooth end of the pump trigger) directed at the smouldering fabric around. Don't direct the jet at the incendiary or it is liable to burst.

Rescue Work: Remember when attempting to get at people imprisoned under the debris of their house that the material covering them or blocking the way may easily be the only support of the roof or ceiling above you.

If you can, approach the debris from the side of the house furthest from the crater; get to the back of a house by crossing through the house next door and climbing over the back fence. In this way investigation may be carried out under partly collapsed floors which are inaccessible from the front.

In many cases it is better to enter by a window. After blasting, most windows of the sliding sash type have the beading shattered all round the frame. The sashes will be loose and the glass broken so do not risk lifting them. Pull the sashes down, cut through the cords and remove the whole window.

If the front door of the house proves too strong to break down and the windows are inaccessible investigate the basement. (NB never take a Warden's word about the impossibility of getting into a house – INITIATIVE OPENS MOST DOORS!!)

If you get some leave try the London Youth Hostel, 84 Highgate West Hill, phone Mountview 1831. Bus or tube to Highgate Archway. 611 bus to Highgate Village. One shilling bed, 1/3d supper, 10d. breakfast or 1d. for gas if you cook your own, 4d. hire for sleeping bag.

SHELTER WORK

Shelter welfare. If you are a resident marshal, endeavour to get children washing and gargling regularly, get them inoculated against diphtheria and see that shelterers remove their bedding, sweep round and beneath their own bunks and spray disinfectant. … Try to form crèche space for babies under two and a children's corner for children over two so that part of the shelter is quiet enough for children to go to sleep. Maybe attempt to form an old people's bay separate from younger people who wish to talk, play darts etc. until later hours.

Suspected infectious or verminous person – contact nurse at district medical post

Suspected verminous bedding, bunks, walls – notify nearest Wardens' post, with details, and whether bedding is abandoned or not.

Burns and scalds – severe: treat for shock. Dry dressing. Send for doctor.

Cuts – If dirty cleanse in weak solution of iodine (1 in 100). Place small strips of elastoplast across cut to draw edges together instead of stitches. Dry dressing.

Shelter Children's Centres – Learn the children's names as soon as possible. … Let each group concentrate on one occupation … but when the time comes to change, do not be too exacting. If a child is absorbed in making something, never stop him as it is far better for him to stick to one thing if he can. If anything is lost, never accuse a particular child of having stolen it. Suggest instead that they should all turn out their pockets and turn out your own as well. … If a child is being a nuisance don't ignore him. He is probably only trying to make himself felt and would rather be scolded than ignored. Try to do neither. Find out what he wants to do and help him to do it. Never scold a child. Just say firmly, 'I'm afraid you can't do that here.' … Children who want power should be given younger ones to look after. Aggressives should be given special responsible jobs to do – collecting up the plasticine or giving out the drawing pads; they will respond to being treated like grownups.

Find out about facilities for organised rambles, excursions etc. which shelterers could join and get out of the blitz area for a few hours.

Encourage people in the shelter to make your own job unnecessary, i.e. for shelterers to run the shelter for themselves.

GAS

Clothing: Ordinary clothes give ten minutes immunity against vapour and slight splashes of blister gasses. But they retain the gas and there's danger of suffering from traces of gas if mask is removed before clothes are taken off. Wet clothes gives protection against phosgene but increase the danger of mustard gas which dissolves in water and therefore remains long in the clothes.

INVASION

The experience of refugee workers in France and in the Netherlands suggests that the biggest danger is the possible herding of refugees into fields, exposed to aerial machinegun fire, so that the roads may be kept clear for military traffic

Shelter, lean-to sheds or tents well under cover of woods or copses rather than on a clear site running the risk of machine gunning from the air. It is more important to ensure a dry surface to sleep on than a roof above one's head.

Feeding – cooking in the open is best done by means of fire trench, built to the leeward of the camp, well away from trees. The line of the trench should be on the line of the prevailing wind. There should be a runway at the wind end with a sheet of tin or wood for use as a damper if the wind is too fierce.

Our days were eventful, most of the time. So you didn't dwell much on what had happened, even quite recently, or what might lie ahead, when there was so much worth noticing here and now. This was part of what might be called an undergraduate approach to life (and death; and destruction). Within the shelters there seemed to be something of the same fellow-feeling; even amongst older people; even amongst those who had lost their homes, and sometimes their relatives. It didn't do to show anxiety. Fear, all-of-a-sudden as you heard the bomb in transit through the upper air, was momentary and afterwards, relief tended to expunge those feelings. Emotions, said the poet I read at school, can be recollected in tranquillity but tranquil was not the word to apply. More often with the likes of us, incomers, young and full of vim, it felt then and after to be the time of our lives.

From the very beginning it was obvious that we were doing something useful, and in its way rewarding. But there was no specific end in sight. So early on I sat at the top of the stairs in Paddy's Goose, where there was a working telephone, and rang my tutor back in Cambridge to explain that I would not be returning to resume my studies. He said it was quite all right, he was sure I would be considered as on *active service* and entitled to return when the war was over.

So that was one link dealt with. The other was a letter from Christine after Term began, saying that she and others had gone round to where they thought I would be in College. After the intense socialising and the transfer to outside digs in the previous year, there had been a chance to opt for a different base in my third year. I had got the promise of a little room over the main archway as you entered College. It was reached by a narrow winding staircase which I thought would be enough to deter most of the people otherwise wanting to stop over to socialise en route to and from dinner in Hall. Now, at the beginning of term, there was my name painted at the foot of the staircase, just as for everyone else's rooms, to show where I would be living.

But I wasn't there. So far as I was concerned that chapter had ended.

Christine's letter got no reply.

Chapter Seven

BREATHING SPACE

May 10th 1941. I had just begun a two-day leave, care of a hospitable Quaker, in a Hampshire village. That evening we stood in his garden listening to the drone of many bombers and the ack-ack barrage, watching the wide horizon turn slowly red as the fires took hold. It looked and sounded the very worst so far and continued until the firelight merged imperceptibly with the dawn.

I got back that morning and found the others in the Unit, a bit bomb-happy, but otherwise safe, and apart from some minor lesions, sound. Some had been out and about as usual, on patrol and at the first aid posts in the shelters. Others, in our top flat, had survived a direct hit two floors down with nothing worse than shattered windows and ceilings, and a pile of debris burying my portable typewriter (second-hand, all of six pounds ten shillings!).

That night's raid surpassed anything anyone had seen before. Many of us began to think that it signalled *the beginning of the end.* We went on expecting more raids on the same scale. Instead, the bombing stopped almost completely. The bombers' attention turned to *the Russian Front.*

As what we had thought was just a pause in the bombing continued, month after month, we began to realise that the work in hand was changing. People were less and less inclined to spend their daytime in Rest Centres and their nights in the shelters. Everyone was changing gear.

Our day and night time jobs got us on easy, friendly terms with youngsters like ourselves. Older people were matey, too. Together we were helping to patch up some of the physical damage, to people as well as buildings.

There were now ten Pacifist Service Units operating in bombed cities, four of them within London. In each we found ourselves up against the aftermaths of the raids.

All these efforts tided things over, until the Authorities got back in charge and tidied their filing systems. But underlying the physical damage and the feelings of social solidarity in coping with it together, there were breakdowns in everyday family life: *broken homes* and *problem families.*

Evacuation plus call-up were breaking traditional family ties. Youngsters, according to their elders, were getting *out of hand*. Husbands, called up, were out of touch.

As an adventurous 22-year-old, I could respond to the physical effects of the bombing, and I could see how some people were losing their bearings. I reported accordingly:

> The contacts we made in our emergency work led to a whole series of cases – destitution, malnutrition, illegitimacy, desertion, wife beating, alcohol poisoning, prostitutes – in the majority of these we were called in, as friends, either by the 'case' or by the neighbours. We are able to advise, arbitrate, intercede with the authorities or local charities. Much more important we aim to get down to the practical work of scrubbing floors, de-lousing, tending the sick, moving house – and by practical example we are persuading our friends to start over again, to raise their standard of living... It is neighbourliness, not the dispensing of charity that we are after. The result has been that both authorities and voluntary organisations have plied us with cases, and at the same time our old cases have been referring their friends to us when they are in trouble.

I could see what was going wrong but I was out my depth when it came to dealing with the damage being done to family life.

Recently we had a new member, Arthur Collis. Coming fresh he could see that we were still needed, but less concerned with danger to life and limb, responding more to the trauma beneath the surface.

We had learned, along with others in the community, to get a grip on the System – the ways in which local and central government were reviving, repairing, replacing administrative routines. We could see some of things that could be done to fill in the gaps which still remained, to spot and improvise the services that were most needed. It was back to the things Ethel Upton had been doing all her working life. I could see that all this made sense, but at the time, it seemed, for me, second best.

The carnage of war was for the most part abroad: at sea, under it, on foreign soil – Europe, the top of Africa, the Far East.

Abroad was where I wanted to be.

At one point, as Lex Miller and I sat together on a bus, I began to unload my feelings. As a fellow pacifist and the Church of Scotland minister at St. Paul's, he was staying on. I was wondering whether to *join up* and get into the RAF like my friend Guy Somerset. But wondering was as far as I had got.

Lex listened, but chose not to comment. Explaining to him how I felt, I began to glimpse the difference between feelings and conviction. That left me still wanting to be up and doing, but deciding it was time to move on.

Arthur Collis gradually took over. Concern was increasingly with young survivors amid the debris of the bombing, and what the aftermath of the Blitz was doing to families, in particular what was happening to youngsters on the loose. Eventually the PSU turned into the FSU – Family Service Units, which have survived, without fuss, into the twenty-first century.

I had come across members of that Quaker-founded Friends Ambulance Unit who were based, whilst they waited for assignments, in a large (and we thought rather comfortable) building just off Commercial Road that had previously served as the Students' Hostel for London University. Locally it was better known as *the Conchie Ritz.*

Previously I had assumed, without really thinking it through, that they would be too closely linked with the military. I began to see from what I heard of the FAU's work in Burma, on the Western Desert and in China that there was a case for co-existence. In the field, where everyone could see what they were up against, the military were inclined to put up with, even to welcome, people who did not see eye-to-eye with them on military action, but who showed they could tackle some of its ill effects.

I made enquiries, applied, was accepted on my record so far, and transferred from the PSU to the FAU. I went as a new recruit, to the Unit's fifteenth training camp and was made a section leader – one of half a dozen sections of ten each very much like the PSU outfit I had left.

The difference, now, was that I no longer had to be wheeling and dealing, improvising under pressure, making the most of the unexpected. I found all this refreshing, like a lull in the bombing. In other respects belonging to the FAU, at this stage, yielded much the same serio-comic commitment. Serious because of what might lie ahead; comic because we were mostly young, off-beat, irreverent, in for a bit of horseplay if things got too dull; and committed, like everyone else in the warring world, to keep going *for the duration*.

Comfortably hutted in our Bourneville training camp, helpfully supported by the Quaker Cadburys, we learnt to stand at ease, or at attention, and to march in step so that we would not look too shambolic if we had to line up alongside soldiers marching in a theatre of war. We did not, however, learn to give or return salutes; but we got used to observing a short quiet time together, each day, Quaker-fashion where we were all, trainers included, on a level.

Our first concern was to become really reliable first-aiders, with a bit of basic fire-fighting and elementary cooking thrown in. In between these doings, we listened to visitors describing what they knew at first hand of famines, routine disasters, and coping with the unexpected.

We kept regular hours, ate and slept reasonably well and could leave decision-making to our top brass, people like ourselves who had mostly *been through it* and knew what all of us might be in for. So this was an unexpected breathing space.

When our basic training was complete, we dispersed to reinforce the learning process with some practical service in one of the hospitals which had agreed to take on Unit members as *ward orderlies*, doing dogsbody jobs, but picking up some of the realities of hospital work in the process.

So the breathing space continued, with all but the most routine decision-making done by other people.

My first assignment was to St. James' Hospital in Balham where several of us were apprenticed to a formidable Ward Sister. Under her rule we made beds, emptied urine and faeces (under rather more hygienic conditions than we had met *Underneath the Arches* in Shadwell) and occasionally laid out the dead. We learnt about *ward discipline*, and also enjoyed the teamwork, particularly with some of the younger nurses.

This led, for two of us, to a spell in the operating theatre, where we cleaned out the sinks, fed the steriliser, and if we were very good, were allowed to *scrub up*. This meant donning sterilised gowns and gloves, facing the surgeon across the operating table, and handing him or her the tools of their trade. So in this way I helped the surgeon to remove an appendix or two, taking the place (under her vigilant gaze) of the Theatre Sister.

She was as formidable as the Sister who oversaw us in the Ward. But as a very attractive young redhead she also had an eye on the socialising possibilities her Theatre might offer. At Christmas an ex-patient who ran a pub presented the team with a case of his best. Our Theatre was twinned with another, and on special occasions one closed while the other kept going. So we invited everyone within reach to a Christmas party in our Theatre during one of its off-periods.

We decorated the Theatre with festoons of bandage dipped in gentian violet or iodine and everything went very well with lots of laughter and some spontaneous singing. I noticed at one stage the Theatre Sister laying flat out on the floor; out, I thought, for the count. Then, with a sudden increase in the local bombing, we were called on to cut short our off-period, and cope with a surplus of emergency admissions.

At this point the Theatre Sister arose, apparently unscathed, put on her sterilised gown and gloves and resumed her job beside the operating table. Business as usual.

Allowing for Emergencies and other excitements, there was still time for everyday life. That included making friends. In particular Maria, a Staff Nurse qualified in Poland, who had fled the invading German army, leaving behind her *best friend*, a German living in Poland who chose to side with the invaders. We got on together, as she told me about him, and then about herself, and began to take a passing interest in me. And so it went on, *walking out* together, getting used to our different outlooks and upbringing, finding ourselves on the edge of being in love.

Then my stint in the hospital was completed. We stayed in touch whilst I went to another hospital for an attachment with a little bit more responsibility, and after that to an *advanced field training* scheme run by the FAU, in borrowed premises on Highgate Hill.

There we were on the *qui vive*, ready at short notice to go to major *incidents* anywhere in the country as part of *Air Raid Emergency Relief.* There were lectures, we did PT in the large back garden, and between times listened to two Donalds (one of them Donald Swann) side by side at a conveniently available grand piano doing everything from ragtime to classics via honky-tonk.

We spent one day by courtesy of Lord Rothschild (who had a Jewish background and Quaker sympathies) on the grounds of his estate, in a *refugee exercise* to simulate what we might expect abroad (or at home if the war went that way) and we had to respond to the real thing.

We shared the exercise with a group of young Jewish relief workers. We took turns in the parts of workers and refugees. The Jewish group had the morning to be relief workers and we became French villagers and returning refugees in *a devastated area*. We entered into our parts as French villagers with zest. We were inclined to get a bit of fun out of everything we did. One of us found a large wheelbarrow and wandered around with it proclaiming to everyone '*Je suis l'entrepreneur des pompes funèbres*', getting a laugh wherever he went. The Jewish relief workers coped with this situation, and went through all the proper motions of sorting us out, identifying needs, making arrangements, with a kind of detached good humour.

In the second half of the day it was our turn to be the relief workers and this time we were placed on the fringe of woodlands in Rothschild's great park. We busied ourselves in sorting out what should be done with the refugees – when we could find them. But there was no one apparent until gradually in ones and twos, they emerged from among the trees, exhausted, bewildered, not knowing where to go or what to expect. And this time it began to be real, not just a staged simulation. For some of them had been refugees, from the war which overtook them where they lived in Belgium, France – and Poland. So they, unlike us, knew exactly what it was all about.

That night they invited up back to a party in which they danced and sang, joyfully and at times sadly, of their longings for a place of their own in a country where they could belong.

We found ourselves for almost the first time in a learning situation.

We went on waiting to know where we would be going and what we would be doing, at home or abroad, not just for once in a while, but as a long-term assignment. One morning, most of the group were called away to a major *incident* in Plymouth. I was regretting being left behind, and then I learnt that this was because two of us were to go abroad, first to North Africa, and then to somewhere in the Mediterranean, where *action* beckoned.

When the course was over we marked time for a little, billeted in a vacant ward of the Middlesex Hospital, waiting to know our fate. Some bright researcher seized the opportunity to recruit four of us to reproduce the effects of blood loss and shock in the Western Desert. This involved lying flat on an operating theatre trolley whilst the researcher inserted a very thin tube in an available vein, and kept on pushing it along until it reached one's heart. Meanwhile another vein was being tapped for rather more than the traditional blood donation. This *blood loss* was coupled with exposure to extremes of heat, and then cold (bare feet in a bucket of icy water). All this was meant to simulate the effects of a body wound and accompanying *shock*. The researchers monitored our bodily reactions, watched us pass out (temporarily) and then revived us with the usual cup of tea and biscuits that rewarded blood donors. There was some risk attached, which allowed us to think that we could respond to *real* emergencies, and be, in a small way, *heroic*.

Maria and I were still going out together, and suddenly this would be for the last time before I left.

During that something-and-nothing period, and for a few months afterwards, I kept a diary. It has stayed unread until I began to write this book. So I have to think myself back and try to recognise the sort of person I was then, a couple of generations ago.

September 2nd 1943 Lyons Brasserie, Coventry Street. Maria

The second time I sit beside a girl whilst she cries. Once it was like some incredible practical joke: a park bench on a misty night in Cambridge, three years ago, me in gown, clutching a tattered square under one arm. Anne leant across a far-from-manly chest, crying because the struggle between dignity and the impact of varsity life was for a moment unequal, because we liked each other a lot, and goodness knows why, for five minutes she had got herself in love. And me? Looking across her hair at a watery moon above the housetops and feeling like something out of a poor and tasteless musical comedy. ...

And now, in the bustle and blousy commotion of these tinsel surroundings, Maria sits and talks quietly whilst the tears gather, poise themselves and flow down one by one. This is, we suppose, the end of our year's acquaintance. ... we have played at loving each other in a mild park-bench kind of way, admitting to each other that we are neither of us in love, and in seeking the mirage of distant or imaginary sweethearts have found an illusionary comfort; a sop to our mutual solitariness. Now, after a day of half-confidings, we sit with a bottle of cheap and nasty wine between us, and begin to talk desperately against time. Our hardness was dissolved before her tears came to melt it and in this moment of quietness and fragile dignity, she cries for the German boy whose love she has lost and I, comforting her, wish only that we could find our ways to love each other. Then leaving the blare of light and chatter, we walk sadly and a little sheepishly to the station and a goodbye kiss.

I joined some thirty other Unit members on a troop train to Gouroch Dock, outside Glasgow, to embark for foreign parts. Most of us were still relatively inexperienced, taking everything as we found it, including the opportunities for anything off-beat. At Gouroch we learnt there would be *just a few hours delay*. So some of us went back into Glasgow by tram to visit the local Turkish baths, managing the whole thing just in time to embark, feeling that all such luxuries would now lie behind us.

This notion was underlined on the voyage. We had to go far out to the Atlantic on a detour to avoid U-boats, and the troops were required to take turns on *U-boat watch*. However the thirty of us in the FAU, being still pretty doctrinaire about alternatives to military service, felt that this crossed the borderline. Our officer in charge managed to negotiate an alternative – taking turns as scullions in the ship's galley. The quartermaster sergeant major cook in charge took his responsibilities seriously. He remained affable whilst assigning us the dirtiest jobs he could find. In particular scouring out the enormous tureens in which the daily stew was heated.

Many of our group retired to their bunks, seasick, but a few of us kept sickness more or less at bay by walking up and down on the deck, hour after hour whilst the ship zigzagged out into the Atlantic to dodge the U-boats.

October 30th, Saturday (I think). Lord know where in the Atlantic

750 dinners of apricots and stewed fat steaks. Alan and I had to go up to the deck once or twice for fresh air and Alan began to part with his breakfast. I had done rather well – two boiled eggs and plenty of cornflakes, and fought a long drawn out battle to retain them in spite of the evident desire by a crude-minded quartermaster sergeant major that I should give up. In the end everything was finished and all my sinks and pans cleaned up. Nearly everyone had gone and I was turning to go when my hour came upon me. I turned on both taps into my newly scoured tureen ...

November 3rd, Gibraltar

When we draw into the Straits, it was almost evening. Tarafia was a soft flat pastel picture on our port quarter. A Czech officer lent me his field glasses and the little town suddenly assumed its third dimension, tower, mosque and terraces of whitewashed houses stood against a purpley-green hillside of granite and scrub. The sun began to go down, a great flaming penny sliding suddenly into its terrestrial slot. Whilst it was still poised on the horizon, the convoy swung into line ahead. We stood and watched from the pig bins in the stern as the line of nearly a dozen ships stood silhouetted in diminishing perspective against that vast red disk, sailing over waters of blue and purple and magenta and green. Behind them the Spanish foothills and the Rock of Gibraltar and beyond, the Mountains of the Moon receding until they could barely be distinguished from the streamers of powder-pale cloud beyond.

November 6th, Algiers

I was an orderly in the galley when we reached our first anchorage and emerged to find Algiers looking like a drop-scene, flat, drab and rather trite. Terraces of white, clean-seeming (but very deceptively so) houses above a series of mock Moroccan picture palaces which turned out to

> be the French Government buildings. Then the galley called and we dived down. When we came up again we had moved into the quayside. The drop scenery had become an incredibly detailed peepshow panorama. Quays surrounded us on three sides with immediately in front of us a huge battlefield of a quayside covered with odd piles of stores and huddles of lorries and men like a vast assembly of uncounted loot. We stood about on deck watching this go on below us for two hours and then filed down devious alleys to the gangway and dry land – to become ourselves a detail in the picture for another three hours. On ground level there was little to see of the Algerian terraces. But for one solitary palm tree growing in a corner between warehouse sheds, we might have been in Liverpool or Cardiff. Especially when it began to rain.

Landing in Algiers the thirty of us formed up to march to our billets, only to find that no one knew where we were to be billeted. The problem was in part that our destination, across the top of Africa, was to be with the Free French in Rabat and in Algiers most of the military and civilian arrangements were in the hands of a different kind of French administration, rooted in the previous regime.

We formed up behind our own Quaker officer, partnered by the French military liaison officer who had been assigned to cope. After a short march through the streets in the pouring rain we came to a halt. There was a lively dispute between the French officer and an unidentified colleague. They were arguing about our destination. It appeared that we were not really expected. So we all marched back again. After some discussion it was decided that as foreigners we were really the responsibility of the Foreign Legion. So we landed up at the Legion's barracks. We were assigned our quarters and told that all visits to the latrines should be in pairs. There was danger that we would be knifed by Zouaves, fellow members of the Legion but looked down on by French personnel; and in turn inclined to take it out on anyone resembling them.

Nevertheless there was some *camaraderie*. Four of us accepted the invitation to go on a tour of the alleyways in the Kasbah, which in those days were more accessible than they are today – so long as you knew who to go with.

November 10th Kasbah, Algiers

> We walked about for a couple of hours, down the main street of the prostitutes, Rue de la Fouchette, curving round the compass, each door marked with a giant number in white paint, and below, the girl who

dealt there, half naked , most already beginning to age and coarsen. One door alone had no number and above it was a dirty card with the legend, Maison Honnête, belied by one girl sitting stark naked inside. Elsewhere there was suddenly a formal classroom, with a class of children packed tight upon the floor, droning their response to the insistent recital of their teacher.

In between, all sorts of tiny shops, and occasional coffee rooms scarcely big enough to house a brood of chickens, Arabs sitting solemn on the floor, watching the world go by.

Up a steep alleyway of steps an old women suddenly burst out of her doorway and shouted at some urchins below; then spat, strong and vehemently at them; and they ran away. In the darkness up three more flights of steps a donkey browsed among the piles of garbage.

At long last we got our Movement Order for the journey across the top of Africa to Rabat. We began to feel that we knew our way around and could cope with the unexpected. This proved useful once we embarked on the train where we were assigned seats in the passenger compartments, but nothing much else in the way of essential services. This was luxury compared with the low-sided open trucks into which Arabs were overcrowded and the covered cattle trucks containing Zouaves, Senegalese and a few French volunteers still in civvies, who had recently been liberated from Spanish prisons and from Corsica. Few had overcoats and all were very cold at night, whilst we, and a section of French officers, stayed warm in our greatcoats.

November 12th

Soon after leaving Algiers – whilst still in its suburbs, we stopped. Getting out to stretch our legs we heard murmurings and saw Frenchmen getting down from the cattle trucks to gather stones and throwing them at Italian prisoners working on the line nearby. The leading spirits were recently liberated Corsicans and when the train moved on stones continued to be thrown whilst most of the prisoners tried to take shelter. As we passed the level crossing one Italian prisoner remained firm and in full view, his arm raised in a Fascist salute.

There were only eight of us in our compartment. That night it was very cold and two French privates from one of the cattle trucks were preparing to doss down in the corridor outside our door. I suggested that we invite them in and after ten minutes debate this was agreed and they were very pleasant company. Next morning the rest of the FAU were worried about our setting a precedent whereby they might be expected to share their own space. Our officer feared that French officers would not approve and after much talk there was a general ruling prohibiting strangers from entering the English compartments. We explained the decision with much regret to our guests. They were very nice about it but we spent the next night with rather more comfort for our bodies and rather less for our consciences.

There were frequent stops, sometimes in open country, more often beside a village from which people came to bargain with all sorts of usually delicious food. The journey took several days and we got used in the mornings at a random stop to ambling up the line to the engine where we could negotiate with the driver for our shaving water hot from the boiler.

One stop, longer than usual, happened, we discovered, because there was a difference of opinion between the engine driver and the local stationmaster. The difference was about our destination. We listened to the discussion as it became more heated and finally intervened to say that so far as we were concerned our destination was Rabat, via Tunis and Tripoli. This confident assertion settled the argument in favour of the engine driver and on we went.

Eventually this feeling of freedom coupled with ability to take the initiative prompted us to go into local villages in search of additional food, and one member got left behind when the engine driver started up again. We discovered this about thirty kilometres further on when we got to Tunis but were able to convince the engine driver that he should take us all back to the previous stopping point to pick our fellow member up.

After that our self-confidence knew hardly any bounds, until we arrived, some days later at Rabat where there was a base camp for the Free French hospital unit most of the others in the Unit were due to join. Here I met up with one of an earlier contingent of the FAU who had been attached to the Hadfield Spears surgical unit and seen real service in the Western Desert. Sam Marriage had been a miller, in a family business in Essex, not used to talking at length, but with an eye for anything a little bit out of the ordinary, especially if it was a little bit comic, not that he would go very far in laughing about it, or even venturing a sly grin. He had no illusions to speak of, having seen conscientious assenters to the war, the soldiers in action in the desert, and knowing that in their way they saw life, and dealt with it, much as we did, although with rather more first hand experience of the worst as well as the best aspects of the human race.

He and I were to be detached for a different kind of job, elsewhere in the Mediterranean.

Meanwhile our hosts were the colonial French, who were a bit of an eye-opener.

November 16th

This afternoon I first saw the French penal system in action. Three Senegalese were loaded with blankets full of earth and marched up and down the allée behind the grandstand. This went on throughout the afternoon until dusk at about 6pm and through most of the next day. Various other Frenchmen looked on and the party was conducted by the Senegalese NCO under the direction of an unshaven ex Legionnaire. To vary the business they were made to crawl, run at the double, stand at attention or at ease, or shoulder imaginary arms. Ken Duck who had seen the business first of all, said that whilst he was there the ex Legionnaire was kicking the Senegalese in the balls when they dropped down and then knocking them down again. Whilst I was there I saw him strike one more than once and I noticed the smallest Negro crying. He also had an ugly cut on the head. I found the whole business unspeakably degrading but stayed dead still at the end of the allée watching in the hope that the more presence of a foreigner would help to cut down the manhandling at least. Whether or not this was the reason, there was no more hitting. … At 8 am the next morning I met the party coming out for another day's 'justice' and I went up to the Legionnaire and asked him why this was done. He replied indifferently that there had been 'quelque bêtise' and I said I had seen that sort of thing in Germany but was surprised to see it here. Short of behaving in a Christian manner and either knocking him down or helping the smallest Negro with his bag of earth, there seemed nothing a good FAU-er could do.

When the FAU Section heard of my action, there were similar worries to those occasioned by our inviting the two Frenchmen to sleep in the spare spaces in our compartment on the journey here. But there were a few who felt even a protest such as mine cleared the air a little. … That night (our last before Sam and I were to leave for Algiers) some of us found a pub just outside the camp. We were joined by a couple of Frenchmen and one asked me if it had been I standing in the alleyway and looking disgusted. I said yes, and repeated that I was surprised at the Allies doing this kind of thing which was more suited to Nazis. The

> FAU-ers, especially Sam Marriage and Fleming, the old-timers, looked a bit worried and Sam rushed in with an involved funny story that kept his end of the table amused whilst I and the Frenchman had a fortunately very amicable discussion. It turned out that he was sympathetic to our point of view, though he stuck to the view that it was 'the only way to deal with the blacks'. However we both listened to each other with some sympathy and no one seemed a penny the worse for our daring to broach the topic.
>
> Next morning I was not so sorry as I might have been that Sam and I were to be off next day. ... It remains to be seen how long the small minority like Ken and Derek and myself can last out without us landing up to our necks in well-intentioned hot water.

The train that Sam and I were embarked on consisting entirely of cattle trucks, with the floor to sleep on. A cattle truck provides a much better view of the countryside when the sliding doors are wide open, and the air circulation is that much better, too. The driver of this train was not so adept at making village stops for refreshment, but we had our rather boring C rations to fall back on. Hard tack, but edible. What everyone principally lacked was an improvement on the water in our water bottles as drink. The first night out Sam produced two battered billycans, one larger than the other, which became a brazier, fuelled by bits of coal from the engine driver, and scraps of thorn bush picked up when the train came to rest. Once the brazier began to burn, it was slung just below the threshold of our wagon's sliding door, maybe half a metre above the rails, where it could get a good airflow. Lying on the floor, with our heads just poking out, we could see to refuelling it to boil up water in the second billycan. Sam, of course, had a supply of tea and milk powder in his dunnage and from then on we had hot tea whenever we chose. At first it was just the people in our wagon that benefited. Then those next door. On the third night, as the train negotiated a bend we could see a line of fairy lights along its length, with every wagon's billycan on the boil.

Chapter Eight

LEARNING ON THE JOB

We hung about until there was floor space in a transport plane from Tunis to Sicily. After the North African desert Sicily was like adventuring across the mountains of the moon. Steep hills, jagged cliffs, hamlets and little townships perched on the cliffs' edge. Narrow valleys with sparse cultivation edging upwards as far as mules could go. Then, the plain around the coastal city of Catania, riddled with shell and bomb craters, where we were to be based.

Back home the Cadbury clan and other *weighty Friends* (as Quakers called their leading lights) had negotiated a working relationship between the likes of us and the military establishment responsible for coping with civilian survivors. So we were attached to what had once been called the Allied Military Government of Occupied Territory – AMGOT for short, until it was learnt that AMGOT was the Turkish word for manure. So now we belonged to the Allied Commission, and for want of anywhere else to put us, we were billeted with the 66th General Hospital, on the top of the hill overlooking the city.

Each day we walked down, through busily reviving civilian activity, to the offices of the Commission. We had the advantage that no one had precisely defined our status, or for that matter what we were going to do. So we were absorbed within the officer class, and even saluted occasionally by Other Ranks who knew no better.

We were replacing two other FAU members who had managed to fit themselves into the system without attracting undue notice, and for that matter without actually being assigned to anything very demanding. Fortunately for us we were attached to an open-minded American major, and later on a British colonel, neither of whom was clear about our functions, and therefore willing to allow us to spell out what we could be doing – and get on with it.

Our be-all was to find out what needed to be done about the refugees, flowing down from mainland Italy in dribs and drabs, sometimes in hordes, and finding themselves foisted on poverty-stricken Sicilian villages already suffering the devastation caused by the Allied and German bombardments during the Sicilian campaign. There were shortages everywhere, and the refugees' invasion made them worse.

Sicilians, based in their mountain fastnesses were looked down on by people from the Italian mainland. In the top half of Italy there was an up-market definition of the difference between Us, living in *Alt Italia* (meaning High or north) and Them – the Other lot, of much less importance, labelled *Altro Italia*. This attitude was up-ended in Sicily where locals saw anyone from the mainland as either fair prey or a faceless bureaucrat. Sometimes both.

Neither the American major nor his British colonel knew quite what to do about the situation, fraught with anger and potential aggro. There were now three of us, with Colin Giffard, detached from one of the FAU's surgical units reinforcing us. We were dispersed, each equipped with a requisitioned car and a driver, respectively to Palermo, Agrigento, and, for me, on the hop between inland Ragusa and Syracuse, Catania and Messina on the coast.

The idea, well suited to the military mind, was to undertake a *reconnaissance.* So I found myself making raids inland to those mountain top townlets where the sanitation consisted in letting it all slip down the rocky slopes to find its own level in the valley below. More often than not these were the places, conveniently far from more comfortably placed military and civilian administrations in the big cities, that refugees were being dumped. (Much as incoming asylum seekers nowadays get shifted away from prosperous suburbs to be lumped with residents on their uppers in *deprived areas.*)

The three of us, each exploring the terrain, free-range, had no problem in reconnoitring the problems on the ground. Not just the problems, but also the opportunities. So almost imperceptibly we became doers, rather than observers, using the vague status conferred by our attachment to Military Government to wheel and deal with each self-sufficient unit of local government. The refugees coming from the devastated areas, shell-shocked, demoralised, assumed that as fellow-Italians they would be welcomed and helped to survive. For the most part, in the early days, there was no such welcome. The British and American Allies had established an Italian government, a shade more than a puppet government, but without much clout. Officially, there were outline requirements for the *host* communities to *accommodate* the incomers. Just what that meant in the way of practical aid was at best known, or partly known, to each local authority, presided over by the Sindaco, a sort of mayor. Getting accommodation, food, basic medication over to the refugees was haphazard. Some authorities did their best, and were appreciated. Others delayed, and tried to get by with the bare minimum of support, sometimes even less.

We went traipsing about the countryside inspecting makeshift refugee camps, finding out how much of the officially authorised support was missing, seeking out retrusive officials and telling them (with the borrowed authority of the Allied Commission) to make amends.

It turned out that the most effective assistance depended on first getting after the local authorities and then the few recently established local support agencies (which also tended to suffer from bureaucratic lethargy); and eventually helping the incomers to form their own self-help and local pressure groups. My Italian vocabulary – first centred on words needed when enquiring about the provision of latrines, bedding, bug powder – rapidly expanded to include phrases of exhortation. I would tell officials, *Bisogna spingere* – it's necessary to push things ahead, get a move on, etc. So I learnt from the friendlier of the officials I met that I had acquired a nickname, *lo spinto* – the pusher, the one who pokes the embers.

Basic accommodation meant not much more than a roof over refugees' heads and the food ration to be issued to refugees from the Sindaco's resources was seldom adequate, and sometimes completely missing.

I found myself giving a dressing-down to the Secretary of one local Sindaco because his local authority wasn't giving refugees a fair deal in food, bedding, care. He was a slightly-built elderly man who took it all with no more than a quizzical look at my outpourings, and then beckoned me over to his own house and said, '*See where I live. No proper water. Hardly any fuel for cooking. See my family's food cupboard. Almost empty. Look at me*'. At this point he lifted up his foot for me to see the gap in the sole through which the bare skin showed.

From the start we wanted to be doing something useful, not just telling other people what they should be doing. Here and there we found locals willing to have a go. We went the rounds of the allied military installations and scrounged old tents and other fabrics. We borrowed 30 cwt army trucks and took the loot to a little colony of nuns who sewed the scraps of fabric together to make quilts. One day, back at my desk in the Allied Commission offices, I was approached by a smartly dressed Sicilian from Messina. He had heard that we were short of medical supplies for refugees and others, in particular plaster of Paris to make casts for broken bones. He explained he was a small businessman, an entrepreneur, and he had dealings with the providers of *gesso*, the lime used on the walls of houses. With a little help, this could be converted. He got the help, reported progress on notepaper with an imposing heading, sent specimens, and ..... faded out. After that we were more careful to check up on entrepreneurs.

Later, wanting to make a case to the friendly, courteous, but not very well informed colonel in charge of the Allied Commission administration for the city of Catania, I talked things over with Francesca who did for me as a cleaner and occasional cook. *'Yes'*, she said, '*we Sicilians have always been poor, for the most part*' (always excepting the Mafiosi, the smugglers, and the members of the *intralazzo*, the informal network of black market businessmen – I thought to myself). Then she said, 'The women are selling off the *corredo*.' '*What's that?*' It was the contents of what in England we used to call the bottom drawer, the treasured bits and pieces put together over the years to become a kind of dowry a girl could take with her when she marries.

In Sicily there was a standard list of essentials, headed by the *lenzuoli*, the marital bed sheets, of fine linen. And these could still command a price on the open market. So with Francesca's help I got details of the market for bed sheets, and produced a statistic of the staggering increase in the volume of sales. I made a beautiful graph and took it to the colonel to convince him that people were actually in need. He alone could authorise and enforce a percentage increase in the level of support for all civilians.

It was the statistic that won him over. It meant rather more to the young women who were sacrificing their marriage portions in order to have enough to eat.

In mainland Naples, in the wake of the Allied advance northwards, the desolation left behind was compounded by a typhus epidemic. There were vaccines to spare in Sicily and I got the chance to combine a week's overdue leave with a trip to Naples carrying an emergency supply. Afterwards, filling out the paperwork in the top floor office of a city tower block I faced an official with his back to the window. Across his shoulder I could see the coast road, in the distance, military traffic rushing towards the war fronts. In the air above Capodochino airport a troop transport circled. Across the Bay of Naples, engineers were still blasting their way through the chaos left by the bombing of the docks. Dominating everything else was Mount Vesuvius with a wisp of smoke ascending from its crater. And then, as he went on talking, I saw the volcano erupt. A vertical stream of fire and dust straining up through a layer of red-tipped cirrus clouds, and then spreading out horizontally above them, coil after coil, as if ejected from a tube of discoloured shaving foam.

For once I was struck dumb, until the official noticed the break in our conversation and turned round to take it all in for himself.

Later, with a few days leave still left I went to the lower slopes of the mountain and watched as the glowing lava, from the volcano's mouth, house-high, advanced hesitantly down the steep mountainside at a snail's pace devouring the villages and vinyards in its path with a horrible deliberation.

I went on to see what had happened when Vesuvius erupted long ago, to what had been the prosperous suburb of Pompeii. There, in the middle of that desolation, I came upon a child. Actually he came on me, for he was playing 'tag' with another urchin, round the narrow alleyways of the ruined town, and he charged into me full tilt. Seeing an *Inglese* he forgot pleasure and turned at once to business.

He produced a batch of dog-eared picture postcards, and then felt deeper in the pockets of his cast-off American fatigue jacket and brought out a battered British Army tobacco tin. Inside it was an eggshell, carefully preserved in a scrap of cotton wool. Earlier that morning I had been nosing round the storehouse in which relics from Pompeii, unearthed by the archaeologists, were jumbled together. I guessed what this specimen was supposed to be.

When the excavators laid bare the ruins, they found that the light volcanic ash had taken the mould of everything it covered: the bodies of the housewives, the pots and pans in their kitchens, the loaves of bread in the larder, even the fish nets hanging on the wall.

I had seen eggshells amongst all these, in much the same state as what this youngster now offered me as *un ricordo* – a souvenir. '*Two thousand years old*', he said, with the understandable exaggeration of a good salesman who likes to talk in round figures. '*Worth at least a lira a year!*' – but, as he watched my unenthusiastic face, '*For you, Capitano, we make it 1500*'.

I wasn't convinced that the eggshell had been there in AD 70, but even if it had been, I wasn't much inclined to pay good occupation currency for it.

All the same, I couldn't resist the sheer commercial bravado he brought to his bargaining. So I bought a packet of postcards, and asked him about himself. Where did he live? '*Oh, anywhere*', he said. But his family? – they used to live in Cassino, pounded to pieces by bombardment (where the Allies and the Germans killed each other '*by the thousand*'), but they too were all dead now, he thought. When the worst was over he had found his way to an American unit which adopted him as their mascot, and eventually brought him back with them, on leave, to Naples. '*Are you still with them*?' There wasn't any answer. '*You got separated?*' – '*I was tired.*' He wouldn't explain any more and sat silent, and a little glum.

I began to ask him about Naples, the city; he brightened up and talked nineteen to the dozen of the great number of people that were there, and how many things to buy and sell, and how many soldiers of the *Alleati* would pay good money to have their shoes shined, or be shown the way to a pretty signorina.

This was the life it seemed, a bit more adventurous, with people a little more like those at home, than in the kindly, but somehow alien atmosphere of the American Mess which had adopted him.

Why was he here in this desolate place?

He looked around him at the bright emptiness. *'I like to come here, now and then'* he said, shrugged his shoulders, dismissed the subject.

'Will you go back?' I asked him, thinking of going back to the Americans. But his mind was on other things, and he was talking about Cassino when he said, *'After the war, when there are houses there again, then I will surely go back.'*

Later, looking for a peaceful spot to put up for the remaining days of my leave, I hitchhiked along the western coast of Italy until I came on a villa built against the cliff, with a little ornamental garden, overlooking a bay of clear blue sea.

There was a thin spiral of smoke coming from a chimney and I pushed through the wrought iron gate and knocked on the door. An old lady came out, big, buxom, face wrinkled by the weather and the years. I asked if it were possible to rent a room. She shrugged her shoulders. *'No one will stop you.'* I asked her about terms. She motioned me indoors to her kitchen. She hesitated. *'We shall continue to live here, will that be all right?'* I was taken aback. She took my hesitation anxiously. *'My husband is a fisherman, it is necessary that we continue to live here. We cannot move again.'* I couldn't understand what she was driving at. She took a deep breath and explained. *'We are sfollati – displaced persons. We do not belong here. The owner of this place was one of our nobility, and a fascist. Recently he left in a hurry. Our home was in a cottage further down the coast. But when the Americans came, they thought our house would be a good place from which to bathe; so they turned us out. They have people on leave there from time to time; but, after their fashion, they are kind. They saw this villa was empty and they said we could live here, for the time being. But we cannot move out again, for there is no other empty house in these parts.'* I mustered my Italian vocabulary again and explained that all I wanted was to rent a room for a day or two. We agreed on terms, and I moved in.

We were fellow-squatters and later that evening the old lady and her fisherman husband, tinkering with his nets beside the kitchen fire, invited me to take a little wine with them.

It was the first time they had to speak with an Anglo-Saxon who was neither a policeman nor a military billeting officer. Gradually they came to talk of the people they had watched pass down the coast road. First, the retreating coastal defence units of the Italian Fascist army. Then these had been taken over, at pistol point, by the Germans. Then, as the Germans retreated, the Italian partisans took over. After that, the French-officered Moroccans arrived, looking like the devils from hell. Then real French, and Poles, and Czechs, and British, and now finally, the Americans.

At first they just listed the bare facts. Then, a little less guarded, they made comparisons. The cold harshness of the Germans, the frigid reserve of the English, the buccaneering Americans, the piratical Fascisti. No bitterness, but speaking with almost pathetic caution of the remote future when there might be peace again, back home.

In the early evening, when the day's work was done, I noticed that the old lady would move off around the bay to the remains of a *rustic* summerhouse, to sit there and twirl her cotton bobbin and spin her coarse yarn. When I asked the old man what she went there for, he was embarrassed, a little contemptuous: '*These women, they have their ideas, you understand. Foolish but obstinate.*' And he changed the subject.

On my last day I came across the old lady on her evening visit. We went along together a little way, and she pointed past the barbed wire barrier with a notice prohibiting Italian civilians from entering. Uphill, on the other side overlooking the sea, was a neat stone cottage, deserted, a few deckchairs and some empty cola bottles still lying about. Sitting and spinning within the little summerhouse, her stolen home out of sight behind her, there was still the great sea stretching away to Corsica, and a touch of salt spray in the wind, just as she remembered.

My leave over, I hitched a truck going south and we found ourselves skirting Monte Cassino. At first it was only recognisable when there was a sudden rift in the clouds and the skeleton of the Monastery gleamed out at us from the summit. The houses of Cassino had been built of stone quarried from the mountain itself. But now we could scarcely make out where the rocks ended and the ruins began. The shells of the buildings reared up like ghosts from the undergrowth and the rubble and the haphazard graves. I remembered Shadwell and the onset of the London Blitz. But then the place still buzzed with people who hung on in the shelters, and those, evacuated, who came back again because there was no place like home.

Here there was no one left. I remembered those *displaced persons*, the child and the fisher-wife, one displaced a few hundred yards from home, the other almost as many miles. I guessed there was the same sort of homesickness which found a kind of healing: the view of the sea from the villa; the ruins and the solitude of Pompeii that were so like the last sight of the little boy's own hometown. In each there was something tangible: like that eggshell fragment it was *un ricordo* – a keepsake.

The time came when the Allied advance northward left the southern half of Italy relatively safe for the refugees to return home. Home too often was just the ruins left by bombardment. The Allied Commission arranged for the refugees housed in Sicily to get back. Their journeys were to be by train over a rudimentary network within Sicily; then by an Italian cruiser, moored at Messina harbour, to Naples; finally along the bomb-damaged roads that led to home.

The three of us had the job of organising the Sicilian end of the operation. We had a week in which to organise trainloads from north, west and south. I was at the receiving end in the Harbour Master's office at Messina.

My vocabulary had extended and I could talk by phone with scattered railway officials as well as my mates in Palermo and Agrigento who in turn were gathering refugees by road from all directions, and packing them on to trains.

As the operation developed we all became, to use a polite word, more emphatic about who should do what and when and where and how. I reckoned to be reasonably fluent on the phone, being a *spinto* for all I was worth, occasionally lacing what I had to say with Sicilian words denoting, roughly, *Why the hell hasn't this or that happened? Bloody well get on with it!*

Standing in the little office, telephone gripped in one hand, receiver jammed to my ear, belting out advice and admonitions, I caught sight of a little group watching from the doorway. There was a small man, evidently a priest, wearing a shovel hat, another, younger priest, and a very beautiful young girl. They were taking it all in, especially the behaviour of this rude Englishman. It turned out that Shovel Hat was a Monsignore, the President of the Vatican Commission on Refugees. The other priest was an important sidekick; and the girl was Monsignore's niece. They had come on behalf of His Holiness to study the refugee problem in southern Italy and what was being done about it.

Learning, rather slowly, just who they were, I was brusquely polite. I explained that with difficulty we were beginning to overcome the problems in gathering the refugees from all parts of the island in readiness to embark them on the cruiser.

The visitors were at first rather reserved. Then, as everything began to work out, and the flows of refugees coalesced, the ice began to melt. There was time to make conversation, and learn a little more about each other and what we were up to.

This changed markedly for the better when all the refugees were on board, mainly below deck in the cruiser and we were beginning to sail along the western coast towards Naples.

Monsignore Baldelli was not a great conversationalist, and did not speak much English, but my attempts in Italian seemed to be appreciated. By this time he had heard quite a lot about what we three FAU members had been up to. This included favourable reports from the nuns who stitched the quilts, and others in local churches where our efforts had got them support (for their own members as well as for the refugees). So we began to get on quite well. Very well indeed with his niece and we talked in two languages linked together on the rails watching the coastal scenery go by. By the time we landed we found each other, I thought, *simpatico*.

On both sides there was a revelation. My Methodist upbringing (a son and grandson of the manse), and later involvement with socialistic Anglo-Catholics, Presbyterians and Quakers in Shadwell during the Blitz had left me ignorant, and suspicious of Roman Catholics. They were the ones, like my first History tutor at Cambridge, who appeared to be on the side of the Italian Fascists who invaded Abyssinia and joined with the German Nazis to back Franco and his fascists in the Spanish Civil War.

Working in Sicily I had a mixed impression of what use local priests might be. Too often they seemed to be on the side of the inhospitable Sicilians, concerned to get their own flocks properly fed, not wanting to spare much time for the asylum seekers from the mainland. The nuns were an exception of course but that, I thought, was because they were women and less hidebound, more naturally sympathetic to humankind.

As for the Vatican – I had been brought up to think (incidentally, not sparing time to bother about it) that Popery was in itself what the authors of *1066 and All That* would have called a Bad Thing. Much of the European history I read up at university featured the machinations of aggressive Popes, asserting power, first over warring factions on the Italian mainland and then gaining influence and prestige by manipulating alliances with military-minded kings, emperors and over-mighty counts and dukes. It was mainly the fault of Pope Urban, wanting to consolidate his political powers that the First Crusaders took off, pillaging and massacring (as I later learnt) all the way across Europe to rescue the Holy Places from the Infidel.

This Vatican-based lot did not fit in with all that. The Vatican Commission was ready to join with non-Catholics, including the likes of us, in getting things done, seeing fair play both for refugees and for the people who had to put up with them.

I went back to Sicily where the work we had been doing continued to expand, and in turn led to a project throughout southern Italy, allied with the newly established United Nations Relief and Rehabilitation team, based in Bari, and a rather more adventurous bunch from the Save the Children Fund.

Our relief work was no longer just for the refugees. It now included everyone affected by the destruction and dislocation the armies left behind as they moved northwards.

In Sicily we had taken heed of Blitz-time experience back home, and got every local group to form its own *do it yourself* committee, bringing together needs and resources, wheeling and dealing with every kind of authority.

We were helping to mobilise local self-help. Plaster of Paris was left on the shelf, but quilt-making and other small enterprises were goers. All sorts of possibilities began to reveal themselves, or more properly to be revealed by local people once they got the idea that they could make things happen with their own resources as a starting point. Soon there was a network of little, semi-co-operative enterprises scattered about the heel and toe of Italy. We were now going to and fro, encouraging people to make their own starts, negotiating with the allied military authorities to get them additional help.

About this time I got a telegram from a man in Rome. His name was Tito Zaniboni. Pre-war, as one of those secretly resisting Mussolini's fascist regime, he got the use of a flat above the piazza, overlooking the balcony from which Mussolini periodically made war-like speeches. He lay in wait with a gun, but before he could use it, he was found out, arrested, sentenced to solitary confinement over many years. When the Allies seemed to be winning the Italian war, with Mussolini's forces, gradually abandoned by their German allies, in retreat, Zaniboni was approached on Mussolini's behalf and offered first, better prison conditions, and when that failed, instant release, provided that he announced his support. He refused both offers. Only when the rest of Italy had been liberated from the Germans, and the Mussolini regime collapsed, did he accept freedom.

Now there was a new, Allied-supported, Italian civil government, given its head to a large extent by the Allies, and already winning over support from the run of the mill Italians north and south. Newly liberated, Tito Zaniboni was offered and accepted membership of the new Italian Cabinet, as Minister for Refugees. Scanning the horizon for information about the refugee problem nationwide, and ways of coping with it, he heard about what we had been up to and his telegram summoned me to meet him in Rome.

When I got there I found his Ministry was based in a vast palazzo, once the home of the rich and well-related. At the entrance there was a receptionist. I waited beside him to know where I should go to meet the Minister, and when he might be free to see me. I did not wait long. Down the imposing staircase came the man himself, tall, craggy-faced with a bunch of stiff grey hair, running down the stairs hand outstretched, greeting me by name in a welcoming roar.

That was the beginning of a fascinating encounter. He wanted to know all about refugees and their hosts, and what to do about their situation. I said half the battle was to make proper use of the new Italian government's legislation on refugees' behalf. So a secretary was summoned and we went through umpteen scraps of legislation establishing local rights and responsibilities. I noted them all down, each with the *protocol number* and the details defining who should deliver this, that, or the other.

Then I went back home to Bari, and we extracted the relevant sections of the recent support legislation, printed them up with their protocol numbers alongside, and distributed to all and sundry so that refugees and their supporters in and outside local government could have the key clauses at their fingertips, brandishing them in the face of any bureaucrat likely to create obstacles.

That was the only time I saw His Excellency Zaniboni face to face, though we had occasional phone conversations in my broken Italian. Meanwhile there were excuses to return to Rome and follow up the links with the Vatican Commission in general, and with the President's niece in particular. She and I walked to the opera together, though trailed at a thirty pace distance by her father, as chaperone.

By the time the European war ended, the work with the refugees had become much more dependent on local initiatives and local support, reinforced by United Nations aid channelled through UNRRA staff. So far as the FAU was concerned our Italian job was over and for many of us it was our turn to get back to Civvy Street. For others, including me, there was still the yen to be involved, at the workface so to speak, as long as the world war continued. So I opted for China, broke the news to Monsignore's niece, went home on leave, heard the announcement of the Hiroshima bombing over the radio, drew a line under my Italian experience and set off in charge of a bunch of eight FAU members heading for China.

The last I heard of Tito Zaniboni, that civilised, self-denying servant of the people, was that, living and working a simple life, not depending over much on government limousines, he died of a heart attack running for a bus.

Chapter Nine

STARTING SMALL

Getting out to China when the European war ended grew more attractive, and demanding, stage-by-stage. The eight of us from the Friends Ambulance Unit, Europe, were now embarked on a Slow Boat to China, just like the song, but minus romance, since it was an all male party. We got as far as Bombay (now Mumbai), hung about for a day or two for the train which took its time over another couple of days to get us across India to Calcutta. Then a few weeks waiting for a plane.

Crossing the Hump (the Himalayas) at that time meant falling asleep halfway because only the pilots got the necessary oxygen supply to keep awake when the plane was high up. When we awoke we were already inside China, and beginning to descend on a muddy field just outside the ancient city of Kunming. This brought us really down to earth. Journeys from now on were by winding, rocky roads in well-worn Chevrolet trucks. These were propelled by charcoal gas, generated by fires below enormous hoppers fixed alongside the driver's cab.

The Friends Ambulance Unit China Convoy, so-called, had bases scattered across China. The main job was to commute between them carrying medical supplies, in the early days during the war with Japan; more recently re-equipping civilian hospitals that had closed down when the war overtook them. Here and there, there were also surgical units, FAU manned (and occasionally womanned) served for supplies by the charcoal gas trucks, visiting the fighting fronts. Now all resources were being concentrated to help revive and staff the civilian hospitals, often attached to missionary outposts starved of supplies.

First in Kunming, and then further inland at Kutsing, I met one or two of the old Unit hands I had originally trained with back home, and began to learn how life in China had transformed them. The whole country was our oyster, and the modest jobs we were doing ranked quite high, simply because there was scarcely anyone else doing them.

We had friends in high places, on both sides of the civil war between

Nationalists and Communists that was gradually reviving. Chou En Lai, Mao Tse Tung's right-hand man, was friendly and influential, and he knew all about us because his nephew, Henry Yu, was one of the Chinese who had joined the Unit.

We did not take ourselves too seriously. There was a duplicated newsletter which circulated a patchwork of jokes and scurrilous ballads at each other's expense (via our own transport), along the mud roads that spanned China.

On the strength of the work I had been doing in Sicily and Southern Italy, I was supposed to be a refugee expert. There was already a major refugee problem up north in and around the province of Honan. Partly the results of the Japanese war now ending, this was made even more chaotic because the southern dykes along the Yellow River had been breached so that the floods might stem the Japanese advance. Year on year the floods continued their work of devastation. And now the damage was about to be extended as the civil war revived.

I waited until a truck was available to get me the first step northward, to Chungking, where the Unit had a base with a thriving mechanics training centre. The truck was piloted by 'Bij', short for Brian Jones, skilled in coaxing Chevs to do their best. He was what used to be called an *Old China Hand*. This was just as well because our truck was on its last legs, due, once it reached Chungking, to be dismembered for the trainee mechanics to practise on.

It took us over two weeks to make the journey negotiating a couple of mountain ranges. This involved zigzagging up the mountainside to allow as much horizontal driving as possible. So *22 Bends* up one range and another *72 Bends* up the next. This made slow going and it was even slower because of frequent stops to mend the engine. Occasionally another Unit truck would stop by on one of its regular medical supplies missions, greeting us with rude remarks or kind enquiries.

Meanwhile I learnt my job as *charcoal boy*. This meant negotiating at the nearest village for the next day's supply of charcoal. I had picked up enough Chinese on the boat coming over to say '*Hello*' courteously, and then '*How much*' in a business-like manner. Each day's supply was stacked in a great big hopper, lashed just behind the cab. My job before starting out each morning was to light a very small fire underneath the hopper and then follow the pipe from it which led all the way round the sides of the truck to the point on the engine where the producer gas being generated could be ignited. To get the gas travelling along the pipe I had to operate a suction fan. Winding this around for several minutes was a useful substitute for doing physical jerks before breakfast. Breakfast itself was on the move, without much conversation.

Bij, having long experience in coaxing charcoal trucks up mountains, was rather taciturn. His most intimate relationship was with the engine, deciding just when, nearing the summit, it stood most in need of a shot in the arm. This came from a five-gallon jerry can mounted inside the cab just above the windscreen. From there it could be led down a tube with a tap by which one of us could regulate the flow, drop by drop, shown on a glass insert in the tube, to supplement the gas supply for the engine.

We slept in our bedrolls beneath the truck with our campfire near enough to appreciate its warmth on frosty nights.

We kept a lookout for bandits. One evening, as our supper was warming up, we heard what sounded like a musket shot and dived below the truck – only to find that it was a stone splitting under the flames. That was the nearest, on that journey, that we got to anything dramatic.

In Chungking our warmest welcome was from the mechanics needing our truck to dismember and play with. Whilst I waited for a plane to take me to Hankow and the road north, I began to learn more about the other old China hands – Americans, New Zealanders, Chinese and British, sharing, more or less, *Quaker views on peace and war*, reinforced with much laughter, and a feeling that we were all immersed together in a lifestyle that had a bit of everyone's background stewing in it.

I took the opportunity to do some language revision. Setting out from Britain I had evolved a cunning plan to make the most of my copy of *The Thousand Character Lessons* , an English version of the manual invented a generation earlier by a Chinese YMCA worker, Dr. Jimmy Yen. This introduced literacy to Chinese villagers who knew all about village life, without being able to read or write. Each *lesson* had one or two new words set in a few sentences about making the most of everyday life together.

Early on it made two simple statements:

Shiatz k'uu – blind people suffer.

Bwu shyh tzh-de yee k'uu – letter-blind also suffer.

That's the lesson which motivates. Armed with their newly acquired literacy, everyone can go on, and on, lesson by lesson, marking out stage by stage how to make the best of one's self, hygiene, cleanliness; and then how the village can get together first to decide things, and then to set about doing what is needed. By the end of the manual you could become language literate, and at the same time discover what it is like to belong to an active community.

Just the job, I thought to myself. It's simply a matter of acquiring words (Chinese words) with the way you would sound them in English, plus the Chinese ideographs which represent them. One at a time, gradually accumulating a command of the language which is there for keeps. So, on the way out from the UK I copied each new Chinese word, one at a time, on to a domino-sized slip of card. One side had the Chinese ideograph and below it the sound it makes, rendered in English text. The other side had what the Chinese word meant in English.

Step by step, on board the boat making for Bombay, in the train crossing India, and very occasionally on the zigzag road to Chungking, I accumulated matchbox after matchbox each filled with the little word cards. I paced the deck with a matchbox in hand, looking at one side of each card, deciding what the other side should be, turning the card over and checking. By the time we had reached Chungking there were a score of matchboxes, each packed with the words I had noted down and learned.

I decided to do some revision. The latest matchbox to be completed: everything remembered – ten out of ten! Then the matchbox before it – nil! I discovered that the process of acquiring a new matchbox-ful had erased all memory of the contents of the one preceding. And so all the way back to matchbox number one. There were no hooks to hang the words on. I began to see that everything, like a baby learning to speak, would depend on listening to Chinese conversation, recognising an occasionally familiar word; then using it where appropriate in return; gradually anchoring this knowledge in the everyday exchanges with the Chinese-speaking members of the Unit; and later on with every other Chinese I came across who was willing to respond when I attempted to say Hello.

The first opportunity to test this out was on the plane to Hankow, but conversation was rather limited, because all the other passengers were busily conversing among themselves and not really into chatting up a stranger. The breakthrough happened on the next stage of the journey when I was joined by Glyn Hughes who besides being a fluent Welsh speaker, had been long enough in China to get the hang of the opening courtesies. These he reinforced with a simple description of who we were and what we were up to.

Our transport was in railway trucks , roofed with tarpaulins. Three trucks each containing forty or fifty passengers, with standing room only. Our engine was the fourth truck, a Japanese lorry refitted with railway wheels. We made steady progress northwards, passing through territory where the difference between *bandit* and *guerrilla* was not always clear. Each lap in the journey began and ended with a short stay in a stone-walled strongpoint, what the Boers would have called a *laager.* It had to be spacious to contain all four trucks, engine included.

Rubbing shoulders in this way made chatting much easier, and I began to eke out my limited vocabulary in support of Glyn's relatively fluent conversation with our fellow passengers. They were agreeably curious about who we were, what we did, and where we were heading. Glyn explained that we were en route to a former mission hospital, the Hwa Mei I Yuan, the Hospital of the Beautiful Flower. This had been evacuated during the Japanese war now ending, staff dispersed in all directions, but now gradually reassembling and we were there to reinforce them. What did we do? We proffered our Red Cross satchels full of first-aid bits and pieces. Everyone nodded appreciatively and in turn told us what they did, which was mainly growing things, and then selling them in the nearest market.

At every stop on the way, not just the overnight resting places, local people came offering to sell us food – just like, I thought, the villagers who besieged the train in which we crossed the top of Africa. But on one occasion there was a significant difference. A woman came holding a little girl in her arms with a damaged foot. The previous day she had been playing too close to the rail track, tripped, and the wheel of one of the rail trucks cut across her foot and almost severed it. During our stop next day the word had gone round that there were two *foreign doctors* aboard – Glyn and me. So now her mother brought her to seek our help.

We were a little taken aback, but we drew on our knowledge of war wounds, and took a closer look, the mother handing her daughter over to us as we sat on the side of the truck. At this point the journey resumed. The trucks began to move, with everyone clambering on. The mother, parted from her daughter, called to us to heal her at the hospital, and off we went with the little girl beside us. We looked more closely at the wound, sprinkled penicillin over it, bound it up well, and did our best to comfort her; Glyn attempting a very basic description of the hospital that would make her foot better.

Everyone else in the truck helped describe the medical wonders that awaited her and cheered us on.

We reached Chengchow in the evening, with muddy streets half lit by lanterns slung from poles attached here and there to market stalls. We found a rickshaw, loaded it with the little girl and all our baggage, and trotted along beside the rickshaw-puller until we reached the gates of the hospital compound.

All save one of the buildings inside were deserted. We made for its flickering lights and announced ourselves and our patient. About half a dozen Unit members had already arrived from other parts of China as the nucleus of the team that would revive the place, and thanks be! they included a doctor and a nurse. So we handed the little girl over. Next morning, December 23rd, when we called in to see her, she was already sitting up and smiling, the hospital's first patient. We explained to everyone that we had brought her to the hospital as our Christmas present.

Gradually the team at the Hwa Mei Hospital took shape, coming by truck or by train from all over China, exchanging the latest gossip, helping to contact and re-engage the Chinese supporting staff who had dispersed, along with the doctors, during the Japanese advance. But I wasn't there as a hospital worker. I was in China on the strength of the earlier work with refugees. There was a massive refugee problem/opportunity in waiting. The Yellow River had been breached at the dykes upriver at Hwai Yang K'ou. Further downstream the river's flood course had overwhelmed the little city of Chungmou. All that was left were the mounds on which the city walls had stood, a mile square. Later on, visiting the place for the first time I noticed what looked like a marble bench, beautifully designed, curling over in a scroll at each end. It turned out to be the top of a ceremonial arch immersed in the all-embracing river mud. Hardly anyone was left. Beyond the city limits, on slightly higher ground there were the remnants of outlying villages, also deserted.

That visit came later. All we knew in Chengchow was that sooner or later, with the help of the newly formed United Nations Relief and Rehabilitation Administration (UNRRA) the mile-wide breach in the Yellow River dykes was going to be repaired. The flooding would eventually cease. People would gradually come back home to the city and the surrounding villages. There would be a new flood, this time a flood of people, returning to rebuild the city from scratch.

Those nominally in charge of refugee *rehabilitation* were the Provincial Government based in the provincial capital, Kaifeng, some forty miles away from us in Chengchow and about the same distance from the drowned city.

Kaifeng was a big city with a long history well aware of its importance and its ancient traditions, with thriving markets, but many jobless people on the loose. So Kaifeng was objective Number One; not only the refugees squatting in it, but all those from throughout the flooded areas who had gone for safety in the provinces adjoining Honan.

The Unit members based on Chengchow were for the time being almost the only people available for the massive rescue operation that lay ahead. And I was the only one known to have been concerned, as a *refugee expert*.

So as the only such expert within reach I was invited to Kaifeng to meet the provincial governor, beginning with at a ceremonial banquet to greet the *honourable foreigner*. This involved everyone drinking toasts, to me and to each other. Each toast, person to person, required, in courtesy, an instant response. To keep count I had previously learned to make little tears along the edges of the beautifully written name card which lay beside my place at the table. A tear for each *kan pei* (roughly *bottoms up*) which I had to drink in response, two tears to each edge. When all eight were done, I just managed to stop responding by actually drinking the toast, and in the lively atmosphere managed to drain the contents of my glass inconspicuously away.

The serious business began in the following days. I was assigned a very polite and unassuming bureaucrat as my liaison officer/interpreter. He was blessed with fairly fluent English, expressed in many courteous phrases. Between us we went the rounds in the Provincial Government, consulting all sorts of departments which might be relevant. Next step was the appointment of no less than six committees. Each would deal with a different aspect of refugee resettlement – once the work at Hwai Yang K'ou was completed, the river dragon tamed, and the refugees ready to come home.

This committee mongering went on for several weeks. We worked out where to site transit camps, how to arrange disinfestation for people who might have picked up vermin, how to mobilise transport, where to accommodate people en route, how to get them fed.

When all these arrangements had taken shape, I suggested to my patient and courteous liaison officer that I should go the rounds and visit these newly established resources. This proposal proved very hard to negotiate. There were all sorts of reasons for postponing, or even omitting such visits. Finally I borrowed a jeep and went on tour. At the site of one of the chosen transit campsites – nothing. Nothing more at each of the other places earmarked for support.

I came roaring back to demand an explanation. The courteous liaison officer explained that none of the arrangements we had made were immediately practicable, and that was why there was nothing to visit.

At this point I forgot all had learned about Chinese courtesy and thumped the table. This was just enough to make the liaison officer abandon courtesy in his turn and come clean. He explained more in sorrow than in anger, that the whole refugee problem had been solved already. The Provincial Governor was using the United Nations subsidy earmarked for refugee resettlement to pay the Governors in the next door provinces to stop the refugees coming back. They were quite good at this, at first. So for the time being, there was nothing further to do.

At this I exploded once again. Why?! had we set up all those committees?

The answer came, polite but firm, shorn of courteous embellishment: '*Of course, we had to honour you as an important visitor wishing to contribute his knowl-*

edge and experience. It was the least we could do to show the necessary courtesy and respect.'

Having learnt this lesson I went back to our base in the hospital at Chengchow, south of the river. We could all see what would certainly happen when the flooded villages and cities became habitable again. Refugees would come back, in spite of official obstruction. And anyhow the payments made to the other Provincial Governors were made one-off, and the incentive to keep refugees back would surely vanish.

I reckoned that the complex administration involved in refugee rehabilitation back in Europe was irrelevant. Refugees, here in China, were used to fending for themselves. They would get back, somehow, to the ruins of their homes. What mattered would be the way in which they could be helped to recreate their own communities. It was still months before the breach in the river dyke could be healed and the next season of flooding averted. So there was a gap in time when things could be tried out on a properly diminutive scale – not an all-embracing, top-down Grand Plan, but some little try-outs in one small spot.

We made enquiries amongst the Chinese who had fled earlier on when the hospital fell to the Japanese, but were now returning to Chengchow. They knew the lie of the land, and one had connections with a hamlet called Shih Li T'ou which stood ten li distance from Chungmou city. It had two advantages: it was on higher ground and had not suffered from the Yellow River floods. And our hospital contact told us about Mrs. Fan, who lived in the village, knew everyone in it, and had a say in everything the village did, or didn't.

With this introduction, four of us set off in an ex-weapons carrier we had borrowed, piled high with our personal baggage topped with the materials we might require in order to set up Something Useful. This something would have a medical bias, because there were no medical resources to speak of within at least fifty-mile radius, distant from the hospital itself which was already overburdened.

The four of us were an English doctor, a Chinese nurse, a Chinese agricultural student who we felt was bound to come in useful sooner or later, and myself as a general factotum. We reached the hamlet in the early evening and were welcomed by Mrs. Fan herself. She cleared one room in her own small house for us to eat and sleep in. At night, lying on our improvised beds looking up at the thatched underside of the roof, we put up with cascades of dust and occasional insects. Later on we stretched a parachute we had acquired from an American dump to create a ceiling. Then we lay and watched the pitter-patter of little feet as the rats crossed and re-crossed above us.

Meanwhile our main concern was to set up a Clinic. Mrs. Fan spared us a space just outside her house. We built walls of wattle made from sorghum stalks laced with mud. (I remembered those little walls we two seven-year-olds improvised on the edge of that brickfield, long ago.) The framework and the rafters were timbers we had brought with us. The roof was a great tarpaulin Unit members had acquired along with the parachute from that American dump, a hundred miles away.

Almost overnight we were in business. Patients came from fifty miles around, walking, or drawn by their relatives, on little carts. Dr. Peter Early and Nurse Jean Liu worked round the clock.

Jean still found time to follow up other possibilities. She was determined to start small, within the scope of the village. There was cotton growing that could be carded and turned into yarn which could be woven to make things to sell. All that was needed was a carder machine and she set about organising a whip round to buy one from distant Kaifeng and get it transported by one of our trucks if and when they passed by and made a diversion. The basis for all this would be a co-operative. We had all heard about Jimmy Yen, who besides getting villagers to read had used his *Thousand character lessons* to promote the idea of *industrial co-operatives* – village-based, not just city set-ups. Every co-operative would mobilise the resources of people and materials that lay immediately to hand, and so compete with the cut-price factory firms.

Alongside the fledgling carder co-operative which Jean set up in her spare time from the clinic, Wang Hsiao Hsin, the agricultural student, set about making the most of another resource right there beside the clinic: people coming from far off, patients and their supporters queuing for hours before it was their turn for treatment. Hsiao Shin decided we should make use of our China-wide network to gather some well-bred animals, mostly males. Between us, in spare time from the clinic, we built huts to house them close by where everyone in the clinic queue could see them. By devious routes – charcoal truck, weapons carrier, even train for part of the way, we acquired a Berkshire boar, a Holstein cow, two Leghorn chickens, a pair of goats. People in the queue could now make good the waiting time, bringing livestock with them, and handing them over to have them duly served. Within the village this service took shape as another very small co-operative.

Once the cotton carding had begun, Jean talked other interested women into setting up a weaving and dyeing co-operative.

The clinic itself brought people to us from near and far, and the more they had to stand around waiting for the doctor the further we could go in

attracting them to explore other possibilities. Besides their animals they brought their children and soon a very elementary literacy school took shape. Jean and Hsiao Shin enlisted other literate residents in conveying to children, and others, the first few of those 'Thousand Character Lessons' which I had studied en route from Europe. We began to see how practical they were just because they dealt in simple ways with villagers' everyday life and the ways they could make the best of it, together.

When Christmas came (my second in China) we all had something to celebrate. Doug Turner, who used to be a farmhand back in Essex, had joined as a reinforcement for Hsiao Shin. Jean and Doug between them persuaded others in the village to create and perform a nativity play. This needed no theatre. The scenery was the village itself.

The part of Mary, the mother of Jesus, was taken by a village girl who had become a volunteer nurse in the clinic. Short, stumpy, bearded Doug was Joseph tramping beside her as she rode on a donkey into the village, along the only village street and knocked on the door of the imaginary inn. From within her own house, Mrs. Fan, as the innkeeper, shouted, *Mei you tifeng! – No room!* And they went on through the surrounding crowd of village spectators in search of a place among the animals where they could lay their heads and the baby could be born.

Chapter Ten

BESIDE THE RIVER DRAGON

In the previous spring, with the clinic and the co-ops doing well, I got the chance to take a look further up the Yellow River where the dyke had been breached.

The man who knew most about what the Yellow River could do was a Canadian pastor called Donald Faris. He got together some Japanese horses and mounted three of us to ride fifteen miles or so from Chengchow to see the Gap for ourselves. Apart from that *slow silent walk* around the clay mixer fifteen years back, this was my first proper horse ride. Going across uneven country didn't help. But when we arrived the soreness was forgotten. The Yellow River as it descended from the northwestern hills picked up the yellow dust which gave its name. At that time when we first saw it, before the flood season, the tributaries which fed it produced something more like a lake than a river. It was a mile across. Where the military engineers had blasted a hole in the dykes on the south side to stem the Japanese advance, that too, where the river divided was now almost a mile wide. Most of the water was coming placidly south. What was left continued along its old course, already diminishing to a stream between great expanses of mud, flanked by all that remained (not much) of the old dykes leading north and east through Communist territory.

Each year, as the winter snows in the northwest mountains began to melt, the river rose, like the dragon that gave its name, and through the Gap its floods spread southeast and southwest throughout the province of Honan and the villages and townships where 40 million people had used to live.

Now the United Nations was sponsoring a scheme to mend the Gap and halt the devastation.

The guy in charge of the UN project was Mr. Todd, known in many parts of South Asia as Todd Almighty, because as an innovating American engineer he had a reputation for diverting rivers, building dams, draining swamps, wherever he went. He was an affable little man, not really superhuman, friendly but with few words and he managed to get on quite well with his Chinese opposite number, General Chao, polite, even friendly, to us strangers, aware that Todd Almighty knew what he was doing and what needed to be done, better than anyone else.

What was being done already looked a bit like one of those Egyptian frescos depicting the creation of the pyramids. There were ox carts on either side of the Gap, bringing rocks and logs, wheelbarrow men with branches and smaller stones, all toiling up either side of the broken dyke to dump their spoils. On the crest of the dyke small groups were performing a set of what looked like folk dances. Each cluster was centred on a big rock attached by separate ropes, like the spokes of a wheel, to each man. Alongside the group was a singer leading each chant, setting the pace rather like the fiddler on board an old sailing ship as they hauled up the anchor. As each man heaved on his rope the stone rose and then thumped down on the earth beneath. The group chorused, and sidestepped so that each thump was on a separate space. On a bigger scale the thumping was done with the help of a tall derrick on wheels, with a pulley at the top. This time the gang were in line, heaving the great stone up, letting it go, edging the derrick further on.

Smaller stones for the walls of the new dyke were coming from thirty miles away on trucks, offloaded into the wheelbarrows, then placed one by one by hand, with logs as piles to reinforce them.

More rocks, mixed with earth and tree branches formed the core of the two dykes, very slowly advancing from either side of the Gap.

There was no more than a trickle of water continuing up the old course. So on the dry ground of the old bed we put up tents and tried to organise support – first aid, not much more because people were used to bringing their food with them wherever they worked. This work was no more and no less than the backbreaking routines they followed every day on what was left of their own small plots.

The real need for the likes of us, we reckoned, would be downstream where in the flood seasons, the river had devastated the city of Chungmou. Later I went to see that devastation for myself.

The boundaries of the old city were a mile wide. Once there had been walls and formal gateways. Now there were just the earth mounds on which the walls once stood. Almost everything else had been flattened. There was a rise in the ground where I came across that 'marble bench' I mentioned earlier. It was just the top of a ceremonial doorway, surfacing in a landscape of mud and rubble. But further up, on a rise of ground, the magistrate's yamen still stood, lapped by the river waters at flood time, but accessible, dry-shod, for the rest of the year.

We were able to make the yamen our base. We proposed to build on our experience in the village of Shih Li T'ou, seven miles to the south. It, too, was on rising ground. The route between, except at flood time, was through a seven-foot high forest of sorghum stalks (the kind we had found so handy as reinforcement to the mud walls of our village clinic).

The magistrate's yamen was just a shell when we moved in, but there was an upper floor with boards strong enough to bear our mattresses and ourselves. The ground floor was divided into two rooms by good brick walls. We made them our living room and our clinic.

We still kept things going in Shih Li T'ou. Now with reinforcements from the Unit in Chengchow we set out to repeat ourselves in the city, in spades. First the clinic, which eventually would turn into a hospital. Then literacy classes that became a little school. An extension of the carder co-op and the beginnings of a market.

We were joined in our animal husbandry work by a bright young agricultural student, Wang An Min, who had been part of the student opposition in the north, and then trekked down to the southwest and joined the Unit in Kutsing. (More about him later.) Now he had come north again to help.

Despite the Provincial Governor's deal with his next-door neighbours in the adjoining provinces, refugees were trickling back, reinforced by people in flooded Honan who had managed to find temporary shelter beside villages like Shih Li T'ou on slopes above the flood water level.

On the southern outskirts of the city there was higher ground. People began to return and rebuild the homes that they had abandoned when the floodwaters rose. What they had left behind were the skeletons of their houses, roofless, windowless, with gaps where the doorways had been. Now those missing parts returned, piled high on ox carts. Back into place went doors and windows, with families giving each other a helping hand with the roof timbers.

We went back to Shih Li T'ou to see the team's nativity play, and followed it up with a Christmas celebration in Chungmou. Over the previous two months several of us had written home to get family recipes for Christmas pudding. We pooled this expert information and gradually assembled and mixed together all the rich ingredients. In all this the unit transport network proved a bonus, picking up different fruits to be embedded in the pudding, and, at last, a bottle of Chinese brandy which would be poured over the pudding and set alight as we took it to the table.

The first course of roast chicken went down very well with Chinese Unit members and co-workers. Everyone began to relax with the help of some rice wine, to await the climax, the arrival of the pudding when it was brought in from the clinic next door. Tim Tyndall, who ran the clinic, and I adjourned with the brandy to douse the pudding. We did that and then tried to light it up. Match after match failed us. The brandy was not what it should have been. But, being in the clinic we had immediate access to an alternative, the alcohol in which we sterilised the surgical instruments. And this responded at once. We re-entered the now darkened living room, with the pudding aflame whilst someone rang an ancient temple bell which had been dug up from the silt left by the river. It all went down very well.

As yet the major repair work at the Gap was only just beginning. The river dragon had still to be tamed. The news that the dyke work at the Gap had begun, and that eventually the whole river would be diverted back on its old course, emboldened the railway authority to resume repair work on the railway bridge spanning the river just south of Chungmou.

In the city when the day's work was over in the clinic and before long, the co-op and the school – we used to go upstairs in the yamen to drink tea and very occasionally something stronger, and watch through an upper window to see how far the bridge construction had progressed.

When we had first arrived and pitched camp in the yamen there was an open space of dry land between us and the river wide enough, we thought, for a five-a-side football pitch. The river was still flooding through the Gap, wearing away the banks downstream, eroding the space beyond the yamen. A few months later it was scarcely wide enough for a cricket pitch, and narrowing day by day. As the flood season commenced the river was no longer placid, picturesque. It was becoming its second self, the river dragon, with crests of water forming like the scales on his back.

One evening, we looked out as usual to see how far the bridge builders had got. And as we watched we saw their work disintegrate. Under the force of the floodwaters the little huts on the bridge framework where they kept their tools and had their breaks, the steel girders of the framework itself, the piers on which it rested – hour by hour – were carried away. Next morning all that was left were a few spars and a bit of the railway line poised above the unlovely brown mounds on which the bridge had been based.

Our work continued through the flood season. I managed to get across, upstream, aboard a local fishing boat and reached Kaifeng by donkey to negotiate with the provincial government and the United Nations' people for more medical supplies.

The meetings went well, and were almost completed when I got an unexpected message from the Gap itself. Overnight the river had risen by a metre. I knew what that was likely to mean downstream and managed to get hold of the man who had brought me on his donkey to Kaifeng. We set out with what I had cadged of medical supplies on his donkey's back and trudged across country towards Chungmou.

Nearing the river, we were joined by two others. They were carrying guns, rather as if they belonged to their everyday working lives, like a spade or a pruning hook. This suggested to me that they could be either communist guerrillas or bandits, or possibly a bit of both. The owner of the donkey had made himself scarce.

It was at this point that the conversation I mentioned in Chapter One occurred. Aware of that click of a rifle bolt from the gun-toting stranger just behind me, I thought to make use of my Chinese visiting card. Offering this in the customary manner, with both hands extended, helped to create the traditional relationship of courtesy, and allow time to explain my connection with our clinic. I mentioned that the packs on the donkey's back were precious medical supplies which only doctors knew how to use, so not of much value to anyone else. We walked on together, politely, even amicably, until we neared the Yellow River bank, the northern side. Almost imperceptibly, my travelling companions drifted away. I found the reason when I climbed the dyke and saw in a sheltered space beside it, the camp of the railway bridge construction engineers. The donkey's owner returned. Arriving at the camp we unloaded the supplies and he left.

(A month or two later I heard again from those anonymous travelling companions. One of them turned up at our clinic, courteously requesting treatment for a gunshot wound.)

The river was still in spate. The ruins of the railway bridge had almost disappeared below its surface. Just beside the engineers' camp there was an eddy of relatively still water in which they had anchored the barge they had used to ferry materials and equipment for the rebuilding work.

It took a lot more pidgin Chinese on my part to persuade them that I should be given a lift in the barge across the river, along with the medical supply baggage, to our clinic in the half-drowned city. But eventually they agreed. We set off to make the crossing with the engine going flat out, and were carried aslant the river the best part of a mile downstream before we reached the other side.

We kept a wary eye on the riverbank, which every day shed a little more mud and dust to stain the Yellow River downstream. I went back to Hwai Yang K'ou to see how the work on the Gap was going. The dykes on either side had advanced to the point where the mile-wide river was pouring through a space about the length of a cricket pitch, spanned by a swaying wire bridge. Beneath, the waters had scoured a hole many metres deeper than the riverbed, and created a kind of whirlpool. And this was still the low water season. The Y-shaped channel which would lead the river back to its old course through communist territory had still to be dug out before the last stage in filling the Gap and making good the southern dyke could be completed.

At this point the Nationalist government, which more or less controlled the country south of the River, came up with a cunning plan. A message was sent to Todd Almighty the American engineer inviting him to an important conference in Nanking.

Off he went.

Then General Chao took over. He instructed the government's engineers to complete the filling of the Gap so that when the floods began they would flow back along their old northern course – before the communists' Yellow River Commission had time to complete the rebuilding of the old dykes.

There were still a couple of months before the flood season. The United Nations Relief and Rehabilitation Administration which backed the whole project, north as well as south of the Gap, made urgent representations to the Nationalist government. It must allow free passage for a convoy of construction supplies into Communist territory to speed up the dyke repairs.

The convoy set out with safe conducts issued by the Provincial Government. As soon as it reached communist territory it was strafed by Nationalist planes under the command of the very same Provincial Governor, and returned to base.

We made a second attempt. It began with my visiting the Provincial Governor, accompanied by Father Frasinetti, the Italian missionary, whose mates had embraced me and drunk deep to hear my news of their home country. He knew all about Chinese protocol, so we set out at five in the morning and reached the Provincial Governor's office via several intermediary offices, just in time for elevenses. The Governor himself was immaculate in full dress uniform and gleaming leather riding boots. He apologised for the 'misunderstanding' that had occurred when his planes strafed the convoy. Then he re-issued safe conduct papers. We thanked him and went back to work.

In a few days the convoy of forty trucks re-assembled, still loaded with the supplies of netting, wheelbarrows, pickaxes and spades which had been carried on the previous trip. The new convoy was led by Donald Faris the Canadian missionary, a fluent Chinese-speaker, like Father Frasinetti long experienced in Chinese ways, though much more sparing in his words.

Along with a fellow Unit member, Brian Sorenson, we set off at dawn and crossed the river waters still trickling through the Gap. By early evening we were in a kind of no man's land. The Nationalist soldiers who had been with us faded away and we waited in open country to meet the communists. So far no strafing by air and only a few distant shots which might well have been soldiers in search of animals for supper. Then in the gloaming we saw one man approach us from what we still thought of as the Other Side. We made contact, shook hands, he climbed aboard the lead truck and guided us on the next stage of our journey. Still no sign of communist military, apart from an occasional soldier visiting his home or foraging for food. After another day's journey we reached the Headquarters of the Communist Yellow River Commission.

It didn't look at all like an HQ. There was a scatter of half a dozen villages, each looking just as they always had been, so not easily identified by cruising bombers from the air. One was the hospitality village where we were billeted, others were for the headquarters of the Yellow River Commission, the Transport Authority, the Social Affairs office. Each was involved in the administration of an area rather larger than the 40 million population Honan Province where we had been based. Every so often this administrative network moved on to another cluster of villages to dodge the attentions of the Nationalists who still had American-backed command of the air.

We were given supper, assigned our billets and during our first night the contents of all forty trucks were unloaded and dispersed.

The next day nothing happened. On the third day a rather weatherworn jeep turned up with a driver and one passenger. Both were dressed simply and almost alike; without insignia or anything special to show that the passenger was the equivalent in communist territory of that Provincial Governor we had gone to see back in Nationalist Kaifeng.

We were greeted without fuss or ceremony and everyone got down to business, whilst the driver smoked a cigarette in the doorway and occasionally contributed a useful comment. The business, conducted between Donald Faris and the Chairman was about further support that the United Nations might one day provide. It was soon done to everyone's satisfaction. We set off at the head of the convoy of trucks now emptied of the supplies we had brought three days earlier.

All the way down the trail that went beside the old course of the Yellow River we could see those materials already in use. In each village beside the riverbanks, there were groups beginning to repair the old dykes which over the years the gales had worn away, already using the tools and materials we brought for them. Two months later, the full force of the diverted Yellow River was flowing down its old, northern course. But the dykes had been built up on either side by a metre and a half. The flood devastation that the Nationalists had planned was averted.

I began to make comparisons between the Nationalists and the Communists. We still got news sometimes from the outpost of the Unit that was based far to the northwest at the communist headquarters in the caves of Yenan. Their news matched the impression I got when we met the Chairman of the Communist Yellow River Commission and his driver, and afterwards, going south saw each of those instant village improvisations that achieved the dyke repairs.

Overall success stemmed from the Communists' ability to involve village people in getting things done. Previously, in the years of the war with Japan, what success had been achieved by the Chinese was largely the result of communist guerrilla activity. The Japanese armies never knew when they were going to be attacked and could seldom trace their attackers as they melted back into the villages. The guerrillas on active service, rather like the American settlers in their War of Independence from the Brits, could rely on a network of information supplied by villagers about the movements of the occupying Japanese. The communists had nothing much in the way of support from any outsiders, Russia included. But they had a song which ran:

'*We've got no arms! We've got no equipment!*
Never mind! The enemy will bring them to us.'

Now, at their Yenan base, word from a handful of Unit members working there reinforced this impression. Initiatives were at or near ground level. Community enterprises were taking shape alongside a co-operative form of village self-government. Decisions were made just as in the guerrilla campaigns against the Japanese. The communist cadres were in charge, overall, but they lived on a level with everyone else, and took to the Unit newcomers and their efforts to help, without fuss.

Back in Chungmou we watched the waters ebb and dwindle until we could see the banks on either side dried out, and a rivulet flowing along what had been the mile-wide course of the river.

The city was coming to life. People arrived with their belongings piled on oxcarts and the backs of donkeys. They enquired about these Chinese and foreign people who had taken over the magistrate's yamen; picked up rumours of what was going ahead already in Shih Li T'ou village, seven miles away. They took us on as part of the new era opening up after the Japanese surrender.

Our efforts back in the village were bearing fruit. The animal husbandry co-op beside our clinic was flourishing. Wang Hsiao Hsin was in his element making fresh contacts with local farmers, backing up the animal husbandry project. Meanwhile, Oscar the Berkshire boar still served the sows brought to him by patients whilst they waited for their own medical treatment. The textile co-operative was expanding and there was a rudimentary food co-operative.

Within Chungmou city there was now the beginnings of a school. A sister clinic based at the foot of the old magistrate's yamen where we had our base, was becoming a kind of information centre, fuelled through the medical treatments for which people came from fifty miles away. We began to think about building a hospital to succeed our clinic. In between times we ate, drank, swapped mildly funny stories, occasionally sang together.

And talked of home.

Within the city boundaries, apart from the magistrate's yamen and the small shops the incomers were setting up around it, the site was just a muddy desert, slowly drying out as the river level dropped. Walking across that drear expanse, on the way to see how they were getting on in Shih Li T'ou, I felt almost as arid as the ground itself. *An expense of spirit and a waste of shame.*

Seven years on the go, some things achieved, some opportunities missed, I felt played out: not just in the work I was doing, but also in the life I led, solitary whilst in the midst of daily activity. Homesick? But, short of battening on my parents, there wasn't really what I wanted to call home, wife, family, neighbourhood. Outside the city limits, making my way back through the sorghum to greet Mrs. Fan and my other team mates, I could see that my journey within the Unit was nearing its end.

Not, however, with a whimper, but with a bit of a bang. The Yellow River and its diversion was making news, and with it the rebirth of the whole city. The word had got round that the projects now beginning to thrive were examples, models even, of the way rehabilitation, at the grass roots, could take shape.

We were alerted to receive a visit from the UK delegation of the British United Aid to China, led by its president, Lady Cripps. Her husband was Sir Stafford Cripps, who after a stormy career as a leftwing MP had become Chancellor of the Exchequer, Prime Minister Atlee's right-hand (or rather left-hand) in the recently established Labour Government back home. With her as one of the BUAC team came her daughter Peggy. They were visiting China to report on the uses being made of the Aid which the British government was beginning to provide, and to look into ways and means for follow-up support.

Alerted to all these possibilities I persuaded everyone that we should put on a show. Every shot in our locker. The BUAC team turned out to be friendly and down-to-earth and took in everything on the guided tour we offered, without fuss and with evident enjoyment. They made no speeches, but tramped around seeing everything for themselves, in the city, and out in the village.

First the flourishing projects in Chungmou city; then by jeep to see what we had been up to in Shih Li T'ou – the carding co-op, the weaving, now some dyeing as well and finally Wang Hsiao Hsin's plot of model crops. To crown all, Oscar, the Berkshire boar and supporting livestock.

Support ranged from the Holstein bull, the Leghorn chickens and the goats to the Chinese sow, literally supporting Oscar who chose the moment of our arrival to perform.

Word of Oscar's contribution went the rounds on the Unit's network and was celebrated in Shanghai by Spencer Coxe, an American friend of mine, with a scurrilous ballad at my expense. Each verse dwelt on my showmanship, detailing a different project *laid on* for the benefit of the visitors allegedly *ad maiorum gloriam Tonii*. It culminated in Oscar's guest performance,

Lay on a sow for Lady Cripps.

The visitors left in excellent spirits, with what I thought was just a polite invitation to look them up when I got back to London.

For me, enough seemed about enough, at least for the time being. I still believed there was a future for the resurgence of China in which I thought the Unit might be able to contribute: always provided that Chinese communism, in the long run, would differ from what had turned out in Russia.

Perhaps after taking home leave (and just possibly acquiring a wife) I might be able to return. With reinforcements.

I went back to Chengchow for a meeting of all the Unit members within reach, and got the opportunity to suggest that instead of gradually winding down we should open a new chapter. Chou En Lai, the communist Foreign Minister had kept in touch with us, through his nephew, Henry Yu, who had been a full-time Unit member almost from the outset. So we were known about, appreciated, and might I thought, one day, be part of a friendly working relationship with the Western powers.

What I had seen and heard so far of the difference between Nationalist and Communist China made me think that the communists were going to be in and the Nationalists very soon out. What Unit members had so far seen convinced most of us that the communists were living out their beliefs. They lived simply. They had popular support. They were able to organise without the need to intimidate. And here was this vast country waiting to be redeemed from generations of corruption and mismanagement.

The other Unit members in Chengchow, like me with an eye on the possibility of completing their stint and getting back home, nevertheless agreed that there could be a future for some of the Unit at least, plus of course plenty of new blood as reinforcements. So I had another reason for wanting to get back home.

I told the Unit headquarters in Shanghai as much and along came a replacement, Tim Howarth, who made his first priority the laying of the foundations for the hospital. I saw the work begin, and made for home. The building went ahead, the clinic was absorbed within the hospital. (Thirty years later mates of mine made a return visit to China, and managed to get to Chungmou where they were welcomed by the hospital staff who whitewashed the outer walls in their honour.)

I got the train, with a seat this time, to Shanghai, hung around with the Unit there joining in, slightly shame-faced, with a full-throated rendering of the song about me and Oscar and the Cripps; and took flight via Hong Kong to what my father at the end of World War I, would have called Blighty.

Almost the first step was to report back to some of the 'weighty Friends' in Friends House in Euston who had overseen and helped to fund the work in China. I wanted them to appeal for more volunteers to come out and reinforce what was already going on and perhaps to strike out afresh as China began to change, hopefully, for the better.

But the wars, in Europe and in the East, were over. Everybody was wanting before long to be homebound. There were not the pressures for newcomers to join up. The American Friends supporting us felt the same. The object now was to tidy up and close down. Until, perhaps, it would be revived again for the *next* world war.

Until then, I thought, China, for me, was out.

Meanwhile I decided to take up that kindly invitation to renew acquaintance with the Crippses. I went to the small upper flat in Whitehall where they lived, was greeted by Sir Stafford from the sink where he was preparing a salad, and chatted at length with his wife and daughter. I wanted to wake everyone up to the new kind of China that seemed imminent. I talked about people like Chou En Lai, the Foreign Minister, and his Chairman, Mao Tse Tung. I guessed that their primary concern was for a kind of national renewal. That would be good for China, and maybe the opportunity for a friendly and mutually rewarding relationship with the West.

This was quite different from the picture presented by most of the media in America as well as back home in the UK. From what they had seen at first hand, Lady Cripps and Peggy shared my own impression. They agreed that the thing to do was to get at the media. I was given an introduction to one of the leader writers for *The Times* newspaper, went to see him and described what had been happening on both sides of the Yellow River. He thought this was newsworthy and was prepared to take it up on the leader page if I would provide him with some notes.

I went home and told my father who said '*Don't do the notes, write the article*'. I did that and they printed it as it stood, two columns, flanking the leader page. Everyone was interested in China but comparatively few people had got further inland than the coastal cities. So for the time being I had the edge. My father and I bought every copy we could find of The Times with my article in it. I borrowed the Writers and Artists Year Book from the library, and sent cuttings of the article far and wide, explaining that this was the kind of article I was currently writing and would they like one for themselves?

So the first one begat others in national newspapers and magazines – via *The Times*, from *The Guardian* and *The Spectator* to *Everybody's* and *Good Housekeeping*; with everything I could think up about what life was like as I had seen it: in North China, South China, North Africa, Italy, Sicily – the lot.

The Cripps family continued to show interest. Sir Stafford commented favourably on an article I had written about British relationships with China. We all attended at the Theatre Royal, Drury Lane in the box reserved for VIPs with the Director visiting in the interval to receive plaudits and pay his respects. There were more such visits, sometimes with Peggy Cripps on her own. At the very back of mind I began to wonder whether I was being considered as a possible addition to the family.

I was still preoccupied with my first love – with filmmaking. I went the rounds of the documentary film units that had flourished during the war, and were now attracting fresh notice as they documented the peace. I flashed at them the articles I had begun to write, and asked for a job. They were all very friendly, and said that as soon as I got a union card, I should come back and there might well be an opening. However getting a union card depended on having a job in films, so this was a problem. Then my father contacted an old school friend who had made a name for himself as a scientist specialising in industrial photography. He had links with Gaumont British Equipments Ltd whose products included filmstrips. He got me a job there as a filing clerk. That, believe it or not, would qualify me to become a card-carrying member of the Association of Cinema and Allied Technicians.

Suddenly becoming, for the first time in seven years, a wage earner was surprising and on the whole enjoyable. Up to now I had been looked after first by the Pacifist Service Units, then by the Friends Ambulance Unit, rather like a prisoner on parole – meals, lodging, travel expenses, standard issue overalls, plus the equivalent of 12_p rising to 25p a week for pocket money. Our motto was G.A.D.A. – *Go Anywhere Do Anything* (so long as it doesn't mean trying to kill people or starve them out).

The bonus then was to a very large extent being my own master, belonging to an outfit that could get on with whatever lay near to hand and seemed needed. Doing what needed to be done, whenever. 'Whenever' tended to be happening anything up to 6_ days a week.

A five-day-week paid for by British Gaumont Equipments took some getting used to. I was still economising but in an enjoyable way. My elderly aunt and uncle put me up free of charge for bed and breakfast, based in the attic of their home in Ealing. I walked to work across the common to the factory in Perivale, using the fresh air, and the variable weather to think about the next article I was going to draft in the evenings and the weekends. The daily walks were a kind of celebration of being on the way in to something new and probably enjoyable.

Being *the* filing clerk (note that '*the*') at work was better than it might sound. There were two congenial ladies in the office, one called a *progress chaser*, whose job was to keep the paperwork moving throughout the factory, the other sorting out most of the paperwork required by the Secretary to the Management. They both thought me an interesting oddity, and allowed me a free hand, first to get acquainted with the system and the paperwork on which it rested, and then, gradually and almost imperceptibly, to revise the filing system. By the time the Management had become aware of the changes in the filing references at the top of all their papers, the system had taken root and no one seemed to be the worse for it.

At this point I went down with a nasty cold and cough. My ever-loving aunt put me to bed and brought up the radio to comfort me. One programme caught my ear. It was part of a range of programmes I had not come across before, the morning and afternoon output of the BBC's Schools Broadcasting Department. It sounded rather good. I looked up the BBC in the Writers and Artists Yearbook, gathered a set of my journalistic cuttings and sent them off.

Back came a phone message, not from Schools Broadcasting, but from someone in the BBC's Talks Department, to whom my cuttings had been copied. Would I like to call in at Broadcasting House for an informal chat?

You bet I would.

Chapter Eleven

AIRBORNE

I had already had a brief taste of the BBC when as someone just returned from the backwoods of China I was interviewed by a BBC regular, the cartoonist Horrabin, for a television series he was presenting. Alexandra Palace was then the BBC's television centre: two studios converted from exhibition halls. Nobody in North London could miss the sight of Ally Pally, risen from the ashes of a fire fifty years back, overlooking the rest of London like a temple on the hilltop.

Studios A and B came alternately on the air in the afternoons and early evenings. Whilst one studio was on the air the other was rehearsing against the clock to be ready when the next-door programme ended. Early on a series featuring the Zoo Man highlighted this arrangement. He introduced the viewers to a buzzard which then managed to free itself whilst the programme was still on the air. During the rest of the day viewers got glimpses of the buzzard in alternate programmes. Between times there were desperate efforts to bring it down from the rafters. The experience made everyone's, including the viewers', day.

Horrabin's programme, buzzard-free, brought three of us together to say what we thought was going on in China, backed up by photographs mounted on caption boards.

In the interval after the rehearsal run-through and before we went out on the air, the producer took me out on to the balcony. As we drank our coffee, he indicated the modest parkland below us. With enormous pride he told me,

'*Our audience, the viewers, could actually fill all that space!*'

At the back of my mind was the memory of my first encounter with a stand-up microphone (no cameras) on Durdham Downs as a twelve-year-old saying my piece to an audience of roughly the same size – maybe half the number that nowadays attend a major football match.

But now what still mattered most in the BBC was Radio. Nearly every household *listened in*, though until that weekend in bed with the nasty cold, I hadn't much time for listening.

Broadcasting House at the top end of Regent Street seemed to me the summit of journalistic endeavour. Going indoors felt like entering the portals of a palace. Making my number with the uniformed custodian at the Reception desk was an experience in its own right.

The Talks producer who had invited me over looked after me like a friendly governess and after my first broadcast for her, proposed another. Meanwhile the Schools Broadcasting department, a mini kingdom on its own, had commissioned a script on life in a Chinese village, enriched with actors from the Schools Repertory group, five strong, but capable of contributing as many different voices as the scriptwriter desired.

A day or two later I was contacted by another producer from the Talks department and went to see her feeling like a traitor, actually having dealings with someone other than my first Talks contact. However I soon learnt that once you were inside the BBC beehive you could quite properly make the most of any and every busy bee in search of a contributor. Without realising it I had tapped into a network of opportunity. Quite suddenly I was on to peddling everything I had in mind with anyone, at Home and Overseas, who saw the point of getting their listeners an earful of what Chinese life was like beyond the reach of VIP diplomats and politicians.

Meanwhile I was raiding every national periodical I could reach, at first with background articles about everyday Chinese people and the lives they led. Before long I was concentrating on one section of the non-VIPs, Chinese students, who were beginning to make themselves heard in protest against the corruption and the 'Thought Control' of the Nationalist government. Some of the news came at first hand from Unit members still in China, with an occasional word about Wang An Min, once again a student leader, now based in Tientsin.

I wrote again and again about what I was hearing of the possibilities for a liberal alternative to the Nationalists, capable of making a deal with the communists which would, just possibly, allow both sides to live and let live.

I mentioned, in passing, that the Nationalist government had received more American military equipment since the Japanese surrender than had been conveyed throughout the war with Japan. I wondered to myself what hope we might have of British foreign policy makers prepared to size up a situation independently of American pressure. At this point, thanks to support from the Cripps's I was formally elected to membership of Chatham House, the Royal Institute of International Affairs, and for a year mingled with some of the politicians as well as some of the academics who reckoned to influence government policy. At the end of the year, however, finding that membership required a 15 guinea annual fee, I dropped out.

There was still a market for all the articles I could churn out, and I kept at it, before long finding it easier to keep up the flow when I booked myself in for a hour or two's dictation at a small bureau in Covent Garden. Saying what I had in mind was better than writing it, because I found myself choosing my words in order to keep the interest of the lady at the typewriter. So lengthy sentences and academic witch-words were out.

I was getting all sorts of enquiries out of the blue because at that time there was a dearth of information about what was really going on inside China. Quite often I was invited to *come for a chat* with an editor and between us we worked out what might be a suitable topic. So this was a very useful apprenticeship in its own right.

The news from the Unit members still in China underlined the dangers that student leaders were encountering. Writing and broadcasting about what I had seen and done in China was one thing. The reality, right now, was centred on Wang An Min, the Nanking agricultural student who had joined us in Chungmou to help build on the success of Wang Hsiao Hsin's village animal husbandry project.

He was born in North China in the same year as me, and his life has been a miniature history of change in China. The son of an officer in the Chinese Nationalist Army, who was mostly away on duty, he was brought up on grandfather's peasant farm. It was like most of the other 100 million farms in China, he told me.

> 'We ploughed for millet and sorghum with a wooden plough. Mostly we had a draft cow to pull it; one bad season we had to sell the cow and the women pulled the plough instead. It was all right next year though; grandfather had rents coming in from a few small plots of land that he let out to poorer villagers. He pushed up the rents and we got enough to buy another cow.
>
> Q. 'How did his tenants manage to pay?
>
> 'Oh, they ate less. Others turned bandit during the dry season when there were travellers on the roads. One cousin of mine sold his small daughter and survived that way. You had to do something to keep going on a farm, or you starved.

An Min began his education at the hands of the village *scholar* teaching him the first 5,000 Chinese letters which he learned to repeat by rote. On the strength of this he got into a Middle School at a neighbouring town, where he had now to learn English in order to follow lessons mostly given by missionary teachers who were *weigoren* – outsiders. He got accepted at Nanking University in the Faculty of Agriculture but his studies were interrupted when the Japanese invaded China. There were about 11,000 students and staff who moved, mostly on foot, across country to South West China where the University put itself together again and studies were resumed, mostly in open air or in huts that they put up themselves.

An Min and others in the Agricultural Faculty spared time to organise evening classes for local peasant farmers but found more to learn from them than could be taught them in exchange. This volunteering brought him into contact with our own heady mixture of the China Convoy of the Friends Ambulance Unit based in Kunming, most in his age group, Americans, British, New Zealanders, and one Malayan. As a newcomer he joined us where we were working in the Yellow River flood area, starting out in our mud hut clinic, setting up a livestock co-operative to help breed up better stock.

Whilst he was still with us I was visited by two officials from the government's department of *Thought Control.* They wanted to know what my thoughts were, but by this time the work in Chungmou had provided some independent status. As courteously as possible I indicated that information about my thoughts was not really relevant. After they had gone I began to realise who they were really after. But Wang An Min had already moved off, to resume his university career. For the moment he was safer in the bosom of the University than with us.

After the Japanese surrender, the whole University had moved from its temporary base in the southwest, to open up again in Nanking. An Min completed his studies and took his degree. Meanwhile he had been elected Vice Chair of the University Students' Union and led protests against government *Thought Control* and the war of attrition between the Chinese communists and the Chinese Nationalists. Now things were getting too hot to handle. I heard from the Unit in Shanghai that his arrest seemed imminent.

I talked this over with the Cripps's and they came up with the suggestion that he should be awarded a postgraduate bursary that could bring him over to the UK. This did the trick, I met him on arrival and took him to where I thought he would find congenial surroundings – Dartington Hall, in Devon, a beehive of interesting, innovative ideas, in politics as well as in agriculture.

When I went back a few months later to see how he was getting on, I began to wonder. He in turn was wondering not so much about Dartington and its ideas as about what seemed to be ordinary people's indifference to the British government's American-influenced international behaviour; to say nothing of our tolerance, even under a Labour government, of the gap between rich and poor.

Back at work in London I kept in touch, but before long he wrote to say that he would be cutting short the period of his bursary and getting back to China. At long last the nationalists were in retreat, and the new world was about to be born.

Back he went and for a little while we corresponded. He had got himself a teaching and research job at Beijing University, and with the tide turning against the nationalist government, was wondering why our foreign policy was still wedded to them.

British politics had room for all sorts of New Look innovations, at least in theory.

My father, verging on 70, and still committed to bringing all sorts of organisations together to get things done (or undone) took up the work of the Churches Commission on Gambling. Just as he had done a generation earlier in organising the Bristol Disarmament Demonstrations, he went the rounds to all the church denominations – Presbyterians, Congregationists, Baptists, Anglicans, Roman Catholics, Friends – the lot. From a tiny office in the Methodist Central Building, Westminster, he and a part-time secretary/typist cornered MPs across the road in the House of Commons, plied every periodical within reach with facts and figures on the behaviour and the profits of the Pools promoters and the bookmakers, enlisting the help (free of charge) of leading journalists and artists, including the Punch cartoonist Fougasse.

Watching him in action I could see the point of being a *lobbyist.* An old FAU mate, Pat Armstrong, told me about his part-time job, labelled Parliamentary Research Assistant, to a couple of Labour MPs, Henry Usborne, Bill Rogers, and a Conservative, James Pitman. They had started up what they called the *Crusade for World Government.* And there could be a second part-time research assistant's job on offer. So, having completed the Gaumont British Equipment's new-look filing system, I packed in that job, and took on this relatively high profile, low-paid semi-parliamentary inside job. We were housed in Old Palace Yard overlooking the main entrance to the House of Commons, and had passes which allowed us to circulate within the corridors of power.

The work that mattered was where power was lacking – 'ordinary people' the length and breadth of the land. On the MPs' behalf we approached every progressive organisation we could think of, coaxed them into setting up meetings, public and private, at which the MPs could tell everyone it was high time to forego narrow nationalism and to embrace the world. We chimed in, occasionally as very junior speakers; but most of our time was spent in ringing people up, writing handouts, following up any interest engendered with leaflets and pamphlets and membership forms. An enthusiastic support group began to help the process along, in the office and at the meetings. Pat and I were becoming minor missionaries.

Afterwards, looking back on that word 'Crusade' I wonder why we ever thought we could get away with world membership of something that at least half the world regarded, historically speaking, as a high-minded excuse for highway robbery.

That was back in the Middle Ages of course, when Europeans thought Islam was an aberration, and believed that in the name of Christendom they were entitled to invade and occupy the Holy Land, with massacres en route and on arrival of any *infidels* they came across. The Crusaders behaved themselves better within the cities they eventually occupied, such as Jerusalem and Acre; but there were still periodic reversions to Christian barbarism, when the locals got out of hand. Our ancestors stayed in charge for a generation or two until the Islamists, as we now call them, edged them out again.

'Crusade' might be a mistaken label, but 'world government' was appealing. The spadework we were undertaking to build a UK membership that would back up the idea was all right so far as it went. But I had some reservations which I did not always have the tact to conceal. World government, if and when it was going to happen, would be on behalf of everyone everywhere; but how would it not become vulnerable to high-powered personalities with the rank and file reduced to a supporting role?

Already we could see this happening in China. Mao Tse Tung was beginning to develop a cult of governance that distorted what some of us had admired in village-based decision-making. I had glimpsed this local initiative at first hand in the de-centralised rebuilding of the Yellow River dykes that saved communist territory from a second devastating flood. At second hand we all knew that it was a guerrilla-based Eighth Route Army that alone stood up to the Japanese, and here and there defeated them.

I was rubbing up against all sorts of more or less like-minded media people, writers, broadcasters, small-time editors, up-and-coming politicians like the young Wedgewood-Benn. We came together in the evenings, eating snacks and not drinking too much, hosted by whoever happened to feel hospitable. In the buzz there were more arguments about the international pros and cons. It was not only the civil war in China, and the stirrings of war in Korea, there were also misgivings on all sides about what people reckoned they stood for. Or stood against. In the States McCarthyism was beginning to fester via the House Committee on Un-American Activities. This was a twentieth century version of the medieval witch-hunt. Any writer or performer from Charlie Chaplain to Bertolt Brecht might be arraigned, denounced, and if possible blacklisted for employment.

Back home there was already a whiff of suspicion, and the words *fellow traveller* were coming into use. In our evening talking-shops, between anecdotes and professional chatter, I argued vigorously in favour of a journalistic free-for-all. No one's contribution should be modified or censored. I said that people's own first hand knowledge and experience was what counted. For instance, I said, there's an old friend of mine who is working in the *Economist* Intelligence Unit, gathering information from all quarters. He told me he is a communist, but that shouldn't be a bar to him devilling the facts for the *Economist* leader writers. '*A communist right there in the Intelligence Unit!*' exclaimed a rather serious-minded young man (who later became a moderately influential editor in his own right), '*What's his name?*' I decided not to aid the potential witch-hunt, and refused to answer. There was a chill in the atmosphere which anticipated the onset of the Cold War.

The editor of one of the more sober periodicals (which reckoned nevertheless to be moderately influential) had been in friendly touch over more than a year, commissioning articles about what was going on in China, and what were the rights and wrongs of British foreign policy. In one article, critical of American policies, I had mentioned ex-Ambassador William C. Bullitt's advocacy of American military intervention against the Chinese communists. This got a furious letter from Mr. B. himself. The editor invited me for a chat and explained that in his official capacity he would have to make an apology, and this could be coupled with my own explanation.

He allowed me a full page in which I was able to go into detail quoting Mr. Bullitt: '*To turn the tide of the war in China requires not merely economic and military supplies, but also American direction and control, exercised by a fighting General of the highest qualities*' (elsewhere specified by Mr. Bullitt as being General McArthur). I backed this up with quotations from others in the pressure group to which Mr. Bullitt belonged, advocating '*combat advisory aid extending to strategic and tactical authority*' (appearance before the Senate Appropriations Committee) and a report in the *Christian Science Monitor* on this '*influential group in Washington*' favouring the provision of a yearly aid budget of half a billion dollars, plus the despatch of ten thousand troops which would be broken down into command detachments. This was followed by the group's principal spokesman Walter H. Judd saying, '*China cannot survive for long without all-out military aid from the United States … it can still be done, but the expenditure of any more money in that area short of total military and economic support would be unjustifiable*'.

I said I regretted any '*mistaken impression*' that '*all-out*' and '*total*' military support via a landing of ten thousand picked officers and men was just '*the beginning rather than the full extent of the military intervention that was favoured*'.

Nothing further was heard from Mr. Bullitt and his friends.

The editor commissioned another article mentioning at the same time that they were also getting a supporter of American policy to write his piece alongside. That seemed fine to me and both articles were duly published. Then came an interval, followed by an invitation from the editor to drop in for a little chat in the Boardroom. The editor and a colleague offered a glass of sherry whilst they explained that the magazine had just received valuable financial backing from overseas, actually the United States, and this created a problem. I had been writing about Communist China and the dubious behaviour of the Nationalist Kuomintang government backed by the United

States amongst others. But enough was enough. So it was explained, reluctantly, over the sherry, that any further contribution of mine would be unacceptable.

It was about this time that we heard again from Wang An Min. He was in at the re-birth of the new China and its repudiation of the West. He felt that any further correspondence from any of us should cease.

By now I had moved to a flat in Mecklenburg Square, in the heart of Bloomsbury, a brisk morning walk from Broadcasting House. It belonged to the rather straight-laced mother of a Unit member still in China. There were two upper rooms to spare, and a makeshift kitchen on the landing, approached by a creaky staircase that went past her bedroom door. I shared with my old college friend Guy Somerset (the one who used to converse from his top window to my ground floor window). He was newly returned from service as a sergeant pilot in the Bomber Command and was beginning a career as an industrial economist. We still saw eye-to-eye on most issues: even our respective involvements as conscientious assenter, and conscientious objector to the war.

We also shared a social life dominated by another ex college friend, Hugh Belcher, who hosted parties that were interestingly different from the debating sessions attended by would-be politicians and by journalists like myself. In those sessions males were in the majority, and females if present did not seem to get much of a word in. Hugh's parties, with any drink available contributed mainly by the guests, were much better balanced affairs; livelier and more widely ranging, with everyone eyeing the opposite sex across the room and before long, close to. There were artists, would-be artists, and enthusiastic appreciators of the arts, particularly the artistry that figured in mildly satirical revue sketches performed at the Players Theatre. Pegging level with everyone else, Donald Swann, just back from the FAU service in Greece and beginning to link up with his old school friend Michael Flanders, Tristan Carey, making his name as a song-writer and ballad performer, and once in a while Peter Ustinov. We chatted each other up, particularly the women, without, as the phrase went, *bumming our load* professionally as up-and-coming newcomers.

Eye contact was more potent than talk. I encountered Lucille where she stood chatting at the other side of the room, and on the instant we each decided to take things further, and closer. She belonged to a well-established Jewish family. At first I made the running by talking about those Jewish relief workers evoking wartime realities when our fledgling team of prospective refugee workers faced them in that mock-up encounter on Lord Rothschild's estate. I still remembered them, not just in the way they conveyed the realities, but also in the way they sang and danced their longings for a time of peace when they could *go back home to the Promised Land.*

For Lucille a lot of that was taken for granted, sympathetically but without much personal commitment. So when we met, and re-met, and eventually trod the squeaky staircase to my upstairs room, we had a lot to say about ourselves, but comparatively little about the rest of the world. In the late 1940s the Promised Land was being recovered at the expense of some 800,000 Arabs forced out of their homes. The view we had at the time was reinforced by others we sometimes met in parties, talking about the courage, joie de vivre, self-help, and self-governing *Kibbutzim* of the first Israeli settlers, creating their own communes. Looking back, it was *Cowboys and Indians* all over again. The incomers were heroic, the locals, gradually being displaced, were the also-rans.

Meanwhile I had a lot to say, over the air and in print, about the places and the people I reckoned I had begun to know at first hand.

Nothing much about the native North Africans encountered inside and outside the French barracks in Algiers and Rabat, and the native French who had taken charge of them and their homelands. Right now, however, we were beginning to witness the process described by Orson Welles (in *The Magnificent Ambersons*) as *come-uppance.* At great cost in lives and livelihoods the French were being ejected and replaced by North African regimes which at least to begin with, seemed just as pig-headed and intolerant.

China, Sicily, South Italy were different, because, I thought, incomers like myself and my mates were trying to help, but not to take over. Even when we operated on behalf of Allied Military Government, everyone knew that we were strictly temporary, and anyhow whatever we tried to do depended on being helpers and backers, not controllers – *on tap not on top.*

More and more of my work was in radio, with an eye on *BBC impartiality,* not taking sides particularly, except in conveying the nature and the strengths of everyday people, at the receiving end.

By the time I had notched up around fifty BBC programmes, I was beginning to feel at home in that previously intimidating Broadcasting House. On the suggestion of one of my Talks producers, I put in for a full-time job as a European staffer. I thought a bit of travelling would do no harm. I got shortlisted and attended the selection panel, but got no further. However one member of the panel was Mary Somerville, one of the BBC greats.

Mary had come in as the privately established British Broadcasting Company (Radio 2LO) turned into the publicly-owned British Broadcasting

Corporation. She was an academic who also knew how to reach everyday people, to be popular without any affectation. She helped to set up the BBC's Talks Department which in turn spawned the School Broadcasting Department. She knew how people can talk to good effect; using very few words herself, but always to the point. After my failed appearance at the interview panel she took me on one side and mentioned that there was another panel meeting shortly to select applicants for a job in Schools Broadcasting. I went for it, and struck oil.

The job offer referred me to the building where the Schools Broadcasting Department was based – Film House, in Wardour Street, where earlier I had trawled the offices of documentary film units. Schools Broadcasting had the ground floor, with desks for 'programme assistants' and producers, open-plan, a den for sound engineers, and a couple of small studios.

Behind the first desk I came across on entering Film House was Christine, giving me a Big Hello.

Chapter Twelve

FRIENDS AND COLLEAGUES

After her vacation job with the Land Army, Christine had returned to Cambridge, and continued for the remaining two years of her degree course. Philip was still in the picture so far as she was concerned (and I had left myself right out of it). Like others in her year she had identified a nocturnal escape route from college, to spend nights with Philip. He had dropped his conscientious objection in favour of assent, and was very soon a junior naval Commander, scouring the seas for U-boats, with regular home leaves berthed with Christine.

It was not clear to me what the situation was now.

Christine had completed three years in the Schools Broadcasting department as the life and soul of the Production team led by the Department's senior Producer, George Dixon. George had been there, in what became the BBC's Home Service, from the beginnings of Schools Broadcasts, when he produced one of the earliest schools music broadcasts by Sir Henry Walford Davies.

In those days being a Producer meant settling in and reassuring the broadcaster, (not always familiar with the microphone – Prime Minister Ramsey MacDonald was a case in point); getting *voice level* so that the engineer at the controls got the volume just right, sorting out and playing, live, the right sections of the gramophone records which the speaker wanted as illustrations to his talk.

George gained local fame when Sir Walford wanted to use a couple of items from separate gramophone records in a studio which then lacked a record player. So as Producer he had to dash downstairs to play them on cue. He got there in time to play the first and sat anxiously waiting for the second cue only to find that he was sitting on the second record. He dashed upstairs to break the news but Sir Walford *didn't bat an eyelid*:

'*Well children, I did promise you an attractive piece by Brahms but Mr. Dixon has just sat on it.*'

George was all that was best in School Broadcasting, knowing exactly how to coax a fledgling broadcaster into giving her or his best, at home with seasoned actors including some of the top notch professionals, getting them wise to the difference between projecting to a theatre audience and communing with the listener. He was a bridge between professional artists and the teaching experts, many of them fresh from the classroom, who initiated and helped to shape schools broadcasts. He loved a laugh, and made it a beautiful sound in its own right, perhaps because in his spare time he was one of the choir at the Temple Church just across the road from Broadcasting House. The Temple Choir had an international reputation and in earlier days had included the boy chorister, Ernest Lough, whose record of *Oh for the wings of a dove* was a best seller. This prompted George's story about the old lady he heard commenting on a playback, telling her friend that *soon after he made that beautiful recording, the little boy passed away.* The little boy actually grew up to be one of George's mates in the Temple Choir, a rubicund little man with a cherry red nose and a friendly smile who joked with us in the pub across the way.

One of Christine's regular assignments as a Producer was a programme *To Start You Talking.* This series brought a carefully selected handful of youngsters to discuss (on script) subjects of teenage concern guided by an older, experienced broadcaster in the chair. Occasionally there were dramatised inserts done with actors from the five-member *Schools Rep* masquerading as youth to illustrate a subject for subsequent comment by the *teenage panel.*

I was making the transit from life within the studio (voicing what I had written, under the guidance of a Producer) to the Production cubicle separated by a soundproof window, from which the production team put the programme on the air. There was a Programme Assistant keeping an eye on the script, and who looked for cuts if the rehearsal overran. The Producer kept an eye on whoever was in the studio – the presenter and sometimes a team of actors in support. At the back of the cubicle were turntables on which the playback engineer manipulated gramophone records containing music, and sometimes pre-recorded interviews. Occasionally these inserts included material pre-recorded *on location.* At the production desk itself was the Programme Engineer, busily twiddling volume controls, and cueing the presenter and any actors involved, by flashing a little green light on a pedestal within the studio.

I spent my time as a trainee observing all these shenanigans within the production cubicle and blotted my copybook once by too eagerly looking over the shoulder of the engineer bent over the turntables, and nudging him so that he inadvertently shifted the needle on the gramophone record and jumped a crucial paragraph.

Meanwhile I kindled to the departmental team, about thirty-strong, chatting at the coffee break or in the pub just across the way, talking sense without jargon at the weekly departmental meetings. Some were ex-teachers, some had moved into the department from other parts of the BBC, some had paved their way as freelance broadcasters and scriptwriters, like me.

The departmental meeting was an opportunity for everyone to hear how everyone else was doing, and there were usually playbacks of extracts of one or two recent programmes, for general comment. It was the time when the feelings of relief and jubilation at the end of World War II were beginning to change. The word *crisis* came back into use alongside talk about a *turning point* in world affairs, centred on Korea. There was strong American pressure at the expense of the North Korean communists (about whom people did not know much) and in favour of the South Koreans who to my mind were much of a muchness with the defeated Nationalists in China.

At one meeting it was the turn of our Current Affairs Producer to chat about his series, and in particular the latest programme on the *Korean crisis*. This seemed to me to follow the government line of acquiescing in South Korea's failings, and, perhaps, ignoring what was positive about the self-help and the decision-making capacities of local people in North Korea.

When the discussion began I piped up with a comment to this effect. This apparently took people aback, not so much because they disagreed, but because as a newcomer I had ventured to say it. It turned out that even the Current Affairs Producer concerned didn't really mind. So people were surprised, but not offended.

And I scored with Christine accordingly. She and I were on increasingly friendly terms, but as yet our contacts were only on departmental ground.

I was apprenticed to various Programme Assistants working on routine schools programmes and after a few months was attached to a colleague entrusted with an experimental series that was to succeed *To Start You Talking*. In *On Our Way* we were to have forty-five minutes airtime, with scope to include roughly the sort of discussion that figured in the previous youth series, this time unscripted and ranging more freely; plus opportunities to lace the programme with *actuality* – miniature slices of teenage life, pre-recorded, and a snatch of music to spice things up.

The first step was to concoct a trial piece of actuality, and rather to my surprise, I was invited to have a go. I took off, aglow with ideas on what a really lively youth programme could be. I went to the Outward Bound centre in South Wales where youngsters were being encouraged to go potholing, climbing, canoeing, music making, and anything else which put activity centre-stage, with talk on the sidelines.

I booked a BBC recording car – a Humber limousine with space on the back seat for the turntables on which gramophone records could be manipulated. On a long lead, with the microphone held firmly by the driver of the recording car, I interviewed youngsters *on their own ground*, supplemented by all the background sound effects we could grab. I took the many-tracked records to an editing studio with Butch Jarman, the friendly tape editor in charge. We spent happy hours putting it all together, feeling like pioneers in the sound equivalent of the groundbreaking documentary filmmakers who had caught my eye all those years back at school.

The edited results were presented to a small panel, chaired by Mary Somerville herself. They listened to the mishmash sympathetically – after all it was a pilot attempt to see what young listeners would swallow – and then Mary led off the discussion with one friendly but terse sentence:

'It wants art.'

In other words, amplified in the discussion which followed, her point was that my ambition to include everything including the kitchen sink, had left out the finesse of the good cook.

However this prentice effort was deemed adequate as a starting point and we were allowed to go ahead with a series which would include all sorts of far-out activities of youngsters, as a way to show what they were really made of. Alongside there were unscripted discussions allowing them to sound off about life in general as well as activities in particular.

The series trundled along and attracted some favourable comment here and there. In particular it caught the ear of the recently appointed Controller of the Light Programme, Kenneth Adam.

He invited the Schools Broadcasting department to venture across the gulf between Home Service and the Light Programme, and launch a new series aimed in particular at the young addicts who were listening to the long-running detective sitcom featuring *Dick Barton*.

Schools Broadcasting department's sojourn, downtown in Wardour Street, was ending with the transfer to more extensive, much better equipped premises in Portland Place, bang opposite Broadcasting House. I had the feeling that the physical gap which had narrowed between us and 'BH' was now being bridged. Kenneth Adam was offering us two, yes two, weekly Light Programme slots, at 6.15 pm with Dick Barton thirty minutes later. It was decided that one, on Wednesdays, should be the revamped discussion programme, to be called '*Question Time*' with an audience of teenagers, and scope for them to respond in their turn, to the answers the adults on the panel made to the questions the audience came up with.

Alongside this, kicking off on Monday nights, was what I was allowed, seeking a showbiz flavour, to call '*Under Twenty Parade*', packed with items that were really *hep*.

This meant going where the younger generation was at, rather more than expecting it to turn up at the studio where their elders were in charge. BBC recording cars were still in extensive use and I began to form quite close partnerships with recording engineers, who usually liked the challenge of getting a microphone halfway up a cliff face, or deep down via a labyrinthine pothole.

Not only potholes and mountain tops, also getting up teenage fashion shows, transforming derelict land into pedal cycle speedways (dads enlisted as umpires), and redecorating premises for elderly and disabled people's clubs. I followed up a couple of teenagers who had been 'Busking Across Europe' and went myself to Hamburg to track down a handful of former teenagers who, whilst the war was still on, had organised their own secret radio network mainly to swap anecdotes and make fun of their Nazi overlords.

These two weekly programmes went out under the general title, chosen by Kenneth Adam: '*The Younger Generation*'. The programmes continued year after year, and begat others, until there was a different production every weeknight and we had become a team of Younger Generation producers allowed free range.

The snatches of teenage activity, far and wide, were meant to be appetizers with quick mentions of contact addresses which listeners could follow up for themselves. Alongside, as alternatives to the magazine items, once in a while I was allowed to include miniature features meant to show teenagers on their home ground, their surroundings, their ways of life. We went up the Swansea Valley where there were two villages side by side, Ystalavera and Ystradginlais, both brimming with activity.

Over and above vigorous sports activities, I counted seven separate operettas in rehearsal at the same time; drawing in older enthusiasts but with most of the zest and momentum coming from the teenagers themselves. Alongside they told me how they felt about their working days. I recorded one young miner emerging from the cage that lifted him to the surface after day's stint down the pit. I asked him how he felt. '*It's savage enjoyment*', he said.

Miniature features allowed scope to put everything together in the editing suite afterwards, without the need for a formal presenter. For the magazine items, flashing from one activity to another, there was at first a professional commentator to scene set the item, and interview the teenagers. I found that even with the moderate programme budget the Light Programme allowed, I could afford to book the top names, in those days: Richard Dimbleby, Wynford Vaughan-Thomas, Audrey Russell; and they kindled to the assignments. It was part of their professionalism to blend with their surroundings, which might include going up the mountainside attached to the rope just below the teenager who was getting his first experience. This was alright for Wynford who liked climbing anyhow, and in between bursts of recording on the way up he would be commenting down to us below on the problem of trying to get bird sounds when clearly '*they're all under contract to Ludwig Koch*' (Ludwig was the BBC's ace birdwatcher/commentator, blazing the trail that the likes of Bill Oddie and Kate Humble have followed since.)

Alongside these recording car excursions, I got the chance to use and almost monopolise one of three EMI portable tape-recorders – the very first in the BBC armoury, which were soon reduced to two when a colleague dropped one over the side in the navy's *Exercise Mainbrace.* I humped the heavy shoebox-sized *midget recorder* everywhere, in the UK and sometimes overseas, to wherever the *younger generation* was up and doing, getting close in, no longer on a lead attached to a recording car. With just me and my shoebox on a sling the situation was freer and easier, less intimidating, with more scope for people to be up and doing, even as they talked about it. No one minded how many tapes we consumed together because everything could be sifted and sorted afterwards.

I spent happy hours in weekly contact with taciturn Butch in one of the Corporation's first tape-editing suites, just up the road from Portland Place. He taught me the difference between what was a broadcastable excerpt – anything from 15 seconds to a minute and a half, and what should be cut out from the original tape spool, and dropped in the bin.

These prentice efforts to reach teenagers on their own ground began to get results: good listening figures, and approaches from other media. David Astor, the innovating editor of *The Observer* invited me, out of the blue, to have a chat. He proposed I should do a series of articles, taking me throughout the UK to report on what young people were up to and what they were really like. And like a fool I turned him down. I was obsessed with what

I was doing already (and also a bit anxious in case my bosses in the BBC would see all this as a bit of moonlighting at the expense of the Corporation job in hand).

The *Younger Generation* production team was growing quickly. Jack Singleton, ex Unitarian minister, well used to getting messages across to and from all sorts of people, joined the department and we doubled up. Jack did rather more of the Question Time discussions, I concentrated on all the up-and-doings. Between us we organised hook-ups with youngsters in Oslo, Hamburg, Paris. Wherever we went we were convinced that youngsters' own capacities were a goldmine.

We decided to make the leap from professional commentators and interviewers to what we were increasingly inclined to call *the real thing* – teenagers all the way from start to finish. Instead of the Dimblebys and Vaughan-Thomases and Audrey Russells we would have teenagers, in their own accents and idiom, presenting the programmes in the studio, out and about doing the interviewing on location, asking the awkward questions and sometimes joining the panel of experts during *Question Time*.

To fulfil this ambition, helped on by some friendly publicity in the *Radio Times*, Jack and I set up auditions, nationwide, for teenage commentators.

In half a dozen city centres throughout the UK we found youngsters coming by the score, sometimes almost a hundred at a time to try themselves out, and have a laugh in the process.

We went together to each city centre, booking somewhere attractive and accessible like a dancehall or a playhouse, passed round the coffee and biscuits, and got everyone to be an audience to each other's performance as interviewers and dummy commentators. The whole thing was as unlike what outsiders might perhaps have feared from the magisterial BBC, as we could make it. A good time was had by all.

Coming back on a late night train Jack and I began to concoct a book proposal that would reach out to every age group, with the message *Adventure for the Asking*. We had the feeling we could get away, so far as the BBC was concerned, with writing up the sorts of activity that we featured over the air, so long as we did it all in our own spare time. We took this idea to a publisher, Victor Gollancz who had already been breaking the mould with reprints and new titles available cheap to the rapidly soaring membership of his Left Book Club.

He invited us to his cramped office just off Covent Garden, pacing up and down whilst he threw out alternative titles, ending up with *The Spare Time*

Book. This had the advantage of allowing us to include anything and everything, in short and we hoped lively sections, without the need for elaborate editorial links. We raided the broadcasts we had been concocting, and followed up every other activity that caught the fancy of people with a bit of time to spare from earning a living. We got good reviews in some of the national papers; *The Manchester Guardian* critic said, '*I cannot over-praise it*'.

This proved a kind of marker, setting up our claim to reach people who could convey their own enthusiasms, without the need for us to do more than show what they were up to, and let them speak for themselves.

At the same time we wanted to make our appeal match youngsters' feelings and attitudes. We couldn't afford to seem too *worthy*.

The opportunity for a bit of a send-up was provided by the Light Programme Controller Kenneth Adam himself. Our production team had two additional part-timers, one specialising in music, the other giving a general hand, and we already had five weeknight slots to fill every week. Now the Controller, feeling munificent, offered us an extra special, one-off, Saturday slot. Not an evening, but all the rest of the day, morning and afternoon, free range.

By this time the mobile broadcasting teams in each Region were getting used to us, and even enjoying the challenge of getting the microphone down potholes, up cliffs, backstage and even underwater, wherever youngsters were showing their paces. So we lined up Outside Broadcast assignments scattered through the UK, which we could feed in *live* throughout the day.

One of the Younger Generation team revisiting St. Paul's school, as a youngish Old Boy returned with news of brilliantly improvised concert items by a sixth form student and his friend. We got hold of them to discuss what they might contribute to offset all those adventurous activities we planned to feature.

No problem. They came up with exactly the kind of offbeat feature we were after, *column climbing*. In the studio we set them going, stage by stage, up Nelson's Column in Trafalgar Square. The junior member of the team was giving *outside broadcast coverage* from an imaginary helicopter, extending the microphone at intervals to the column climber himself to broadcast his feelings as he progressed. He fended off inquisitive birds (going one better than Vaughan-Thomas on the cliff face), stopped halfway up to adjust his climbing irons and take brief refreshment, reached the top, and at the feet of Lord Nelson set up his primus for a proper meal. At this point, carried away, in a burst of enthusiasm, he broadcast fraternal messages to *all the other column climbers* – in St. Mark's Venice, the Brandenburger Tor, the Arc de Triomphe, collectively celebrating their art on this auspicious day.

We taped the entire performance and cut it into chunks which we relayed throughout the day. At intervals during the live and genuine activities of the younger generation all over the UK, our teenager link person would refer listeners *back to Trafalgar Square for a progress report on the Ascent.*

It went down well with everyone, including the Controller. It was no surprise that ending his schooldays the following year the young column climber himself, Jonathan Miller, was the life and soul of the Cambridge Footlights and before long teamed up with Alan Bennett, Dudley Moore and Peter Cook in the groundbreaking *Beyond the Fringe.*

The work itself didn't seem to me like work. It was a vocation, absorbing, tantalising, and most of the time, fun. It left little time to think about anything, or anyone, else. Christine, however, was becoming an exception. Every day when I was at base and coming up for air and a cup of coffee, so was she. She had an excellent reputation as a scriptwriter as well as a producer, and she was at home with actors, ex-teachers, scriptwriters as they came and went. We talked a little shop together, went on to gossip about colleagues and ex-colleagues; occasionally I dropped in on her basement flat in Bayswater for a further chat.

It dawned on me that there could be a recap, with perhaps a better outcome than ten years ago. I said that we ought to talk further; she saw where I was heading and invited me for an evening visit.

When I got to the flat she was there looking a little more formal than usual, but not so as to put anyone off. There was coffee on a small table and she poured us out our cups. So I popped the question once again.

Once again the answer was 'No'. But this time she went a little further and talked about Philip. He had been out of the picture, to my knowledge, at least during the time since we had renewed our acquaintance (not yet, and it would appear never, our relationship.) She said, in very few words, that he still mattered to her.

That was all, we parted. I walked back, desolate, across the almost deserted park in the shadowy autumn twilight and on through the London streets to what still had to be home. I was not sure how to interpret my own feelings. Frustration? Anger? Release? But next day being, as ever, inclined to fall back on action, the first thing I did was to find where Philip lived, ring him up and tell him what I thought to be Christine's feelings for him.

In all this, half of me felt like the second lead in some hackneyed tragi-comedy. The other half didn't quite know what it was all about. Anyhow I thought the answer was to lay all before Philip and talk things out. We arranged to meet, on my suggestion at a rather upmarket bistro at the top of Regent Street (appropriate background to this kind of mini-drama). But Philip failed to turn up. He had got my message that Christine was on for him, but I now understood that for him, Christine was off.

The winter months that followed left me trying to sink personal feelings in the everyday work, preferably away from departmental coffee breaks, on outside assignments.

Meanwhile having faced, once again, the possibility of *settling down, making a home, raising a family,* I could no longer banish the notion from my head. I thought again of the young women I had encountered here and there over the years, and decided that Monsignor's niece, the girl in Rome, might still be sought after, though it would be a very long shot. Five years back but I remembered the break in her voice when she said, '*You're going to China?*' as if that ended a hope she had. Odds against her staying as she was; but why not try one's luck?

My summer leave was almost due and I began to sort out my travel arrangements. Christine heard about them and when we happened to be standing together at a bus stop she said, not quite in passing, that there was a rather good holiday place on the coast of Brittany. Still in that rather non-committal way she sometimes had, she wondered briefly whether it might not be fun to go there together.

And we went.

Chapter Thirteen

MAKING A GO OF IT

In those spring days 'platonic' was the in-word. Getting on together, it turned out, was enjoying ourselves splashing each other in the sea, drowsing on the beach, but otherwise remaining at arms length. *La donna è mobile*, I thought to myself, maybe she'll move further if I don't push too hard. At the time I didn't quite know what to make of it. What was she really up to? Looking back, my guess is that she wanted to see whether we were *compatible* – our outlooks, jokes, backgrounds. Her father was a schoolmaster, just retired from the revered deputy headship of the local high school. She had four sisters and a lively mother, all full of fun, all interested in the performing arts, or at least in teaching youngsters to perform. After all, it was Christine's talent to perform that first brought us together, long ago, in Cambridge.

So what? Maybe on her part it was making the best of what's available. Having tested our common ground we seemed gradually to be coming to the same conclusion – we could maybe make a go of it. A colleague lent us his flat for an overnight encounter. On the strength of this we decided that (with perseverance) we could make a match.

Guy Somerset was to be my Best Man, but was called away for a work assignment in the USA, so Christine's brother-in-law Johnny, a great friend of us both took his place. I moved from the Mecklenburg flat to temporary lodgings, pending the time when our married life would begin elsewhere.

At the Wedding – the Family took over. They had already launched three of Christine's sisters into matrimony, so tackling a fourth went without saying. My ideas of an exchange of marital vows in some small country church, far from the madding crowd – to be followed later on by a super-duper party with all our friends and relations joining in – were written off. We had the Full Monty in the family church with a large congregation of local well-wishers. I stood with Johnny, clad in our hired suits from Moss Bros and watched Christine come up the aisle looking, I thought dimly, into the middle distance. We assembled in the porch for a group photograph, and went on to the family home for a splendid garden party, with Christine's and my appearance rather delayed whilst the photographer tried to get us looking relaxed and joyous. His efforts proved in vain and the Family destroyed the pictures when they came out before either of us could see them.

One of our senior BBC colleagues had given us a week's honeymoon booking in a Hampshire village as a wedding present. The wedding itself was up north and so we decided to stage overnight in Christine's Bayswater basement flat. I organised a bunch of flowers to pick up en route care of the pub we frequented in Wardour Street but when we arrived, the owner of the flat had already put it in the hands of the decorators and their ladders and dust-sheets decorated the bedroom. Christine thought that being together there would not do. So I went back to the lodgings I had left two days earlier (rather surprising the owner) and resumed with Christine the following morning.

At this point the outlook brightened. Our train journey was on a country line (later cancelled by Dr. Beeching) with an old fashioned coach to ourselves, where we walked up and down hamming it up as members of the squirearchy.

The place our kindly senior colleague had booked for us was owned by a very talkative friend of hers who greeted us at the entrance, involving Christine in what seemed to me an endless conversation about life in general and the locality in particular. By the time we got past her to the flatlet upstairs, the honeymoon bloom had faded. Over the next three days we went for walks, quite often in line ahead, and finally came to the conclusion that we badly needed company. We rang up the Best Man and his wife, Christine's younger sister and closest friend, bowed out, and took bus and another local train to stay with them instead. After that, with some of the pressure off, and a lot of shared laughter, things began to improve.

We went back to work and to an upstairs flat in the Albert Bridge Road, overlooking Battersea Park. Life together got better, partly because of our friends whom we visited – Donald Swann was just down the road and round the corner. He had just reunited with Michael Flanders, to work up the act they had first put together whilst still at school, pre-war. Michael had enlisted in the Navy, was then struck down by polio, and spent the rest of his life in a wheelchair. He and Donald made their debut as would-be professionals to an invited audience in Whistler's Ballroom, Cheyne Walk, Chelsea. Christine and I were among around thirty media contacts invited. With some backing by two other theatrical friends, the Flanders and Swann Act took shape, and all us were instantly aware that we were on to a very good thing indeed. Soon afterwards the show opened in a West End theatre, en route for the rest of the world.

As a country we were emerging from the restrictions of the War and its aftermath, released from uniformity. So Flanders and Swann were a part of a series of theatrical send-ups of everything and everyone, including an Arts Theatre production featuring the two Hermiones, Baddeley and Gingold, with a rousing number called, *Don't make Fun of the Festival.*

The Festival of Britain was the Labour Government's gesture in favour of sweetness, light, and a good time all round. Christine and I were assigned to do a programme together about the main Festival site on a derelict stretch of the Thames south bank. Temporary buildings were springing up like an herbaceous border, and we could just glimpse them in the distance from our top floor flat. Groundbreaking architects and entrepreneurs had been given their heads, allowed to experiment. The new buildings had all sorts of displays reflecting Britain's past and intriguing present. After the rigours of the War there were sights to celebrate and enjoy, and invitations to the sightseers to join in. Most of all, we liked the building devoted to English eccentrics, fronted by a life-size effigy of the White Knight on horseback, from *Alice in Wonderland.*

This off-beat outlook was reflected in the parties hosted by Michael Flanders. In his wheelchair he got everyone performing a variation on Musical Chairs, Musical Hats, distributing from his exotic collection, a different hat for each person; all of us dancing in a conga line to the music, with Michael removing one hat just as the music was about to stop. Then everyone had to grab the hat on the head of the person in front, leaving one of us hatless, and out.

It was here that Gerard Hoffnung was persuaded (without difficulty) to relate his memorable story, featuring the Ladder, the Pulley, the inadvertently descending Bucket of Bricks, and the inadvertently ascending Bricklayer.

Christine and I returned hospitality with our own party, hauling Michael in his wheelchair up the narrow, twisting staircase and all went well; Christine holding back a little in the kitchenette to see to the refreshments. No room to play Musical Hats but plenty of laughter, some singing, and perhaps an underlying suspicion that we were none of us as young as we used to be. Sidney Carter, another ex-FAU member was gaining fame as a ballad singer who could shift the mood from joy to sadness. He wrote the music for Donald Swann to sing himself:

Oh the youth of the heart
And the dew of the morning
You wake and they've left you
Without any warning....
The wisdom of winter
Is madness in May.

As often happens it was our friends and workmates who kept us going. And of course the work itself. Back at the ranch we resumed our different jobs in the Department. Christine continued with her Schools Radio programmes, plus a weekly ten-minute sitcom *You're Only Young Once* (YOYO for short) which I popped into the *Under 20 Parade* as a device to bridge the generation gap (and grab some older listeners alongside their sons and daughters).

Our *Question Time* broadcasts allowed us to draw on a range of celebrities, recognisable by young listeners who were now joined at home by older members of the family, intrigued to learn what the younger generation was getting up to. We varied the pattern, with youngsters taking some of the limelight, putting awkward questions, and in turn sitting on the panel themselves to face audiences of their elders.

With Light Programme backing, we had taken off abroad and staged hookups with teams of youngsters in the UK interacting with their opposite numbers in Norway, Germany, France. Different kinds of youngster, but on the whole the same capacity to draw on their own common sense and hard-won experience, and in their answers make some of their adult audiences sit up.

We continued at home with mainly adult panels, grabbing all sorts of celebrities to face the teenagers' music. One panel contributor was Gilbert Harding. In the 50s this middle-aged *enfant terrible* had become everyone's favourite bugbear, saying whatever came into his head on television quizzes, radio interviews and commentaries, all in an endearingly insulting fashion. So he went down well in Question Time, with teenager audiences doing their best to cheer on the panel celebrities or shout them down.

Off mike and away from the cameras he seemed to me a moderately endearing personality, lonely in some respects, asserting his own public personality as a kind of fence within which to stay safe. We had talks from time to time about forthcoming programmes, sometimes during his own tight schedule. (One briefing conversation took place in the women's clothing section of an Oxford Street department store, whilst he was choosing a night-dress as a gift for his elderly sister.)

I managed to interest him in an idea for a new kind of confrontation, on the air.

How about a Trial with Gilbert as the Defendant, defending his right to be very rude about young people? Sounds interesting. How to do it? Well, there's *What's my Line?*, a panel quiz in which Gilbert often figures, and for which everyone tunes in. The panel has to guess the jobs of various unknowns brought one-by-one before it. Enough said. If an opportunity should arise during one such programme, Gilbert was prepared to make a rude remark about young people, and we could then nail him for it and get him on trial for Defamation.

I quietly contacted the producer of *What's My Line?* and he agreed to include a youth worker among the next batch of strangers to be quizzed.

When the programme went out, live on air, Christine and I were viewing it in Gilbert's flat because we had no television of our own. I was a bit anxious because the youth worker was the last to appear on the programme and everyone else as well as Gilbert was busily talking their heads off. Gilbert had other subjects on his mind besides the one on which I had previously primed him. He went on talking to the newcomer and the world at large until the programme was almost due to end, finally he remembered us, and got out the comment he had up his sleeve – a characteristically explosive remark about '*this spineless and spoon-fed younger generation*'.

A sigh of relief from the two of us in the know, and in the next day's *Younger Generation* programme our young presenter announced to all the world that we would seek the trial of Gilbert Harding on a charge of defamation. Date to be announced, and place – on the air, our own *Younger Generation* air.

Gilbert's notoriety meant that lots of journalists watched *What's My Line*? So we got immediate publicity and I was undeservingly praised for spontaneously taking the initiative, no one apart from the *What's My Line?* producer knowing the real truth.

We built up the *furore* (increasing listening figures!) over several weeks with the nightly *Younger Generation* programmes we were running, announcing each step on the way – the Playhouse had been booked for the trial – a controversial ex-magistrate celebrity, Claude Mullins, would preside –Wynford Vaughan-Thomas as counsel to lead the prosecution – Gilbert Harding Himself, would undertake his own defence. A host of witnesses, some young, some *mature* like the distinguished political old hand, The Honourable Violet Bonham-Carter were being sought. Amongst them were teenagers and commentators we had recruited through our mass auditions, and some of the innovating youngsters we had been tracking down on location.

Meanwhile there was a briefing meeting between Gilbert, Wynford and me. It was hosted by Gilbert Harding at the Caprice, a restaurant much further upmarket than I had ever entered before.

In fact the programme format, as a *show trial* following the usual courtroom procedures, needed very little briefing. I wasn't going to tell either of the principals who the witnesses for the opposite side would be. So the conversation ranged widely as the drinks went down. Wynford became even more effervescent than usual. This promoted Gilbert's desire to prick the bubbles. As Wynford went on about broadcasting in general, and an occasional mention of himself in particular, Gilbert began a needling process of small, at first inconspicuous remarks which a later generation would call *snide*. Before long this had its effect on Wynford, who went rather red in his already ruddy face and launched himself into a powerful rebuttal with the words, '*Fuck you, Gilbert....*'.

Fortunately at exactly that point he was interrupted by an American visitor from a tourist party at an adjoining table (just out of earshot) where everyone had recognised these two celebrities and wanted their autographs.

This brought about a ceasefire, and we ended up going home on a round trip by taxi, all smiles.

When the time came to set Gilbert Harding up as a teenagers' target we could draw on plenty of teenage witnesses ready to challenge him, a stream of youngsters who had been climbing mountains, rescuing small animals from the depths of potholes, doing occasional good to the housebound and the elderly.

On the night, in the Playhouse, we had a capacity audience for an almost totally unscripted and completely unrehearsed show. In view of all this uncertainty I decided to leave a colleague in the production cubicle, and to act as Clerk of the Court. This allowed me scope to move around from Bench to the witness box and the seats of the opposing Counsel, announcing each one in their turn (with the opportunity to do a bit of prompting if, as seldom happened, it was needed).

Claude Mullins read out the indictment and the opposing Counsel, Wynford versus Gilbert, went into action with a vigour and commitment that (I thought) derived partly from their earlier encounter in the Caprice.

Our witnesses in turn proclaimed the achievements, or the shortcomings of young people. Distinguished witnesses for the prosecution included Lady Violet Bonham-Carter who in ringing parliamentary tones praised young people in general and in particular. Gilbert, cross-examining, invited her to compare all this with any recollection she might have of *the heroism of old ladies keeping up everyone's spirits in their bomb shelter during the Blitz.*

Back and forth the battle went. We exhausted one programme, and adjourned to the next week (meanwhile building up listening figures even further).

The Verdict? – That of course went to the Jury, sitting not in the Playhouse, but as eager listeners back home.

After it was all over Jack and I and our colleagues had another audience with the Controller of the Light Programme. I produced a graph showing the listening figures, not just for the two Defamation recordings, but for the accompanying youth programmes in the evenings before, during and after: all related to our usual listening figures. So the graph began horizontally, and then suddenly ascended to the Trial mountaintops with the other weekly programmes gaining height on the slopes between, and a gentle descent to a slightly improved level over the following weeks. Kenneth Adam said it was *all rather phallic* and we went back to our desks feeling that we had, BBC-wise, made the grade.

Christine and I were now living in Hadley Wood, up-market compared with the Battersea flatlet. We had been visiting George and Violet Dixon and their family in their Barnet home just south. When they learnt that our first child might be on the way, they put us on to a suddenly widowed friend of theirs who wanted to move out. Our joint salaries from the BBC, eked out by a loan from my uncle, enabled us to negotiate a twenty-year housing loan from the Co-op. We moved into a house and garden that at first felt desolate. My father-in-law, on a parental visit to size everything up, commented, '*Well you'll have **thirty** years of being **happily busy** getting it to rights*'. Thirty years! – and, roughly, so it proved. For both of us the work in hand was a married life-saver. Christine got at the garden, I got at the garden hut and the fabric of the house indoors. I began at the top improvising a kitchenette on a sort of platform projecting over the staircase well. Then with a plumber's help converting the landing at the foot of the attic staircase into a mini-bathroom so that we could eventually make ends meet by letting the attic as a flat.

For the time being half the attic became Christine's work base, having now turned freelance, and being plied with Schools Broadcasting scriptwriting to keep her busy. The other half housed an *au pair*, which the scriptwriting helped to fund. Christine's transformation of the garden plot developed alongside the production of our firstborn, delivered, as we thought proper, at home.

I planted a cherry tree to celebrate (though not being much of gardener myself it didn't last long). But Judy, and a little later her brother Andy, completed the process of turning a house into a home. The children themselves, as they grew, dealt with each of us in their own sweet ways and gave us friendly links with the rest of the street, particularly the parents and children next door.

I continued to career about the country seeking out and featuring doings of the younger generation. I still had my eye on the possibilities in television, both for entertainment and as a parallel to the Schools Radio programmes that Christine still served, and that I had done my time on as a newcomer. At intervals in the meetings of the Schools Broadcasting Department we all heard that the high-ups in the BBC *had in mind* to create a parallel service in television. But it was taking a very long time.

Then I was offered a temporary spell at the Television Centre, to learn the ropes, in case there might be an opportunity for a permanency later on.

Back in the Ally Pally the basics were still there as I remembered three years back from my first, half-day encounter, discussing China with Horrabin in the chair. There were the same big cameras on ponderous dolleys, each cameraman aboard, pushed along by an assistant, with the focus-puller sitting in front or walking alongside. We still alternated between the two studios, with rehearsal time in A more or less matching transmission time in B. Any more detailed preparation had to be done elsewhere, with the essential props, but without the settings. So most of the time was spent in getting individuals to give talks with occasional photographs to help them along.

The really interesting part was bearding them on their own ground beforehand, in order to coax them into having a go. Sir Compton McKenzie, in those days a best-selling novelist, received me one morning at his home in Edinburgh, sitting up in his four-poster bed beneath a flamboyant canopy to match his embroidered smoking cap. He decided he would talk about *Islands*, including his own getaway in Barra. In the studio we showed photographs of islands he had visited far and wide. That set me off, with the yen to see some of them for myself. Were they really places, as he implied, where people got on with their lives individually and sorted out problems and opportunities together, shaping their own surroundings without fuss or unnecessary blether?

For the time being, the job in hand took over. There were other VIPs for whom my job as producer was little more than chatting up the speaker on the floor whilst waiting for the time, five minutes before transmission, to nip back to the producer's cubicle. All the real work was done by the Studio Manager, overseeing the two camera teams on the floor, and the Vision Mixer in the cubicle, cueing the cameras as they alternated from mid-shot to close-up or from subject to photo caption.

Everything opened up when I did a programme featuring Michael Balcon and the studios from which he brought us all the classic Ealing Comedies. Strictly speaking it was the Ealing team who did the job, everything filmed on the spot, with Balcon backed up by a range of actors, producers, and studio hands. (One such *hand* who came over well on interview had previously been borrowed by the production team to appear as a passing jogger at intervals throughout the filming of *Passport to Pimlico*.)

My chance to create a programme myself came shortly before my training secondment ended, when I was allowed to stage a proper programme with actors of my choosing, and some action to boot. The subject was *How to Behave* which I based on Victorian books of etiquette. As compère, we had Leonard Sachs, the Master of Ceremonies at the Leeds Variety Theatre for *The Good Old Days* of music hall. He and Daphne Oxenford had to demonstrate what a genteel person should do in various circumstances, with an appropriate commentary from the wings to point the moral; and a gaggle of young people to say what they thought of it all. This time I got the cameras moving around, and felt I had become a real producer, aglow with a friendly review of the programme in the *Radio Times*.

Back on the sound track, still pursuing younger generation talent, I heard of a place that had stuck in my mind ten years earlier – the Island of Iona. Not just an island to attract the likes of Compton McKenzie but the stamping ground of George McLeod, Doctor of Divinity, radical socialist, friend of Lex Miller whom I had worked alongside in the East End Blitz. When I had met him in Lex's living room, in 1941, George had seemed to me almost aggressive in his conversation, forceful, you might more politely call it, but agreeably stimulating. Not a sitting-down sort of person: back to the fireplace, legs apart, talking to the point and listening with a searching eye. Afterwards shaking hands with a memorable grip.

He had begun as a minister in Govan, a downtown Glasgow parish where most of his congregation were out of work and at odds with the rest of the world. He coaxed them to take a break with him to visit Iona, an island in the Inner Hebrides on the west coast of Scotland. Fifteen hundred years back, St. Columba had landed and made it a base from which to travel all over mainland Scotland winning people over to a pretty basic Christianity. He confronted and entered fortified towns, converting their feudal overlords as well as village clanspeople.

St. Columba had a lot to say about what Christians could be doing, and how they behaved to each other, and rather less on the intricacies of doctrine as set out in the writings of the early Fathers. After his death his admirers and followers on the island built an Abbey with local timber. It became a base from which to promote his kind of missionary work throughout Scotland. Later the work was taken on by the Benedictines, and a great stone building constructed. For a while the missionary work continued. Then the momentum was lost, people moved on, and the great stonewalls began to crumble.

George McLeod's idea was to reclaim not just the Abbey buildings, but to make the island once again the take-off point from which to do great things where they were most needed – in down-and-out parishes like Govan in Glasgow. He had already a reputation in Scotland as a thinker and a doer. Now he was able to overcome the forebodings of some traditionalists and attract other, younger, ministers who joined his own parishioners each year on a working holiday; enjoying the island beauties, in between gruelling stints on the rebuilding of the Abbey.

The trick that made all the difference was that those young ministers found themselves cast as unskilled labourers, working under the supervision of George's unemployed Glasgow craftsmen. So they got relationships – between words and deeds – right from the start.

The summer sessions continued year after year, and before long there was a small team on the island all the year round to help promote not just the rebuilding, but the ideas which underpinned it. That was all I knew, at a distance, about what had become known as the Iona Community. Now, a dozen years later, I could take the opportunity to find out more. I was free, more or less, to choose the subjects for the BBC programmes I produced, so long as they had a bearing on the younger generation. I learnt that there were now summer youth camps, reinforcing the work on the building, with a rather greater proportion of the time spent in exploring the island, the seas around it, and each other.

Off I went, with the BBC paying the fares on the train and the boat. A paddle steamer called *George V* set out from Oban, and ambled round the northern coast of Mull to the Iona Sound, decanting its passengers into small red boats to cross the shallows and approach the ramshackle island jetty. I clambered ashore with my boot box tape recorder slung on my shoulder and there was George striding down to greet me. We walked, laughed and talked up through the little village street to the Abbey. I put up at the Community's base nearby.

The current guests of the team which maintained the Abbey were teenagers from Govan and other parts of Scotland on their own working holiday, camping out, exploring the island, having fun, talking about themselves and the rest of society, and in between helping the small group which kept the rebuilding process going. The radio programme mirrored all this, plus bits of the Sunday service in the abbey, with everyone taking part in singing their heads off, and listening hard to what was said, in short bursts between the singing, from the pulpit and the reading desk. It was what I felt to be a rumbustious occasion, not sedate, but brimming with energy and an underlying commitment.

I called the programme *Laughter in Church* because people felt able sometimes to guffaw when participants, George included, cracked jokes in order to make their point about things worth getting committed to *doing*, Here and Now. A favourite story of his was about the stained glass window in a church somewhere else where a strong-minded teenager had aimed a small stone. The legend above the saints in the window was 'GLORY TO GOD IN THE HIGHEST'. The stone had neatly knocked out a single letter so that it now read 'GLORY TO GOD IN THE HIGH ST.'

The island itself was glorious in the sunrise and the sunset; in between it had a homespun beauty of its own. It seemed to me to reflect this rugged, exhilarating encounter with George and his young Scots. Everyday life went on in the village and outlying crofts, with the fishing boats based within the little rocky bay where long ago they had built the jetty. I wasn't there a day before I rang home to say to Christine, *This is where we could spend our summer holiday*, and I booked our bed-and-breakfasts with the Misses McDonald in their small home just up the street.

Later that summer I returned, with the family in tow. There was just room in the back garden for baby Andy and toddler Judy to take their turn in a tin bath on the grass when, sometimes, the sun was out and burning brightly.

Year by year we returned on holiday, later on moving with our next-door neighbours in London to share a barn that the farmer up the hill on Clachan Corach had equipped with bunks, basic kitchen gear and a chemical toilet.

Back home in London there was a long gap whilst the powers-that-be negotiated for the introduction of Schools Television as a regular part of the BBC's output. Meanwhile the radio programmes for the Younger Generation kept me busy, enjoying each as it took shape and went on the air, but still lusting after the particular joys of Alexandra Palace, and its successor Lime Grove. At long last my former boss, Richmond Postgate, got the go-ahead for what he explained to us would be some *experimental programmes.* Half a dozen schools in the area surrounding Alexandra Palace would be linked by closed circuit to receive twenty programmes, shared out between a team seconded from the Schools Department.

Each of us was free to choose subjects and treatments. So, joying at the idea of *experimenting* free-range, I decided to try out a different style and approach for each of my own programmes. One script was about lighthouse keepers. For it I commissioned a lighthouse keeper turned novelist who had just written a vivid piece about what the life was like. He submitted a script which consisted almost entirely of a lighthouse keeper telling a small boy about his life. He then fled to West Wales, leaving me to try, not very successfully, to get some visuals out of the script to buck things up. By the time it went on the air it was a mish-mash, with the talk punctuated by whatever I could dredge up from the BBC's film library to show a lighthouse, with the sea breaking around it, and a visiting boat bringing the lighthouse keeper's relief. Nothing to speak of about the inside of the lighthouse, because insights into the lighthouse keepers' life in cooking, maintaining the mechanism of the rotating light, getting in a bit of fishing from the rocks on which the lighthouse stood, – none of these were on film, and the set provided was little more than the rocky platform on which the lighthouse stood and a seat just within the entrance for the keeper to tell it all to the little boy.

Another programme proved to be neither one thing nor the other. I suspect it was so boring that I chose to forget it entirely. But the next two in my set did us proud. I decided one should be about volcanoes, bearing in mind my wartime grandstand view of Vesuvius erupting. I spent many hours in the BBC's film library viewing a magnificent array of eruptions worldwide, picking out the juiciest to go alongside what I hoped would be the key element in the script. This was to be a reconstruction of the descent by an Italian vulcanologist, Giuseppe Imbo, down into the crater of Vesuvius at a time when it was still dormant. Oh yes, and to include the necessary teaching element in the programme I booked another vulcanologist to comment on the process afterwards, and discuss it, on air, with some interested teachers.

We managed to get the studio for a longer session than usual, to allow time to set up a big model of a volcano, about five feet high, with dry ice inserted from below and released to provide at the right moment a spiral of 'smoke'. In another part of the studio there were twin caption boards mounting a succession of Imbo's photographs taken of the interior of the crater. Camera One panned slowly across one photograph, and then slowly went downwards as the vision mixer changed over to Camera Two continuing the process with the second photograph. Then back to Camera One on its caption board, panning and mixing to a third photo substituted on Camera Two. Then the same process back and forth between photos three and four. All this gave us 'the descent' into the crater until we cut to Camera Three close-up on a small patch of 'lava' – cinders laid out on more dry ice to suggest the smoke arising through the crater's floor. A foot, clad in a very heavy boot, is seen gingerly testing out the surface. Cut to Camera One, released from its photographic duty, on another bit of lava floor, and a gloved hand appears resting a thermometer on it.

End of descent into the crater, and cut back to Camera Two on the studio commentary team. Cue discussion, aided by a caption to which the vulcanologist wanted to refer, showing a zigzag graph of the behaviour of the volcano, at rest or in action.

All went pretty well until the vulcanologist began to speak, and comment on erratic volcanic behaviour with the help of the graph. Unfortunately, on transmission, he developed a stutter …

Afterwards, with the stuttering volcanic eruption dominant in my mind, I felt that we had a cold potato. But next day I was reassured, when a teacher observing the programme from one of the monitoring schools grabbed me by the arm and told me, '*That descent into the crater it had the children on tenterhooks*'. The rest of the programme – worldwide film clips, big volcano model and follow-up discussion – got by strictly as support for the *descent* (four photographs, a boot, a thermometer, two bits of dummy lava and some dry ice).

The final programme I called Black *and White in an African Village*. We had a ball creating lifelike mud huts and surrounding jungle at one end of the studio, with a neutral space at the other end for some commentary. Most of the 'actuality' was done close up (to make the most of limited scenic resources). The idea was to show how in earlier days it was the white man who introduced new elements to village life, hypodermic injections, new strains of crop to plant, useful utensils, even crystal radio. But 'nowadays' such innovations, along with many more, were undertaken by the people who lived in the place. So the hands in close-up changed from white to black.

In between these short sequences we had a conversation led by a young Nigerian over here to complete his medical studies. He was partnered by that earlier contact I'd had – the cartoonist Horrabin. His role was to make comparisons such as viewers might be used to making, between *primitive African natives* and the *civilised* white newcomers. Okesandu, the young student, could challenge those notions, and put us all in the real picture – cut to the other end of the studio and black hands doing the crucial jobs. I briefed Horrabin to question some of Okesandu's claims about villagers' ability to rival, maybe improve on the work of the white man and as I hoped that lit up the conversation. I had a big close-up of Okesandu's face, in profile responding to a probing question, with the vein throbbing on his temple.

As programmes go, although a bit 'black and white' in terms of its message, without the intermediate shading that ought to have been blended in, it was still a modest success. My BBC boss literally ran into the studio after the transmission with some of the observers who were monitoring the programmes to show them the surprising fact that all this was not a film done in Africa, but a vivid reconstruction. They surveyed the set and for the most part being not very familiar as yet with a television service that was still on the cautious side, they said the whole thing '*was a real life experience'.*

For me, what stuck in the mind's eye was that vein throbbing in Okie's temple, as he talked about the changing relationships between Us and Them, and the *independent* shape of things to come.

Chapter Fourteen

CONFRONTATIONS

When my BBC boss announced that there was to be a short series of *experiments* in Schools Television, I had taken him at his word. There were four of us, each allowed to choose what to tackle and how to present it. So my choice as you will have seen ranged widely, with all the risks and rewards attending. We had all assumed that these first programmes were to be a curtain-raiser, and that full-scale production would follow, straightaway.

As I was completing those experimental programmes I was invited for a little chat with one of the pioneers in post-war BBC TV. Mrs. Grace Wyndham-Goldie had a shadowy, but influential role. Alongside routine television programme production she was a sort of talent spotter, with scope to groom promising newcomers for bigger and better things. Our little chat mooted the possibility that I might stay on after my temporary secondment had been completed, and work with her and one or two other, apparently promising, protégées, one of them Donald Baverstock.

But being entirely wedded to what I thought was the immediate prospect of Schools Television I explained to her that I was already committed – little knowing that there would be at least two years to go before the high-ups finally decided that Schools Television could be a goer, nationwide. (Meanwhile commercial television got there first, which possibly delayed things further.)

So back I went to Schools Radio and the Light Programme's *Younger Generation*. By now we had settled into what might be called a routine, although our object in life was always to innovate. But we knew where to look, and how to get the microphone within the reach of innovating teenagers wherever they happened to be.

Up to now we had been after youngsters with time to spare for adventurous leisure. (Hence the *Spare Time Book* which now came out in a second edition published by Penguin). We began to extend our range to feature the work opportunities that might be within youngsters' reach. The '50s were opening up all sorts of possibilities – new technologies, new ways of dealing with long-established products and services. So at Victor Gollancz's suggestion I put together another book, about *Jobs and Careers,* which just matched the issue of an influential government Report on young people by Sir John Wolfenden. He wrote me an enthusiastic foreword which probably helped to attract some favourable comments in the media – perhaps because '*youth*' was becoming an in-word, tending to displace people's reverence for the elderly and wise.

In between these activities, I began to learn about youngsters at first hand with the upbringing of Judy and Andy, seen to mainly by Christine and Hilda, a much loved nanny, with Christine's scriptwriting helping to make ends meet. I got the enjoyment, without much of the hard work, day by day. This was not the best way to bring up a family, but we managed to achieve a sort of balance by concentrating on the surface of everyday activities, whilst ignoring the fault lines below. When the strain got too much for us we escaped for a weekend with Christine's sister Ruth and her doctor husband Johnnie who had stood in as my best man. Being with them, as friendly observers without making any adverse comments, we all behaved ourselves much better, and returned home refreshed, feeling that we had been taken out of ourselves.

I had the advantage (or maybe the disadvantage) of going off on production jaunts, two or three days at a time, to see, and record, how other people led their lives. I was beginning to fill the Monday night slots with *feature* programmes, attempting to convey just what it was like to live and work (or sometimes be jobless) in other kinds of neighbourhood. The area that impressed me most was the Swansea Valley, where earlier I had gone to get one or two interviews with teenagers to form part of wider-ranging programmes. Now, I wanted our listeners to feel at home with youngsters and their families in places where they belonged, and which belonged in a special way to them. Mining communities have always had that special identity, the feeling that they are up against almost insuperable problems, at the coalface, and with the outside world. And that they always have survived, always will overcome: *who's better*!

I met a former industrial correspondent of the Daily Mirror who had escaped to the Swansea Valley to take on the ownership of the local paper *Llais Lavour*, the Voice of Labour, renamed the Swansea Voice.

We swapped ideas about the ways in which people could be given a voice – a say in the way the authorities dealt with their surroundings – some echoes of everyday life – words and pictures that could give a taste of what it was like to live and love the valley, and celebrate belonging to it.

I had the same feeling about places that were frequented by people from near and far, but created for them a miniature neighbourhood, literally over the weekend. The Youth Hostels Association had the knack of attracting young people, plus older ones who were still young at heart – without imposing formal routines (apart from lending a hand in the washing-up, and observing Lights Out at the end of the day. Everyone could talk easily about the way they had come, and where they were heading, and swap tall stories of previous encounters. No one had to stand on ceremony or seniority. So people were at home with each other. We made frequent use of such gatherings to glean material for the Younger Generation programmes and had an extra special celebration in the Edale Youth Hostel to mesh in (not too smoothly) with a broadcast by the Queen. There was an excellent turnout with everyone full of beans, and a tendency to overlook the timing. But we got away with the programme and, more important, I fell in love with the Edale Valley, leading up to Kinderscout. Back in 1932 it was invaded by a mass trespass and has been free for all ever since. Its summit every good hiker aspires to conquer, perhaps singing:

I'm a rambler, I'm a rambler
Down Manchester way
……
I may be a wage slave on Monday
But I am a rambler on Sunday
I've been up on Kinder
And baked to a cinder
I'm a rambler from Manchester way.

I rambled down from the hostel to a friendly farmer and got a promise that I could come camping one of these days on a patch of his land. So when, later on, Judy and Andy were older enough we got ourselves there by train and bus, and camped out with a recently acquired ITISA tent, so named because when first introduced on a big camping site, its peculiar shape made people ask just what it was, with the response from inside, '*It IS a tent, it really is.*'

It suited us three, with just room to sleep abreast, and an odd entrance space where we could mount our primus and cook. My ideas about rambling throughout the valley took years to mature because the children's first and continuing love was the muddy brook which ran across our little field. (Just like I felt at their age, spurning the seaside on the Isle of Wight for the delights of the brickfield inland).

Eventually we got round to the Ascent, and found the top rather boring, a flat space with a little monument. But the way up, and the way down, and the view of the Mam Tor across the valley when we paused for breath, stayed in the mind.

Teenage groups were travelling far and wide, often to encounter their opposite numbers abroad. Bob Gunnell, a recent recruit to the Younger Generation team, interviewed a bunch on their return from a visit to Moscow and got their candid comments on what they'd seen and heard and argued about with Russian teenagers. Bob put together an edited version and as usual checked it with a senior member of the Talks Department. He was told to cut the contribution made by one of the party. She was talking quite critically about Russians, and Russian communism, but she happened to be a member of the Young Communist League and that made her *unacceptable.* We all knew there was a Cold War on, but this kind of discrimination seemed to us beyond the limit. Jack and I went to the Head of our Department, a friendly, sympathetic, dedicated man whom we all liked and admired. We were very Angry Young Men and showed it, almost thumping his desk. He referred us higher up, noting for the record that our *tone* (particularly I suspect, mine) was not what it should be. Meanwhile I had unearthed quotations from the founding documents of the BBC:

26th September, 1949: Letter from Director General Sir William Haley to BBC Staff Association. '... *The BBC's main trust is towards its integrity and impartiality. If a member of staff imperilled or damaged these, then the Corporation would take appropriate action no matter what the cause.'*

BBC Year Book 1955: *'The BBC's obligation is* ***strict political impartiality'***.

Armed with this we set out to get an official disavowal of that bit of censorship. Stage by stage we worked our way up through the Corporation hierarchy. Finally we reached the Director of the Spoken Word, whose office was next door to the BBC's Director General (and we got the impression that he too was aware).

Jack and I put our case. At the first meeting, whilst Harmon Grisewood was sizing us up, he indicated that our own positions as staff members might have to be reviewed. He explained that cutting out the contribution of the Young Communist '*was an example where expediency demanded that strict impartiality was temporarily suspended'.*

'What kind of expediency?' We persevered.

I had two more meetings with him, on my own, each lasting an hour or more and he began, I thought, to see that because of our loyalty to the BBC we were not willing to let anyone else let it down. At the end of the third meeting I was able to report to my own boss that Mr. Grisewood *would urge on the Director General that some kind of statement is made that would* ***encourage producers to be bold*** *in tackling tough subjects and speakers, not avoiding them for fear of policy difficulties.*

Previously, in the throes of that series of interviews with the hierarchy, I had mooted to my boss the possibility that I would resign (with the implication that I would then be free to tell the world). But now, it seemed, we were winning.

Rather pretentious memo to my boss:

'In the hope that these counsels will prevail I am suspending my own negotiations for the work outside the BBC as it looks as though the 'war' will no longer take place. And very glad I am if this proves so!'

It took nearly a year to get thus far and meanwhile there appeared to be no statement to staff about being bold. I began to think that the BBC, so much looked up to and enjoyed, was letting everyone (not just us, not just that Young Communist) down.

Life was becoming a see-saw of ups and downs, not neatly separating between home and work. There were pressures at both ends, alongside something like the *savage enjoyment* which those young miners talked about: the kick to be had from getting something done – broadcasts that came across the way they were meant to be; home life responding to the challenge of children growing up, battling with each other and their parents, celebrating the good times as well as the not so good.

They helped us to get to know some of our neighbours. In particular Edward Blishen, just down the road from us, who had a winner with his almost documentary novel *Roaring Boys* based on his tempestuous teaching life in a series of secondary modern schools. He survived early years of hubbub and derision and gradually got on terms with his pupils; even getting them to work for more than five minutes at a time. The great leap forward for him was when he set his form a project which required more than words and numbers: *How I would re-build my school.* A few were fanciful, most buckled down to draw on their own day-to-day experience. They made plans, drew pictures, became *committed.*

Edward and his family saw eye to eye with us, sharing views about what the younger generation was up to and capable of. He and I also shared a background as conscientious objectors to the still fairly recent World War II. Now the Campaign for Nuclear Disarmament (CND) was gathering strength with peaceful demonstrations attracting concerned people far and wide, and beginning to worry the powers-that-be.

The biggest so far, scheduled to take place in Trafalgar Square, was formally banned. So everyone concerned, and within reach, including Edward and me, decided to go ahead regardless.

Our wives saw us off, each armed with safety razor and toothbrush, to allow for arrest, but so many people turned up that the authorities held back, and let us all get on with it. We returned to our families in the evening, leaving the Square occupied by a resolute few, who then got arrested in the small hours. On another march, this time from Trafalgar Square to Hyde Park, young Andy came along too, and this time no policemen interfered.

I went alone to another Hyde Park demonstration. Afterwards walking back along Oxford Street, en route for the Bond Street Tube, I noticed two young men, Asians perhaps, who had been seized by the police, and put up, hands stretched above them, faces pressed against a patch of wall. They were being searched, in what looked like an aggressive fashion. I remembered my feelings long ago, watching the French colonials giving the Senegalese a going-over. I crossed the road for a close up observation, in particular to note the numbers on the collars of the police concerned. I stood beside them, not interfering. This move was not appreciated and I was immediately arrested, driven to the nearest police station, caged with other suspected wrongdoers, charged with obstruction and after a couple of hours, released pending a summons.

At the Magistrates' Court there were several waiting in the queue to be dealt with. Two or three of us who had been involved with the CND demonstration were approached by an official with the offer that if we pleaded Guilty, we could be Bound Over and suffer nothing more.

This seemed to me a bad idea, so I took my turn in court and told the magistrates exactly what had happened and why I wanted, *in the public interest*, to establish the identity of the policeman particularly concerned. But – fancy that – the policeman concerned was on duty elsewhere and unable to attend. *Case dismissed.*

At long last the BBC gave the go-ahead for Schools Television. I went with three others to be interviewed, but was turned down. Being too *experimental*? Questioning authority? Or just not good enough to launch and sustain Auntie's the new venture? There was a song at the time *Seven years with the wrong woman is more than a man can stand* and I felt, unreasonably, that it was time to separate. The man in Swansea had been hinting at a combined operation. I began to see him in the role of Orson Welles' *Citizen Kane*, who had started from scratch to become a media tycoon. I thought this Swansea innovator might be on the way up, and figured that I might make a better job of an alliance with him than the fall guy in the film. So now, feeling disillusioned with the BBC, I said I would take him on (that's how I felt about it, though actually it was him taking me on).

We had a house, a family, a steady BBC job. On a return visit to the Valley, I found a place we could lease. Back home Christine and I found a family who would lease our house for a trial period. With her courage and commitment that I didn't fully appreciate we agreed to go for it. I put in my resignation to the BBC, signed up with Citizen Kane and went, in advance, to Swansea to start the new job.

Full of enthusiasm for *actuality* and firsthand contributions by real people, I went up and down the Valley interviewing local residents, and came back with a basketful of quotes that could feature in a series of articles. Citizen Kane suddenly realised he was on to something quite different from what he had expected and we parted company. I went back in the train already beginning to think about life as a freelance, and the programmes I might concoct. Fortunately for us it wasn't wishful thinking. BBC colleagues were sympathetic, knew what I could do, and in a few weeks were offering assignments. So I was back again with Auntie, independent-minded, but making a living, and able to choose what I did (not that anyone offered me dangerously political subjects to cover!).

After that there was plenty of scope, not only in this country, also abroad. I was commissioned to do a reconnaissance in Germany and Austria for a twelve programme series on refugees. Yes, there were still refugees, thirteen years after World War Two ended. This could be an eye-opener for viewers back home who overlooked the fact that wars have aftermaths.

During the war years I had met and worked for, and sometimes with, refugees at home and abroad, and thought that I knew enough about their situations to understand how they felt. I learnt now the difference. In wartime you think ahead to *When this Old War is Over* and you can go back to everyday life. The difference now for many of the people I met was that they lived in a kind of limbo.

This time I met people who were still at the receiving end of World War Two, not on their home ground, but in the *temporary* accommodation, varying over the years, where they improvised and endured. For each of a dozen visits I set out in TV terms: The People, The Story, and The Pictures. Here are a few of those notes to be going on with:

AUSTRIA: RIED

STORY: *In the refugee Camp Ried, a blacksmith who had once been its terror was converted by Pastor Naumer visiting the camp by bicycle twice a month from Linz (four hours cycle journey each way). The blacksmith got together a group of refugees among the different Protestant dominations. One of his converts was a drunken carpenter who had been, as a soldier, a guard at a concentration camp, but because of his decent behaviour to the prisoners, they spared him though they killed most of the other guards on the day of liberation.*

The group decided they must build a church for themselves outside the camp. For years no money could be found... The carpenter exchanged several letters with an American contact living in almost equally poor circumstances, and happened to mention the group's dream of building a church. The American sent $5 to the American Methodist headquarters 'for the new church in Ried'. He died soon after, whilst headquarters were still corresponding with their Austrian contacts to find out where this church was...

Ried is the centre of a conservative, narrowly Roman Catholic agricultural district, which at first was suspicious of 'Protestant infiltration'. The only plot that could be got was a 45 degree hillside. In 1956 a World Council of Churches Work Camp gave a month's work to helping a local contractor cut out a niche in the hillside big enough for church and community centre. The campers built a concrete retaining wall nine feet high by 75 feet long and two inches thick along the bottom of the hill. An American ex-GI who had attached himself to the Naumer community in Linz (q.v.) persuaded the American Methodist to raise another work camp team for a month's work in summer 1957. Meanwhile, without any prompting or official support whatever, a young girl Methodist who had been on the World Council Work Camp recruited a bunch of other young Methodists, and brought them out to give a second month's work, much of it done in pouring rain. The Anglo-American wall 1957 was 30 feet high by 75 feet long, six inches thick at the base tapering to 1 _ width at the top. Within this vast concrete niche in the hillside, in 1958 a second American work camp followed by a second British work camp, which had drawn in Norwegians, English Baptists and Austrian Roman Catholics, with the help of half a dozen local craftsmen, built the first two storeys of the church centre, and made a good beginning on the third.

The impact of these efforts has been considerable. In Ried the leading magistrate invited campers for a dinner and a discussion on religious and political subjects; the headmaster of the local school took them round the sites; shopkeepers recognise each camper at once and knock ten percent off all prices; refugees in the camp, where the volunteers have lodged, are preparing meals and helping on the site.

PEOPLE: *<u>Uncle Thomas</u>, gap-toothed, ruddy face like a comic cork in a bottle-stopper, a good smile, no English. The carpenter whose letter began everything. Could* *be shown at work on the big window frame of the church, or on the rafters.*

<u>*Auntie Thomas*</u>*, a weather-beaten cottage loaf; Yugoslav – Volkes Deutch. Ample, amiable, always handing people something to eat or drink and serenely carrying on with her cooking in the tiny family room in the refugee barrack with everyone meeting all round her.*

<u>*Emil Paul John*</u>*, a first generation American from the Levant. To Austria as a GI. A genius with a baseball or basketball. Started playing games with refugee kids who used to pinch Army games equipment, Helped Pastor Naumer's group to build the Linz kindergarten, went home, trained as US Methodist missionary, returned for three-year stint, based in Linz. Oval, olive face, blue chin, big dark eyes, high forehead, lanky, shambling gait, horn rim glasses, engaging GI personality. Was promising local paper journalist in New Jersey. Writes and talks Saroyan-style, sees and lives almost every situation as a human interest vignette.*

<u>*Helmut Naumer*</u>*, aged 25, one of Pastor Naumer's sons. Handsome, Viking face, with a good curly beard which he may shave off on returning to resume theological studies in Frankfurt unless we give him the word to keep it on. It looks good. With his brothers and his father he helped to build the first Methodist church in Linz.*

PICTURES*: A patch of steep green hillside; pan left to show where the church building is rising out of the same terrain. A view from north-northeast about fifteen yards above one corner of the site where a cross made of two branches was set up. It dominates the building construction, although it's quite small. A view closer to the top corner of the site to show the sheer drop to ground level and the narrow gap between the thick concrete lining wall and the brick wall of the church.*

Maybe it would also be possible to get a shot of the poor-house in America in which the donor of the original $5 lived and died. He never knew what he had begun.

AUSTRIA : BADGASTEIN

STORY*: 'Bad Girls': Many young Hungarian refugees came across unaccompanied by adults. Some were just out for adventure. In camps demoralisation was rapid. Villa Edelweiss is a small pension in the Badgastein tourist resort, staffed by two young volunteers and a middle-aged motherly Hungarian who cooks and helps solve problems. These can include overnight absence on the tiles, acute depression, refusal to work or learn, or (on the day of my visit) assault with a broken bottle on two of the customers at a swish café where two of the girls are waitresses. But crime wave is decreasing sharply mainly because the two young volunteers, in spite of linguistic difficulties, 'talk the same language' as their twenty-two charges, join in whatever's going on, and when they teach (English and German respectively) do so with informality, zest and an endless capacity to invent new ways of getting on with the job to suit whatever mood the girls are in.*

PEOPLE: *Anne Jensen. Dane. Came first to help in Vienna soup kitchen at time of 1956 Revolution. Beefy, blonde, quivering most of the time with laughter at own mistakes. Yet firm as well as friendly. Glasses. Overcomes with animation what she lacks in looks. Has taught herself a working knowledge of Hungarian since starting this job. Fluent, clear English. Could interview well. Aged 25.*

Mrs. Ilana Vierag, middle-aged ex-midwife. Refugee from Hungary. Lost husband. Cooks and teaches everybody including plump Anne to dance Hungarian-style. Quiet peasant face. Kerchief round head, ample skirts.

Brenda Luce, 27. Ex journalist from Orpington, Kent. Good voice, phrasing and perceptive cheerful appreciation of problems and opportunities in the work. ... Knows everyone involved with the intimacy that comes from twelve months work without a half day off. Good features and poise would make her valuable in studio too.

PICTURES: *Bedroom number 5 seen from floor level of stair head, looking across narrow corridor and diagonally into bedroom showing the head of one two-tier bunk and the foot of the other. Four girls needing four different treatments – even to the way Anne gets them up out of bed in the morning – cajoling, kidding, commanding. Good view of this but cutting out the face of Susan, at 13 married to her mother's lover and the mother of his child. Other girls are: Margit, small, sharp, pretty and nimble, 14-year-old who stopped being a number one problem within a week of arrival; Gyorgyi, a 19-year-old Hungarian shop assistant with a little English; Weaner, 21-year-old Yugoslav girl held up from emigration because of TB contracted whilst a refugee. Fluent English.*

Lessons in dancing in the garden, and in the common room (17 ft square) with superb Alpine view through 3½ft by 5 ft. window, everyone singing the tune. Also tobogganing outside, snow permitting.

GERMANY : STUTTGART – LUDWIGSBURG

PICTURE: *'There is a green hill, far away, without the city wall' – as the old hymn has it. This green hill took shape thirteen years back. It shows up, grass-covered, as the skyline. It consists entirely of rubble from the ruins made by Allied bombing when the city was almost completely destroyed. Most of the buildings now to be seen are new. This is the 'hard core' of the refugee problem. The housing shortage is still acute, thirteen years after the bombing. The skyline is a reminder.*

The refugee camp is being partly dismantled with a few hard core families still left in their barracks and a glimpse of the new Siedlung tenements going up in the background. A top shot from e.g. a light mobile crane at work on a site adjoining the camp, to show the way it has become a self-contained peasant hamlet, with green stuff and livestock everywhere round. Pan round sharply to show the new ultra-tidy blocks of flats which will replace the barracks.

***STORY**: The German authorities are dealing justly and efficiently by their foreign refugee populations, giving them exactly the same scales of public assistance, and the same priorities in getting flats, as the rest of the population. In spite of the magnitude of the problem, it is slowly being solved so far as food and shelter are concerned. – At least for refugees who came into West Germany during and immediately after World War Two. But among this foreign population there is still a residue which remain in the camps, despite everybody's efforts to get them out. These are (a) the aged and crippled who can't get lucrative work that would pay for rent normally asked for the new flats that are being built for artisans; (b) people whose long sojourn in a succession of camps has demoralised, so that they're drinking or doping themselves; (c) peasants, particularly from the Baltic and the Ukraine, who can't accustom themselves to urban flat life, and who much prefer living on, even in cramped conditions in wooden barrack camps, where they are less severely regulated by the social workers who supervise the flat-dwellers, and where they can keep pigs, chickens, and grow their own fruit and vegetables.*

Officials can't spare the time, and often lack the imaginative sympathy to appreciate this problem. They are just driving ahead to close the barrack camps, and substitute neat, well-ordered tenements. .... The job is to try to coax the deadbeats into pulling themselves together; to make special provision, or obtain extra grants, for those who cannot afford flat rents; and to find alternative accommodation in private houses for some of those peasants who can't fit themselves into flat life.

***PEOPLE**: Mrs. Kirvo, 30-ish, blond, smiles wryly, but almost beaten. She and her husband and two schoolgirl daughters share two 12 ft square rooms. He has TB. Scanty furniture ... because of the bedbugs that find their way from dirty rooms into clean ones in the barracks. The last official she went to see could not even say which year she could hope to get accommodation outside the camp.*

Mrs. Melders Latvian, suffers from cardiac asthma, lined ivory face, prematurely white hair. Lives with husband and two children in two barrack rooms. She takes drugs and has attempted suicide; says she will do again before long. Eldest daughter emigrated to Canada but came back (in fact because she practiced as a prostitute).

Herr Ernst Grünupp, a refugee ex Silisia, now a World Council of Churches case-worker. Speaks Russian, German, and halting but adequate English. Small, quiet-spoken, balding, gentle eyes, complete lack of officiousness and pep. But has a shrewd assessment of people and needs, though he doesn't volunteer his opinions. Gets on well with refugees, in a direct and sympathetic fashion.

Mrs. Komoroff, neat, dark hair, quiet-spoken, in many ways shares the qualities of Grünupp. Left Russia 1923 as a toddler with her parents. Settled in Lativia. Fled again in 1939 as the Russians invaded. From 39 to 51 lived successively in seventeen different refugee camps. For half a year shared one room with 62 other people. Recently married a Russian Army officer who decided to seek political asylum ... She likes Germans, gets on well, but knows how different they are to the Russian temperament (husband!) and what a hard job it is to fit in. NB she must be given a pseudonym if filmed.

Mrs. Schultz , middle-aged Latvian who left her home in Riga with family at a few hours notice in 39 as Russians moved in. Contracted polio, partially recovered but it has slowed down her movements so she can't work much. Since 1945, has been in six camps. Husband has job in another province. She and daughter share barrack room 12 ft by 12 ft. with one 3 ft by 4 ft window. She goes periodically to one of the two German officials who between them must cope with the housing needs of 22,000 refugees. She is not surprised that they seem unable to cope. But she is tired of living in one room.

Back home, I had joined the local Anglican church, largely because it was a focal point for many of the children in the neighbourhood. It was run by a young, hardworking clergyman whose evangelical theology left me cold. And arising from the very few serious discussions we had, he felt the same about my beliefs. But he worked hard and to put it as I thought then (in a rather condescending way) he meant well. So I backed him up on the church committee and helped at some of the church events.

This gave me just enough leverage, when I got back from the refugee camps to suggest a variation on the usual Sunday service.

The word got around that something special would be happening so we got a packed congregation, seated as usual in the pews, but confronted on the steps leading up to the choir stalls and the altar space by a makeshift hut. Grey sacking represented the walls and the roof, enclosing a space twelve feet square (just like the home of Mrs. Schultz and her daughter).

There it stood during the first half of the service, with the usual hymns and prayers and the first and the second Bible Lesson. But when the sermon was due there was no one in the pulpit. Instead, in complete silence, there was a nine-year old from the Sunday school entering through the main door in a drab dress carrying an empty bowl, walking up the aisle, turning in the doorway of the hut, to tell us, *This is my home.*

Nothing else was needed to make the point. I can't remember what was said and done when the service concluded. But it made its mark because it gave a makeshift glimpse of reality: something to see, not just hear about or read in the newspaper.

It was the little girl whose message came across. She wasn't a heroine, or in any dramatic sense a victim. But people could feel for her and with her.

Whilst I was waiting for the BBC to give the go-ahead to get the refugee series on the air, I was rung up by my previous BBC boss. He had just been appointed as Director General of the Nigerian Broadcasting Corporation. There was to be a new policy, that would mirror the transition from colonial rule to genuine Nigerian Independence. He invited me to come with him to Nigeria *to help change from white to black and from radio to television.*

For me, too good an opportunity to miss. For the rest of the family? It was going to make a change, and the two children, only just of school age, not too settled in, the prospect for them was something new and exciting. For Christine? She didn't really let on. Maybe she thought that the change would do us good. Maybe she was just carried away by the prospect of settling, for a little while, in a new land.

We managed to find a couple who would take on the house on a short lease, enjoy the garden, and the neighbours, and pay us enough to cover the rates and the upkeep.

Meanwhile I handed back the European TV assignment, took the plane to Lagos and was immediately immersed in the process of changing over from old style broadcasting to what we hoped would be something to match the joyous and experimental feelings of the Nigerian broadcasting staff; and offset the more traditional approach of the old colonial hands.

At first I was expected to take over a training centre for newly-fledged Nigerian staff, which consisted of a one-storey shed with a blackboard at one end, and desks and chairs arranged in front of it. People had been coming on courses to be lectured at with occasional illustrations played to them through a large loudspeaker on the rostrum. Telling them what to do took up most of the training programme, with intervals for 'practical' work, pairing off to interview each other and then sitting back to listen to the recorded results through the loudspeaker.

Broadcasting was centred on talk studios, dispersed in fifteen provincial radio centres throughout Nigeria. Here and there, particularly in Eastern Nigeria were go-ahead Igbos contriving playlets, carefully scripted and often related to English set books as part of the schools' curriculum. In Igboland they were already beginning to break loose, with mini dramas based on local legends, and increasingly done ad lib. It was all still talk, but beginning to talk unscripted, free-range – even within the studio where usually the written script was king.

Harking back to what we had been up to with teenagers back in the UK, it came quite naturally to edge people out of the studio, out of the training centre, arming them with portable tape-recorders which at long last were becoming available. Actuality forever! Scene-setting, still with words, but on the spot – in the market, on the riverbank where young people were building their village a bridge, on people's doorsteps where they could be at home, point out what mattered in their surroundings, what needed to be changed, making music and dance around the village threshing floor. In Eastern Nigeria the Igbos had a long tradition of village self-government, with the village *leader* pretty much toeing the line set down for him by everyone else. That meant that everyone else had more than a say in what should be done. They were the ones who decided just how and when and where to do it.

You couldn't precisely script such goings-on; they had to be followed up, gone along with, the words conveying the scenery and the action.

The younger Nigerians, eager to break new ground in this relatively new medium, kindled to this process, and they began to notice and exploit sounds for their own sake, and to use them along with words to convey the sights in the mind's eye. Lecturing about the process, if it was needed at all, was in the form of occasional suggestions on the spot, as the would-be commentators and interviewers tried themselves out.

The young would-be doctor, Okesandu Ogan, who had made his mark, way back, on that television programme about *Black and White in an African Village* was now at the top of his career, delivering the babies of the new Nigerian Cabinet. I was invited to the christening party for the birth of his own fourth child, Obasi. This was the way in to Nigerians at home, not just displaying their wares in the studio or on outside broadcasts.

Soon afterwards Christine and children arrived, welcomed by 'Okie' and family but limited for any follow-up because of the ex-colonial home life awaiting them in Ikoyi – a sort of Reserve though not officially labelled as such. It felt like any moderately well-to-do housing estate back home, housing mostly white families, with some up-and-coming Nigerian families settling in.

The new life was not entirely boring. For any moment now we would become the inhabitants of a new nation. Independence was just round the corner.

Chapter Fifteen

SEEING AND DOING

Independence Day was to outdo the Fourth of July, Bastille Day and the winning of the World Cup. Ceremonies to describe, dignitaries to interview, rejoicings to overhear, with Nigerians themselves, not visiting outsiders, conveying those sights and sounds throughout the land.

The celebrations were to be centred, rather on the lines of the Festival of Britain, on a vast derelict site, with plots allocated to every kind of Nigerian achievement – manufactures, arts, faiths, sports – the lot. Each outfit had either to claim its allocated space free of charge because it represented a government department, or to pay for it as an outside organisation wanting to advertise its activities or its wares. On their spaces they were free to erect whatever they could afford, marquees, huts, even substantial buildings.

There was one exception, an enormous shed of corrugated iron which had once housed herds of cattle en route for the market. As a cattle shed it was well designed, as an exhibition venue it lacked impact. And this was the building assigned by a possibly jealous government to the Nigerian Broadcasting Corporation for its exhibit. The buck was passed to me and my Nigerian mates to make something of it, without of course incurring too much expense. Fortunately someone had come across, further inland, a man who had a love of abstract art, plus a firsthand knowledge of the way Nigerians had traditionally made interesting and exciting patterns – on the clothes they wore and the sheets they hung within their houses to wall off sleeping space. We put to him our problem: what to do about our eyesore, how to make it, at the least, presentable. And what to do about the empty space around it, because the government had made up for the cattle shed it lumbered us with by giving us a patch of muddy ground about the size of a badminton court to front it.

The solution which emerged was first of all to mask the cowshed by erecting an enormous fence, two storeys high, which in itself was an eye-catcher. The fence was made up of different shapes, like the pieces in a jigsaw, spaced out to make a truly Nigerian pattern. You were tempted to admire the pattern, and then enter through it, in a gap provided, and find yourself suddenly within what was no longer a cowshed but a hall of mysteries.

We were able to spend all our resources on the inside of the shed, with a recording studio where visitors could be interviewed and then hear themselves played back, going on to admire photo displays of the celebs and the outside broadcasts that we had begun to feature far and wide.

That still left the large muddy patch outside. We wanted to get across to everybody the notion that we were for everyone in the country, that our fifteen provincial outposts were not in competition according to whether they happened to be Yoruba, or Hausa or Igbo or any of the lesser ethnic communities we served. But all we had was a lot of wasteland. That set us thinking. So we dug it over, reshaped it, and transformed the muddy patch into an enormous 3D relief model of the country of Nigeria. On it we planted, at next to no cost, the provincial radio stations shown as toy buildings with radio masts. Everyone could see it countrywide and know that wherever they came from they were part of one whole, served by the national network.

Then we had to decide how to make the most of the one and only television camera that we had so far acquired. We mounted it on a little platform beside our beautiful jigsaw fence so that it could show Nigeria entire, wide-angle, and then pan round, swinging the lens turret to close-ups on the spectators, seeing themselves for real, on the big screen beside the camera.

To crown it all we managed to attract the Prime Minister, Tafawa Balewa, as he toured the whole exhibition and took a dutiful look at our exhibit. We managed to entice him on to the platform, thinking he would be making a little speech, but he found himself in charge of the camera. He was a good man, prepared for innovation, so he swung the lens turret, and panned the camera around to show the whole country laid out below, and his people beside it, cheering him on.

I had bought a car, my very first, taken minimum instruction, passed my test under the tolerant eye of a Yoruba police inspector and was all set to 'get out' to the furthest flung provincial studios, taking with me the most promising of the Nigerian radio engineers to show the world what the future of Nigerian broadcasting would be like, and who would be at its heart. The first trip was to the far north, Kaduna, and Mike Ejiofor, the Igbo engineer went down very well with the Hausa staff. On the way back however, full of job-satisfaction, I took a turn too fast over the brow of a little hill, skidded on the powdery laterite, and turned us over, with me safely clutching the steering wheel and Mike thrown out through the passenger door and breaking his leg. So back to Kaduna, and the hospital (to which Mike's Igbo family later journeyed across country to rescue him and get him looked after by what they thought would be proper doctors back home).

Meanwhile I returned home, and got back to work. There were occasional parties hosted by colleagues and their families and I got used to hearing the first two lines (never more) of a little song that began

The Commissar of Potters Bar
Has bought himself a nice new car...

I never learned the payoff line, but knew what it would be like, and rather slowly began to realise that I had a reputation. It was a bit like the impression gained by local officials in Sicily who spoke of me as *lo spinto* – the pusher. Not an entirely favourable impression. I had my eye on the ball, without taking much notice of the rest of the field. In particular, my own family, marooned in the predominantly expat suburb of Lagos, Ikoyi. Christine had followed on with the two children, already expecting number three, arriving a couple of months after I had begun to dig in. We had a bungalow with every mod con, and someone to do the cleaning – just like all the other expatriates, and a few recent upcomers among the Nigerians, with their families wishing to peg level with the English, by inviting each other occasionally to tea, and an exchange of friendly chatter about their children and the local (mainly expatriate) primary school.

So while I was rushing about in our family car, Christine was stuck at home with nothing to do apart from seeing to the children after school hours, and making occasional shopping trips by courtesy of a neighbour. She was getting bored and I was getting exhausted day by day, while still obsessed with the job in hand.

We made one trip as a family, trusting me as driver in spite of my track record, retracing the northern journey all the way to Hausa land with the two children fairly cheerfully enduring travel along trunk roads through scenery which seemed to them much the same, and then twiddling their thumbs on arrival at the guest house in Kaduna whilst I shot off on the job. The best moment was halfway home again when we stopped by the wayside and found that a chameleon had climbed the front wheel and taken refuge just under the mudguard. Andy coaxed him out and all was, for the time being, very well.

Back at base the work went on as usual, and so did the boredom back home. Christine's baby, still on the way, began to worry the doctor, and she was moved into the hospital for a caesarean birth which had to be done sooner than was expected. I got the message whilst at work, came quickly to the hospital and was shown to the side ward where I had been visiting her. The bed was empty, stripped of the bedclothes and the mattress. I remembered that was what happened, in the hospitals I had worked in back home, when someone had died.

I did not know what to think or to feel and then a few minutes later was re-directed to the ward where she was up and resolutely smiling, with young Giles, technically a Nigerian citizen, in her arms.

The new arrival, like any other baby, was a handful, and left little time to be bored, when the family was back home in suburban Ikoyi. But it also meant that excursions like the last one were not on. My work continued to be absorbing – *challenging* as people like to put it. Christine's was getting to be humdrum. The children at school had their own school friends to get on with, but without much scope to follow them up out of school hours. Then Judy began to lose her normal zest, and seemed to be suffering from some kind of illness which the doctors could not identify. She was off school, out of sorts, and week by week her normal health seemed to be breaking up.

So it was decided that she should be taken home, where there would be wider ranging medical resources, and whatever had gone wrong could be more easily identified.

We took another ride in the car to the airfield and I watched them go up the steps into the plane, wondering if I should see them all again.

A month later I learnt that she was back in her usual good spirits, whatever had gone wrong was now going right. This apart from the fact that Christine with baby number three as well as his brother and sister to cope with was now living in the attic of the house we had left in the hands of my brother and sister-in-law, and the lodgers we had brought in to help make ends meet.

Meanwhile the work continued, with more and more excursions away from the Lagos base to see local broadcasting teams in action, set up mini-training schemes on the spot, and in between times see rather more of everyday Nigerian life in the cities and in the countryside.

I got a fortnight's leave and Okie made it possible to spend the time back in Uzuakoli; not in the government Rest House, but with some of his relations in their family home.

I drove across country, along the bumpy laterite corrugated roads, and arrived, dried out, to be welcomed at the doorway with the gentle ceremonial exchange of small pieces of kola nut and sips of palm wine. After that, a day-to-day enjoyment of ordinary things. No great sights to see, but lots of politely curious neighbours to chat with, and sometimes follow back to meet their own families, and hear about the jobs they did to make a living. And, as a celebration of their coming of age, twenty-year-olds bridging a stream, shouting their joy, doing it all in a single day.

There was a free-and-easiness which seemed to stem from local pride in seeing to the essentials of everyday village life – the roads, the water supply, the crops, care of the orphans and the very old. Nothing idyllic, but for the most part practical, and good humoured enough for everyone to swap jokes about anyone else who happened to be in authority and too big for their sandals.

At this time people seemed at peace with each other, and (subject to occasional wisecracks) with all the powers-that-be. This peaceable feeling rested on enjoyment of their own ability, and ingenuity to do things together in their homeland, and as incomparable traders to go further afield, rubbing up against everyone else, cracking jokes, making bargains.

Back in Lagos the jobs in hand took over. More coaxing of the programme makers to make the most of local talent, and match broadcasting to local needs and opportunities. More journeys across country to meet local programme makers on their own ground.

Then my boss introduced me to a visitor from the UK, Commander Proud, recently detached from warlike service to help further the UK government's interest in overseas development. In particular, broadcasting. He was now closely linked to the Director of the Nuffield Foundation, who was looking for new worlds to conquer and had settled on the idea of introducing *educational television overseas.* The Commander was on a headhunting jaunt and it was my head he seemed to be after. Nigerian contract completed, I took him on (or was it the other way round?)

The Nuffield Foundation, backed by the UK Government, wanted a set-up which would help people overseas, particularly in the Third World, to develop their own educational television services, in their own style. They had a base in Regents Park which included a big building with a modest concert hall including a little balcony once used as the musicians' gallery. All now available for conversion to a television studio, overlooked by its own production cubicle. I managed to recruit half a dozen lively minds with whom I had had dealings in the BBC and elsewhere and we set ourselves up. To make what kind of programme for the benefit of fledgling units overseas? They were already served by the big television organisations in the UK and abroad with copies of the educational programmes designed for use back home. We had to devise alternatives which would better match local needs and opportunities.

So this was no longer a matter of putting together programmes, ready-made. We decided to offer a kind of do-it-yourself TV pack. Each subject had a selection of useful insertions – film clips, photo captions, small objects for display – that someone on the spot in Africa or the Caribbean could put together with their own linking commentary, making the most of their own knowledge of the ways their viewers might come to understand what it was all about.

We got this service going, and I went to see how it was received abroad, first in Ghana, where people jumped at the opportunity to shape programmes in their own way, then back again to Nigeria where broadcasters went along with what we were now offering, but were already capable of devising most of their own schools programmes entirely for themselves. Afterwards to what were then the two Rhodesias, and then on to Kenya.

There was a problem with the Southern Rhodesians (in what is now Zimbabwe) in charge of broadcasting, all whites, and not fully appreciating that the problem was themselves, still in charge. I was invited to friendly and hospitable parties to greet me as someone coming to them from 'back home'. Everyone, all white, was full of what they were doing, and their enjoyment of the country in which they were doing it. I asked to meet local teachers who were black, and who might have a hand in educational broadcasting. The first to be brought forward was left lurking in the passage outside the office. I went with him to a neutral spot where he could be hospitable and we could talk freely. But he couldn't see how to take things much further, whilst 'They' were still in charge....

In Northern Rhodesia (now Zambia) the atmosphere was different. Opportunities were still limited, but here and there people saw light ahead. Not necessarily at once. Up on the copper belt near Kitwe there was a very friendly and much respected white professional, admired all round for his good working relationships with black co-workers. He confided to me that things would be changing. '*In fifty years we shall have Independence!*'

Kenya was different again, with black teachers already coming together, using my visit and the materials I brought, as a stimulus not a substitute for what they were beginning to do already.

Then the good times in Nigeria foreseen by Tafawa Balewa abruptly ceased when he was assassinated and there followed a series of coups and counter-coups. The Igbo military leaders had been involved in the hope of gaining control of the whole country, when they failed, and General Gowon, a Northerner, took over, he faced Lieutenant Colonel Ojukwu, the Governor of the East Central State, who declared for an independent Republic of Biafra, extending across the Igbo heartlands to include the oil-rich regions around the Delta. The country was potentially reverting to the frontiers that existed before the white men came to colonise and amalgamate.

General Gowon was able to mobilise not only the Yorubas in the West and the Hausas in the North, but also the support of the French and the British, who supplied nearly all the arms required to put down the 'rebels' (and keep a hold on the oil supplies and the international market).

Most observers thought it would be a pushover, with international support enormously outweighing anything the Biafrans could command. Not so. From May 1967 to January 1970 the Biafrans held out, because with Igbo ingenuity they improvised munitions and food supplies to overcome the blockade and repel the invaders.

They turned tractors into tanks, milk churns into bomb containers, distilled salt from brine, operated a radio service from a Land Rover (moving around to dodge the bombing), improvised their own cholera vaccines and hung on for dear life to the oil refineries along the coast.

At the height of the war I got a message from Okie. Still in Lagos, where he could use the phone network, he was planning to move back home, with his wife, but perhaps not his children. Tuning into the BBC's World Service he happened to hear my voice in a series I was doing in what I laughingly called my spare time.

Okie could see that the war was likely to continue, until his countrymen were beaten to their knees. His message was to know whether our family could look after his children. We said yes. I met Amma, Nenna, Obasi and Ameche at the airport, bundled them and very little baggage into my Renault van, bundled Ameche off to his uncle and got the others back to our home on a chilly day when snow (which they had never seen before) was beginning to fall.

We were not complete strangers because I had been at Obasi's christening party, years before. But the girls took over, with scarcely any fuss, thanks largely to Christine and Judy, who between them reorganised sleeping quarters and got them admitted to the school and (to use a more recent word) *embedded* in the neighbourhood. Obasi joined Giles, one step up, at the Junior school.

We continued to churn out the do-it-yourself packs. But I began to wonder about our dependence on the newly established commercial television stations which were now at the receiving end. Schools Television seemed to be tucked away without much commitment, just enough to provide a hint of *public service* to justify commercial take-overs. Precious little opportunity for teachers themselves to take charge.

I was also finding that commuter time getting to and from Regents Park during the rush hours, and the periodic absences abroad, were bad news for normal family life. I had contacts with schools and teachers in my own home county. Members of the Hertfordshire Education Authority had caught the educational television bug, heard what I had been up to both at the BBC and with the Nuffield Centre, and gave me the opportunity to set up an educational television unit for the county. It matched the mood and the pioneering fashion of the 60's so jumping from Nuffield to Herts was a stimulating alternative.

There was a large disused greenhouse on offer. (I remembered a similar challenge in the shape of that Nigerian cattle shed.) With a like-minded colleague, Alan Thomson, and the promise of money to buy equipment, we converted the premises and began to attract teachers from near and far who wanted to take hand in television production, and convert it to use within their own schools.

We began a modest re-think about what television could do for teachers besides providing them with programmes – readymade by someone else – to show to their classes (and maybe allow a breathing space for the teacher).

We were creating a workshop rather than a production unit. We had two cameras, some lighting and a cumbersome video tape recorder. What were the teachers expecting to do with it? They kindled to the idea that they should be the programme-makers in their own way, without too much fuss, and not necessarily confined to our greenhouse studio.

Before long they were recording useful short sequences, loading my little Renault van with the video recorder to replay them as parts of each teacher's own lesson.

Then we all went one stage further, including cameras and microphone on the visit, so that not only the teachers but the children themselves could take a hand.

Age and seniority no longer mattered much because the children produced ideas of their own. We began to see the point of letting them put a programme, or parts of it, together almost without us. I watched a seven-year-old director right there in the middle of the classroom, standing between the two cameras, turning alternately to each of the operators (no longer us, but the children themselves), directing them of what they should look at and whether it should be wide-angle or close-up.

So far as the subject matter, the world was their oyster. Or in particular their locust which someone had discovered at the local greengrocer's in a crate of bananas, painstakingly captured, and brought into school as something to look at. Looking at it was not just a once-off. That particular class went on right through the term looking at the locust every time we visited, long-shot, mid-shot and very big close-up where one child, previously labelled a 'low achiever', discovered and pointed out to the rest of us that you could actually see the locust's tummy on the move.

Seeing how insects, animals, even people did things became a useful part of education, without the need for much guidance from the teacher. Back in our makeshift studio we began to experiment with programmes which showed how you do things, looked at from the *craftsman's viewpoint*. Woodwork, cookery, handwriting, looking after an animal (or dissecting it) – seeing the experts' hands as if they were your own. This tended to tie up a camera, mounted high, to look over the craftsman's shoulder, which rather cramped our style.

We were also experimenting with do-it-yourself animation – a sheet of tracing paper resting on a sheet of glass with a camera placed at floor level to view its underside. So whatever you chose to draw on the top, appeared by magic seen from the underside of the tracing paper. Diagrams, sketches, cartoons gradually taking shape. But we were landed with Camera One stuck in one position. Meanwhile Camera Two just looks straight ahead at the presenter full-face.

We rigged a second mirror on a frame behind the bench on which the presenter could be showing some handiwork. So now we were back to a single camera, facing the presenter and the bench and all the operator have to do was to tilt up to the top for a mirror image of the craftsman's viewpoint, half way down to get the presenter full-face, then down again for the mirror image of whatever he chose to draw. But no words handwritten because of course the camera sees the mirror image.

Drawbacks: two of the three shots back to front or upside down.

Problem/Opportunity!

At the time I was also anchoring a BBC television series on *Social Workers* – nothing very exciting, but a great deal of show and tell. In the interval between the studio run-through and putting the programme on the air I watched the cameramen checking their gear. I noticed that each tinkered with a couple of switches – one reversed the picture from side to side, a mirror image. The other switch turned the picture upside down.

Mirror image to correct a mirror image! A choice to reverse our own view of the mirror above the presenter, or to look straight at him, or to pan down to reverse the upside down view of the mirror below the bench. So now with the help of the reverse line and the reverse frame switches on Camera One, we had three shots for the price of one, all the right way up.

Doing this in the experimental programmes we made, at first for the Hertfordshire schools, later for others interested, began to teach us ourselves something about the relationship between the camera operator and whoever was the subject of her operation. She was the real mistress of the shots, without the need for a production cubicle elsewhere with a producer and a vision mixer cutting back and forth between several cameras each positioned for an appropriate shot. And besides those three shots, she had only to pan the camera to one side or the other to show anything or anyone that the presenter wanted the viewer to see; with our second camera now linked to a film projector for 'telecine inserts'. No need anymore for the production cubicle. The vision-mixing and all the shots are at her fingertips on the little switchboard attached to the camera tripod.

This in turn helped to produce a working relationship between the operator and the presenter, each knowing what the other had to offer, playing a programme almost like a doubles pair in tennis. And now we had not just a one-eyed television studio, with a single camera only capable of one kind of shot, but a modest range of shots all supplied by what became known, far and wide, as the Mini Studio.

Before long we were approached by a delegation from the University of London Goldsmiths' College, wanting the Mini and her operator to show their paces.

Goldsmiths' had a record of innovation in teaching methods, far beyond its London catchment area. But Greater London was now the subject of the delegation's visit. Ken Livingstone (later Mayor of Greater London) was then the leader of the Greater London Council which had this great idea of equipping every school in Greater London with the means to do their own television thing, using video in the same way that they had learned to use the blackboard or the slide projector.

Goldsmiths' College was about to become the focal point. They had two buildings recently vacated plus backing from the Joseph Rank Organisation to provide us with cameras (plural!) to turn them into Mini Studios where teachers could learn how to use video almost single-handed, to make the kinds of programme that they thought would fit the kinds of classes they were used to teaching.

They asked me to put these notions into effect. I was back on the road again, zigzagging between home, the Hertfordshire greenhouse, and the Goldsmiths' project a mile or so south of the Elephant and Castle.

Hertfordshire Education Authority was very helpful, and tolerated experiment in all directions. The ex-greenhouse was attracting teachers from all over. Alan Thomson, living nearby was happy to take over most of the work. I explained to the Goldsmiths' people that experimental television benefited by making comparisons between experimenters ringing the changes each on their own ground. There was a deal which allowed me to bestride two television set-ups some thirty miles apart.

Driving backwards and forwards across London left far too little time for the family back home in Hertfordshire. The family, particularly Christine, put up with the situation. Three days in the week, sometimes four, I drove the van across London from Hertfordshire to Camberwell and back, two hours each way when the traffic was bad. The rest of the week, sometimes including Saturdays, was a half-hour drive to and from the converted greenhouse.

The strain affected everyone, although nobody mentioned it. We just found that there were mini-problems that got people at loggerheads, and needed someone (I thought it would be me) to sort them out.

Our three children had an age range of from four to about ten – individually and collectively they were a very lively handful. Full of frequently conflicting concerns and opinions. We were now big enough as a family (including Christine's godmother now living with us) to take up rather more space at mealtime than our rectangular table allowed. So Andy and I went off looking for an alternative. We came back, £15 spent, with a round table, just over a metre across, carried on the roof rack of my little van. The table's shape now accommodated everyone sitting round it, shoulder to shoulder, but with enough elbowroom to wield our eating irons.

I could see what King Arthur and his knights were after. Everyone sitting at his Round Table was on the level. No one had special *status*, to use the academic word. So I thought to myself that when we had a family problem to sort out, the thing to do was to sit round the table and let everyone have their say.

I can't remember what it was we were going to discuss, first time round. We sat at the round table, shoulder to shoulder, in theory on the same footing, but we were also individually and collectively face-to-face. What actually happened was that Democratic Dad had his say, and everyone else mumbled, yawned or opted out.

However it just so happened that on the following Sunday, after Christine had done cooking and serving the Sunday lunch, and begun a chat with her godmother over the cups of tea, the children and I went into the kitchen to do our weekly stint – the Washing Up. Four-year-old Giles sat on the sink top receiving dishes for the rack from Andy. Judy dried, I put away. Whilst we were all at work I happened to mention the thing we had been trying to discuss a few days earlier. No problem. Everyone chipped in without the need for a Chairman. Eyes focused on the jobs in hand, we all talked to each other out of the sides of our mouths. No face-to-face confrontations, just a conversational buzz which nevertheless kept to the point while the washing-up work went on.

This made me think. Talking whilst you are doing something seems to ease things up, eyes on the job in hand. You feel that wherever the talk may lead, at the very least you've got the dishes washed and put away. But supposing that the subject matter of the talk coincided with the things you were actually doing?

It stayed in the back of my mind.

Chapter Sixteen

D.I.Y.

The great advantage of broadcasting is that it is airborne. It gets to people, wherever they are. The drawback is that you can't pin it down. Apart from videotapes and sound recordings there's nothing that you can get your hands on and say, '*Look, this is what we've done. The real thing, not just a picture or a talk.*'

Buried in most of us there is the desire to create something tangible, worth a second look, an end product. That's why Primary schools tended to whet their children's appetite for history by introducing them to *Man the Maker* – tools, weapons, chariots, ships – oh yes, and homes to live in.

Coming up for air on our summer trips to Iona I kept thinking about building, or re-building what might one day become our permanent base. Christine and the children had already fallen in love with our holiday surroundings – not just the island of Iona but bits of Mull on the other side of the Sound. Suppose that one day we could move to this part of the world for keeps? Using our holidays to 'prepare the ground' or to be exact – to build or re-build a permanent base?

So each summer, in between doing nothing on Sandeels Beach, ten minutes out of the village, I went in search of a derelict building which over the years, as part of another kind of working holiday, we could gradually convert. Absolutely no luck on Iona itself and further afield on the Ross of Mull (the long peninsular extending towards Iona) no luck either. There were some ancient crofts with a few walls still standing, but the Duke of Argyll, who owned the sites was, according to his Factor, unwilling to disturb anything. (Unlike his 18th century predecessors who undertook the Highland Clearances and rid their land of local farmers to replace them with more revenue-earning sheep.)

Up on the little hill at Clachan Corach, down on the Sandeels Beach, we kept looking across the Sound of Iona to the 'mainland' island of Mull, and beside it we could just discern another island, so small it hardly got on to the tourist maps, Erraid. All that we could see were its rocks and, just visible, a row of terraced houses. We heard they had been built when the island was used as a base to quarry stone, and transport it out to a distant reef on which they built the Skerryvore lighthouse. Afterwards they housed the families of the lighthouse keepers. Now the lighthouse base was on the mainland; so who was living, if anyone, in that little street?

On the last evening of our holiday, Christine and I boarded the local ferry, crossed the Sound and walked a mile or two to the coast that faced Erraid. On the other side of the water we could see the terrace more clearly, and just above the water's edge we made out what we thought to be a village woman shaking a blanket. So there were inhabitants!

Next year twelve-year-old Judy and I went back again, put on our bathing costumes and swam across. Landing, we were confronted by a large Glaswegian businessman who said, '*What are you doing on my island?*' We learned that he had bought the island, lock, stock and terraced houses from the lighthouse authorities, and was using it as a convenient rendezvous for members of his extended family, and, important, his business associates.

We explained that we had just wondered whether there might be accommodation available which we could rent next year round for our summer holiday. Impressed, perhaps, by my daughter's very fetching appearance, Mr. Dawson Bowman said that the end house in the terrace was vacant and perhaps we could come to an arrangement. It turned out that the village woman we had seen shaking a blanket was Mrs. Dawson Bowman, a very up-market lady, who nevertheless took pains daily to walk up the street and down the brae to where the last of the member of the lighthouse keepers' families still living on the island survived in a croft house, which had taken its toll over the years, as she had. So every day Mrs. D.B. would go down to see if Miss McGilveray was doing all right for herself, and maybe take her something to supplement her meal. Her home, the Croft, dated back a long way, probably even before the time when the quarrymen came to the island to cut and shape the rocks to piece them together, like an enormous 3D jigsaw, on a huge reef far out to sea, for the Skerryvore lighthouse.

The man in charge of the quarrying belonged to a famous family of lighthouse builders, whose work was scattered across the world, the Stephensons. At the time of the quarrying there was one family member who was not really into the family enterprise, spent his time scribbling, and much later made his mark, worldwide, as Robert Louis Stephenson, the author amongst many other books of *The Black Arrow* and *Kidnapped*. As a teenager he spent a holiday on this island, care of his uncle. He thought the place and its surroundings was almost out of this world, but he put its location into the story of *Kidnapped* (that I remembered reading long ago in Miss Rust's English class). This of course included the information that if you chose the right place, and the right time – low tide, you could walk across with nothing more than your feet wet. So Judy and I could have reversed David Balfour's footsteps and gone round by the back door instead of swimming across.

In all sorts of ways it has been one of those magic islands that Stephenson himself describes:

> *Few men who come to islands leave them; they grow grey where they alighted; the palm shades and the trade winds fan them till they die, perhaps cherishing to the last the fancy of returning home … no part of the world exerts the same attractive power.*

No palm trees as yet on the Isle of Erraid but lots of other attractions.

Next year we spent our holidays in the end cottage of the lighthouse builders' street. There was just room to sleep and cook and eat indoors, and an outhouse from which, daily, a full bucket had to be fetched. D.B. explained that the best plan was to empty it some little distance out to sea where there was a convenient reef surfacing at mid or low tide. He gave us the use of a rowing dingy which had seen better days. So most days, when the summer sea was fairly calm, we rowed with bucket out to the reef and Judy kept the boat steady whilst I got out, stood on the reef, and cast away the contents. (Much later we learnt that the custom set by D.B. for his own family and business associates was for them to take their buckets and chuck them down the back end of the jetty.)

Mr. and Mrs. D.B. spent much of their time either sitting out in the street with some refreshment, or motoring off in their boat in search of fish. We were busily exploring the rest of the island, which is not very big, at its widest no more than a mile and a half across; but full of ups and downs so that you can get enjoyably lost for an afternoon, trying to find your way home after visiting the Atlantic coast on the other side.

Then, the following year old Miss McGilveray took ill, was taken to the hospital on the mainland and died. No relative was interested in taking over the Croft. D.B. gave us the opportunity to move over and make it a holiday home.

There was a stream coming down the brae towards the sea which ended up in a mass of rotting seaweed where the beach met the little hump on which the building stood. Indoors there was room for improvement. Originally the building was what used to be called a but and ben – a living room and a bedroom. We early learnt the little drinking song beloved of husbands straying from their wives for a night out and getting one more for the road:

Just a wee doch an doris
Just a wee drap that's a
Just a wee doch an doris
Before you gang awa
There's a wee wifey waitin
In a wee But 'n Ben
If you can say
'It's a braw bricht moonlicht nicht, the nicht'
Then you're a' richt ye ken

And can show the wee wifey that, speech-wise, you are not entirely pissed.

The family which had lived over several generations in the Croft had made an extension of corrugated iron, rather smaller than you could swing a cat, to make a kitchen, and another much larger to provide sleeping space for an extending family. The roof overall was corrugated iron and leaking here and there. The floorboards were beginning to rot. The windows were a bit draughty. But coming into the place was a joy, unmatched, for everyone in the family, and the friends who over the years dropped in, sometimes bringing tents to cope with an overflow.

On the first day that the family moved in, marvelling, I noticed that son Andy, who was approaching the teenage years when anything and nothing goes, made a beeline for a discarded brass tray, with a pattern embossed on it, rather the worse for wear. He found a duster to polish it and got immediately to work. This was a symptom of something that overtook all of us from the start, and still continues. There has always been something to do, which someone has noticed, and got on with it, usually without bothering anybody else.

We all confronted the morass of stinking seaweed into which the gentle stream disappeared. At this moment Andy suddenly began to cut a new channel exposing rocks which became banks down which the stream could flow, carrying some of the seaweed with it, and allowing the rest of the seaweed to dry out and with a little help become part of the beach.

Giles sprayed Rentokil insecticide throughout the loft. He and I renewed most of the floorboards. We all re-painted window frames. Andy master-minded the expansion of the kitchenette by a good eighteen inches and we all helped to add a modest extension. Judy re-panelled the walls of what now became the sunroom.

After years of carting buckets from the outside latrines to a convenient patch a couple of hundred yards away, we got round to digging a much bigger hole and installing a septic tank. Everyone helped to dig at the time, and has contributed to the flow from the indoors bathroom and the lavatory (which over time is also due for a face lift, if that's the right word).

Eventually with Andy in the lead, we broke the back of a rocky patch of gorse and heather, and begin transform it into a sort of allotment on which Christine and Judy worked to turn it into a thriving vegetable garden. Andy planted some saplings which have grown into trees that shelter it from sea winds.

The corrugated iron roof, painted a dull crimson like most other buildings of its vintage, looked good, but needed replacement, we decided. But not until six years later we got round to commissioning Charlie McDougal, from Fionnphort, the village on Mull at the receiving of the ferry, to do the job, with whatever unskilled help the rest of us could provide. It was done over one holiday and we were all proud of the result, until a few years later we learnt that the building sheets we had carefully chosen, and which seemed entirely suitable at the time, consisted of an asbestos compound. By that time we had got used to having the roof there and there were no signs of asbestosis so far. So we continued to live with it, each holiday, until long after we could afford to replace it, once again as a combined operation, with healthy slates.

We had an amateurish go at digging out what we liked to call a reservoir, further upstream, so that the rainwater could collect in times of drought. Over the years the family and all sorts of friends and acquaintances, largely on their own initiatives, made improvements. Giles went up the brae and dug channels as tributaries to the stream. We cut back some of the gorse around the *reservoir*, dug deeper the channel leading from it; eventually we installed a holding tank which effectively replaced it.

Getting our house to rights in Hadley Wood, over the thirty years my father-in-law predicted, was a chore, absorbing while each job lasted, good to look back on, a sigh of relief when it was all done.

Not so on Erraid. This may partly be for the reason that set Andy polishing that brass tray on the day we moved in. You can't help seeing things that might be worth doing (that probably need doing, sooner or later) and the feeling catches on. Over the years friends, relations, casual acquaintances have dropped in (if you can use the word 'drop' to describe the last stages of the journey, across Mull, and over the sea or round the rocky backside of the island).

Once there, and after recovering one's breath, it would be possible to stick around relaxing. But nobody seems to go in for this for long. You can't help feeling that it would be interesting to do something about the stream that flanks the Croft and borders the patch on which we play a primitive form of football; or something about the wind and the tides that threaten the pitch with sand and seaweed. Or for that matter something about the walls of the Croft – they could do with a whitewash, or the interior – the bunks, the kitchen shelving, the yielding floorboards. At first, there were priorities. Later, nobody seemed to mind much who did what or when. But nobody has to be organised, detailed, put on a working rota. *Man the Maker*, usually preceded by *Woman the Maker*, come into their own.

Back home, as teenagers, Andy and Judy, and before long Giles, made the point.

While still at school Andy was good at getting together with others to do things – running film evenings, gigs, events, visits to all sorts of festivals, raising funds for third world charities, and in the meantime helping to promote a radically-minded school council, with staff and students more or less on the same footing.

In his fifth year I went on a routine visit to hear about his progress from his teachers. It was explained to me that, '*He's very sociable, but he really isn't sixth form material*'. Nothing was said to me about any role he and others might have taken on in promoting the students' (and teachers') rights.

So that was the end of his schooling. And the beginning of a series of innovations elsewhere. He found an outfit that was looking after other youngsters who had been in trouble, was brought in as a helper, got them up to doing interesting things like climbing mountains, going down potholes, designed really impressive graffiti in aid of people in need. After a year his boss invited him to stay on as Deputy. Andy told me '*that seemed like going into a long tunnel*'. He decided instead to get around a bit and got a job as a van driver first, and later on went with a friend to Erraid and they boxed and coxed between them serving alternate days as crewman on a fishing smack and digging out and cultivating the vegetable garden on our plot.

Then, without any formal qualification he put in for a job as a youth worker in a tough area of Sunderland. He got the job which was supposed to start with manning a coffee bar to attract teenagers. There would be someone else as a helper. On arrival he found that there'd been a hitch in the funding so there was no coffee bar and no helper. Everything had to begin, and develop over the next twelve months or so in the streets, coaxing other youngsters into doing interesting things and going to interesting places.

Then he and a colleague called a public meeting. Over fifty teenagers turned up and decided that their most pressing need was somewhere to rehearse rock music without being thrown out by whoever owned the premises. They went around on a reconnaissance, found a garage with a broken staircase leading to an empty room with broken windows and a door that needed repairing. Between them all they fixed it up, and began hiring it out at 50p an hour to all comers wanting to make loud music.

After a while this got too much for the garage owner and his clients, but by this time the group had a reputation with the Council – and there happened to be a school recently closed down, and available for temporary occupation. So now there was room for other activities besides the music rehearsals – a gym and a rudimentary canteen. When the Council in its wisdom decided to replace the school by a car park, the group was sufficiently well thought of to get premises in a derelict bakery. Besides the music rehearsing there were now venue space, a café, more P.E./keep fit and a punk fashion shop, run by the girls adapting clothes they got from charity shops.

The place now known as The Bunker, became a hive of ideas and opportunities which attracted support from various charities. This became the Key Fund which dished out small amounts of money to any and every group of youngsters who could come up with a bright idea capable of getting them self-propelled, learning on the way to cope with bureaucrats, money problems, and each other. A year or two later, with much the same thing happening elsewhere in the North East, including what outsiders might call a notorious area of downtown Newcastle, Andy mentioned that he was thinking of registering with the University so that he could pick up a degree. He did this and went on to help set up a unit loosely attached to the academic system, which could watch over what was going on, join in and learn on the job.

Judy had no difficulty in being typecast as *sixth form material.* She soon qualified as *university material*, entered the University in York and shared a house as a base with others like-minded. As their three-year course went on they decided that the bookshops in York were falling short of what was really needed – *progressive* books about what people were up and doing, or could be doing sooner or later, plus a range of children's books there in their own right, not just tagged on to what the grown-ups liked reading. They decided to become booksellers themselves as a co-operative, sharing in the work and making all the decisions together. They got the chance to do a bookstall (boxes of books on sale or return) at an important CND conference that was taking place in the University.

Success!

On the strength of this they began to build up a stock of books which they trundled round on a borrowed canteen trolley, first within the University, later on transporting it to various conferences elsewhere. By the time their degree courses were done, they reckoned there was enough momentum to borrow money, and buy a shop. It was well placed in the tourist-browsing centre of the city. For the next five years the shop developed and thrived. By that time the big commercial booksellers had cottoned on, added a more progressive range to the books they sold, and the group members individually decided that it was time to explore fresh fields. So they packed it all in, celebrated their achievement and moved on.

Meanwhile twelve-year-old Giles was getting used to taking all sorts of electronic equipment to bits, in order to see how it worked. He made friends with a shop that sold such gear, and let him take home items that no longer worked, and find out how to make them behave. He got involved with a youth theatre, teaming up to assist the lighting engineer, getting a lift from me when available, in between hitching his way there and back. On the strength of this, and later in his teens, he got a part-time job in the youth theatre based in Leicester Square; but by now besides learning more about backstage technology, he was getting paid part-time, 'front of house' helping at the refreshment bar.

Television, amateur video and professional broadcast, was opening up all sorts of opportunities, particularly for younger people with ideas and energy of their own. So, still in his twenties, he set up his own company to help choose and supply equipment (and ideas on how to make the most of it) to budding TV entrepreneurs, and before long to some of the biggies.

Some or of all this might sound at first like a doting father quoting special cases. But the late sixties and early seventies were a time when all sorts of people, especially younger people, had the feeling that the world was their oyster, and they were quite capable of prising open the shell and tasting what was on offer.

Much the same zest for innovation came across in the encounters I had with teachers wanting to have a nibble at ET – *Educational Technology*, in particular closed circuit television. Before long the do-it-yourself TV courses we had begun to run were attracting a range of teachers, from elsewhere in the UK and overseas as well as from London itself. Between them they could pool experience of teaching youngsters at every stage from first year Primary, up through Secondary, to sixth formers and beyond. Each teacher on the course had opportunities to concoct programmes on subjects of their choosing, in whatever way they could make the cameras behave. They were a lovely lot, full of ideas appropriate to the children they taught, egging each other on to try out new ways of putting information and ideas across – and getting new angles, new viewpoints as they went on.

Alongside the programme productions in our *Mini Studios*, once again we bundled a couple of cameras into the back of my van and went out into the sticks – the schools where teachers were grappling with the problem/opportunities their kids were offering them. Our course students used the cameras to show what teachers and children were doing together. In the Secondary schools this tended to be the teacher showing and telling the class, and then extracting from each youngster a suitable account of what he or she had been told or shown. This process was often echoed in the top years of the Primary schools, where children were being readied for the text-dominated, exam-oriented Secondary school world. A bit further down in the Juniors there was more scope for what teachers liked to call 'project work'. (I remembered just how it felt as a fifteen-year-old when 'H.M.' gave each of us the opportunity to do his own particular thing – a subject to find out about, work up, put across in words and drawings, with pictures from magazines or borrowed from the library to back it all up. A solo effort, to put yourself as well as your subject, across.)

Going further down the age range to the four and five-year-olds, was an eye-opener. Here a lot of the lesson time was spent in what the teachers called *activity*, most of it free-range, but centred on what in a theatre would be props and scenery. There might be a counter, with all sorts of dummy products for a would-be sales person to sell to 'customers'. On one visit to a Primary school where this sort of thing was happening, one student cameraman concentrated on the goings-on inside a Wendy House. This is a simple structure, dead easy for anyone to put together, at home as well as in a school. I made one for Judy and Andy out of two sheets of plywood, a metre or so high, one with a window cut out and some little curtains to draw back and forth; the other with a door that had a letterbox and a knocker. The two pieces hinged together fitted in a corner of the room so that they made a private place within which two or three little people can invent a life of their own. By the way, there's a shelf inside with a dummy telephone and that does marvels.

In our case it was the letterbox that featured. They looked through it and shouted messages, and posted pretend letters. In between times they used the telephone to talk about whatever came into their heads. Occasionally one became an outside visitor plying the doorknocker to be admitted.

In the school we visited there were three children making the most of their Wendy House. One of them, it turned out, had been in hospital for a leg injury. That was their starting point. They used the dummy telephone to ring up the doctor, the hospital, the chemist. They crossed the classroom to visit the 'shop' and buy imaginary medicines and dressings. They discussed whether their patient (one of themselves) needed rest or entertainment. All this went on for nearly forty minutes and then they drifted off to sample other activities in the time before the lesson ended.

Meanwhile the teacher was usefully busy with other groups in the classroom, having the sense to let the Wendy House lot continue entirely under their own steam. It was only at the end of the lesson period when all the class got together to *tell and show* what they had been up to, that they heard, from the lips of the Wendy Housers, the full story.

This kind of education, played back to the rest of the television course in the studio, was a bit of an eye-opener to some of the teachers whose jobs were with exam-oriented teenagers. To some of the others, used to teaching younger children, with a bit more leeway in letting rip, it was a reinforcement. But even these were surprised at the staying-power of those children in the Wendy House, dominated by their own desire to tackle a problem of their own choosing, pooling their experience, deciding between themselves what needed doing and how to get it done. All without a shred of intervention by the teacher.

Television comes in handy in observing this process, without interfering. So video recording can help people to see what's already there in children, waiting for the chance to make the most of it. Everyone on the course agreed that that was quite different from the role television plays in conveying information and arousing interest, with the viewers just spectators – not doers.

We went on doing it both ways. Seeing what children were capable of doing for themselves. Seeing what teachers could do for them. Or to them: in programmes that opened viewers' eyes to things and situations which they hadn't known much about before.

It was still a matter of telling and showing them something interesting, whilst leaving them still passive spectators. Watching other people as they made something happen. Not yet being part of the action.

Then along comes one teacher on the course who wants to make a programme about Sir Christopher Wren and the building of St. Paul's Cathedral. She's done a script outline that begins with Christopher as a boy who liked playing with models he made of imaginary buildings. Then there's a bit about the destruction by fire of the old St. Paul's Cathedral, leaving a derelict site, and the invitation to Sir Christopher, now famed as an architect, to design a new cathedral. So he gets to grips with the site plan, and submits his design to the Bishops. But it doesn't quite suit them so he goes back the drawing board in the final part of the programme, and produces what any Londoner today can see from the top of Ludgate Hill.

Four stages in the programme, each with possibilities, we thought, for children to become involved after the programme was over. But wait! How about splitting it into those four parts – maybe three or four minutes each of the video and backing it all up with things that the viewing children could do, on their own?

There were half a dozen local schools that welcomed occasional try-outs of the programmes made on the course. We offered them the four-part

Christopher Wren, along with additional materials that the children could use in their own ways immediately after seeing each section of the video. So this was no longer a quarter of an hour's passive viewing with the rest of the lesson period just follow-up talk. Each three or four minute episode triggered off activity by the children themselves, supported by the materials we asked the teacher to hand out.

After Episode one, cardboard boxes of different shapes with scissors and sticky tape available for the children to experiment, just as Wren did, as they invented different kinds of building for themselves. Episode two – Wren and his site plan for the new St. Paul's. The children get copies of his site plan so that they can use the materials in hand to rival Sir Christopher with their own designs for the new cathedral.

Episode three shows what Sir Christopher submitted, but explains that it wasn't good enough for the Bishops. So he has to adjust his designs accordingly. How will he do it? And meanwhile, how could the children themselves re-design on Sir Christopher's behalf? Episode four shows what Sir Christopher ended up with.

Quite suddenly we were on to something different. We are not handing out something readymade for the viewers' instruction. We're letting the television contribute to the children's own decision-making. And still allowing them to take stock of their own achievements, and compare them with what Sir Christopher finally managed to get done.

When we asked the teachers of the schools that had tried out the programme we found they had been making comparisons, too. They told us of their surprise at the staying power of all the children in the classes that undertook the project. They went on and on. And, to the teachers' surprise, it was not only the academically bright who kept going. They were rivalled, and occasionally surpassed by children whom the teachers reckoned were *slow learners* or *under-achievers.*

In a way we were following in the footsteps of the teacher who promotes children's *activity* work. But we were also giving the activity the spur of collective decision-making, which in itself helped to stimulate the children's imagination and experiment.

About this time, I was also anchoring another BBC series, *Growth and Play* about three and four-year-olds and what their behaviour showed to the people most interested in dealing with them. So there was a lot about the kind of activity we had been observing as part of the teachers' television courses. To back it up there were comments from some of the experts on *child behaviour*, explaining some of the ways in which children were responding to each other and to their surroundings, pointing out how gradually from babyhood onwards, human beings see and touch things for themselves, discover what happens, reach, and maybe revise conclusions. And alongside, how they get used to each other's ways and responses. Eyes and hands do the work, long before tongues.

Back in our own studios we were trying to get the best of both worlds. We could see the scope for youngsters' initiative, and the need – the opportunity – to provide a framework, a setting, which would help to give purpose and direction. We wanted to strike a balance between situations which are interesting, even intriguing – and the courses of action which children themselves decide on to make the most of what's on offer.

This meant starting out on the common ground of children's own experience. So we cast about for a subject on which everyone, teachers, children, ourselves, have a head start. *The neighbourhood.* Not just a Council map, but a place within which we work and play, including our own immediate surroundings – our street, our home, even the rooms within it.

The pack we designed we called *Living Space.* It had different assignments round which groups could form, and then go ahead under their own steam with the bits and pieces appropriate to each assignment that we provided. One group got some cardboard walls, windows and doors, and a polystyrene base, together with some samples of paints, curtain fabrics, carpeting, and a few bits of furniture in 3D cardboard. All they had to do was to decide how to decorate their room, and how to lay things out (including, incidentally, the TV set). Nobody told them what to choose and where to put anything. So they worked out their own colour schemes, and experimented, amongst other things, with the right place to put the TV (not bang opposite the window!). Plenty of maths involved in measuring, scaling up, and afterwards shopping around (local price lists) and deciding the best bargains.

Another group had a long frieze strip to pin up on the wall representing the back end of a town and the landscape beyond it. They had house cut-outs to issue all round the class so that everyone in the class could decide, each on their own, where they wanted their house, and pin it on the landscape accordingly. Result? The destruction of the landscape! So that particular group had to negotiate with each potential householder in the class, to shift his or her chosen site. Once the housing was consolidated there might also be room for a youth hostel, a bus shelter, perhaps a wayside café. And still leave most of the countryside unscathed, to enjoy.

Another group had a rather unappealing layout of a derelict inner city area, with a main road marked on it and some houses still left on the outskirts. They also had cut-out houses (stapled together in 3D this time and about the size of the wooden houses you get in a Monopoly game). Where will these new houses go? What garden spaces, park spaces could there be? (Sheets of green paper provided, ready to cut up.) How about side roads to serve the houses, and maybe some paths as well? (Supply of string and some green wool.)

The action groups concerned had everything to themselves to decide. They became a kind of local authority who reckoned to know best how this new housing should be laid out. And what would make it nice to live in? Each group had a very simple work card which did nothing more than set them off with their own set of materials. When each group had completed its assignment, the work card said: *Ask your teacher for a Red Card to follow up.*

The Red Cards contained what you might call a spanner in the works. For instance the bunch with their inner city housing estate were asked to invite everyone in the class, themselves included, to choose a house on their layout. Easy-peasy? Not quite so. The class teacher had been briefed when issuing the materials to count the number of children attending the class that day, and provide three fewer houses for the group to lay out. When everyone came round the layout to pick a house that suited them – it turned out there was a Housing Shortage. So what does the housing group do about that, eh?

Well it so happens that there's that group clustered round a green sheet representing their own Greenfield Housing, well out of town. They have plenty of room to lay out houses, roads, paths, gardens, sports field, play areas – all sorts. So how about the inner city group negotiating with them to deal with their own housing overspill?

That could go on quite acceptably to both sides, although the Greenfield group might also be a bit preoccupied with the spanner in their works provided by their own Red Card. This asked them to consider the neighbouring village, already marked out in the top left hand corner of their layout, which had been there, long before they started up their new housing estate. What do those locals think of the incomers? What could be done to share some of the amenities, or even to modify the new layout? Call a Public Meeting of the whole class, with some assigned to be newcomers, and the others the people already living there. Maybe do some placards representing different views (opportunity for people not very good at reading and writing to think up slogans that use very few words and still look good).

Back again to the teachers for their reactions. And again they express their surprise – the *passengers* pegging level with the *bright* ones, and all of them wanting to go on and on.

The news of these experiments got around, and attracted the attention of the doyen of educational research, Dr. W.D. Wall. He had previously directed educational research throughout the UK. Now he was Dean of the London University Institute of Education. He asked me over to tell him about the responses of the children, hands on, and how they had surprised their teachers. I thought it was a one-off conversation but he renewed the invitation half a dozen times as the Living Space trials progressed in the local schools. At the end he said that the project '*had at least three PhDs in it*!' and deserved a longer-term, more extensive piece of *action research*. He reckoned the person most likely to share this view of what we were doing would be the country's leading expert on Piaget, Dr. Eric Lunzer who was at the time the Head of the School of Education in Nottingham University.

The upshot with Dr. Wall's continuing help, was a base in Lunzer's Department with the funds, from various national sources, to introduce the neighbourhood packs not just to six teachers in their respective schools, but, it proved in the long run, some two hundred, in eight different Education Authorities in England and Scotland.

The first thing to do was to find schools and teachers within them who were willing to take part. And, most important, who could be seen by everybody else as reasonably representative, 'run of the mill', not specially trendy, not noticeably backward. So first of all, before we ever mentioned the packs, my job was to locate likely schools, and interview likely teachers.

I had reached a turning point, though it did not seem like that, at the time.

Problems, opportunities – all very well to consider at one remove, devising ways in which other people can sort out what they are up against, and what needs to be done – Now Soon or Later. Back home with a 25-year wedding celebration behind us, we found both the problems and the opportunities coming close. Christine had done her stint as a scriptwriter, alongside caring for the old people who landed up with us for their last resting place. The Nigerian youngsters taking refuge from the Biafran War had come and then gone back home.

Away at Nottingham University I had a bed available as well as an office, and could drive off with trial materials to schools and colleges near and far. In between at the weekends, I got back home and had a glimpse of the family. But gradually the house was emptying. The old uncle died, so did Christine's godmother. Judy and Andy had already quit the nest for jobs far away in the North. Giles was beginning to create a job for himself, and a company to sustain it, south of the Thames.

We still had Suki, a friendly black dog whose unlikely parents were a Great Dane and a Scottie, so that when you saw her running through the tall grass, head aloft, it turned out as she emerged that it was the short grass because she had inherited little legs to go with her handsome head. She had grown up with the children. One morning she greeted Christine as usual beside her bowl, wagged her tail and quietly died.

Christine went off to Erraid and the vegetable garden and the handful of enthusiasts from the Findhorn Foundation commissioned by the owner of the rest of the island to look after it. They were soon dropping in on the Croft every other day to tell a listening Christine about their ups and downs, drink tea, and go back refreshed.

But in Hadley Wood the house had lost its moving spirits. We took on a lodger in the attic flat with her small son, and occasional visits from an occasional partner. Then she and the toddler moved on to join him. But they left behind their little cat. Over the years she had taken her individual way among all of us. Now she was left with just me.

The work in hand continued to take me to mini projects scattered all over England, and occasionally in Scotland, with an excuse to drop in – and then drop out. So there was not much time to stay at what I still called home and look after myself (and the little cat). The next-door neighbours helped out by feeding her when I was away. Coming back she always gave me a welcome in her own way. From her adventurous middle years to her pensive final days.

Afterwards I wrote about her.

My small black cat comes silently as snow
I look towards the window – and she's there!
Ledged halfway from the rooftop to the ground below
Tail-tip just stirring in the tingling air;
Wide-eyed, intent, returning stare for stare

A shy young princess, carried shoulder-high
She clings and sways with me in mid-career
Entranced, surveying all that passes by
Distilling every sense to Now and Here
Pouring contentment in my inner ear.
Poised on my lap, her contemplative gaze
(Intrusive fore-paws marking time) presents
Matured reflection on her dateless days
A calm enjoyment of the present tense

No coming hither, and no going hence

Alone and old; keeping an empty house
Her food provided by a neighbour's hand
Alert no longer to the furtive mouse
I visit her and face her mute demand.
She dimly sees, but does not understand.

Now, at the needle-point of time and space
She scarcely questions what the vet's about.
Spell-bound, still seeking answers, face to face
We two, held fast in wonder, love and doubt;
Without a word her little life slips out.

I put away her epitaph in a folder marked 'Ups and Downs'.

Once again, I found myself spending time that might have been devoted to family life – on the road.

During the next four years I met Anthea, a long-serving Primary school teacher, survivor of a broken marriage, bringing up her own children. We fell for each other. I wrote to Christine hoping that, already living apart, we could continue as friends. She rang me and said, '*I've been a stupid woman. I love you and I am going to fight.*' Over the next few months the three of us pulled our relationships apart and ended up going our separate ways. Christine returned to the island, with me and our children looking her up at holiday times. All dealings with Anthea cancelled for the next quarter century until two years after Christine died, with me in the room beside her, Anthea and I came together again.

In the years between the work took over.

Chapter Seventeen

EXPERIMENTS

We got advice about *run-of-the-mill* schools from Her Majesty's Inspectors. I visited and re-visited 84 Secondary and 128 Junior schools in eight different Authorities, none of them specially good or bad, just average, and with at least one teacher willing to spare a little time, outside classroom hours, to tell me how she or he tackled their job. That was the only question I asked, but it spawned individual responses which went on and on, sometimes for more than an hour as they described what they were up against, how they sized up their children, how they got them going.

After each interview was over I mentioned to the teacher that we had a pack about the neighbourhood. Would it be possible to spare a lesson, perhaps a double period, to try it out? No problem. And get your assessment of the children's response? Fine, the children's environment – that's beginning to come on to the curriculum. Interesting to see what the children might make of it.

I learned what I had suspected, that teachers are good at talking, and rather like doing it. I came home at intervals with taped transcripts of the introductory interviews. They ranged widely:

> Mr. S. *'Well I'm old fashioned. I have been teaching for thirty years and I find it hard to take on [the new intake from the Primary school]. They are friendly, very cheerful, but noisy and they cannot concentrate very long. I find that they're –* ***wilful*** *is the word I would use. Obviously they haven't been used to being made to toe the line discipline-wise. You have to spend a lot more time getting their attention and dragging it back after it has been distracted. …*

By the time the children reach their fourth year some of his hopes are near vanishing point.

> *'This morning I have a Fourth Year class and there's perhaps a third of the class which wants to work; there's a third which doesn't care very much either way and the other third, or perhaps less than a third, are really determined they won't do anything. … Sometimes I could kill them, but mostly I just ignore them provided they don't disturb me.'*

At the other end of the spectrum, there's Mrs. B, nine years' Primary teaching experience behind her with a varied career beforehand though no formal teacher training.

When she takes over a group of children of whom everyone else seems to have despaired, she has things that people can handle.

'I took an old motorbike in and we called him Horace. I got these boys to dismantle it. It's lovely, provide a few spanners – and they're not difficult to lay on your hands on – and they're off. All that led to the topic of transport, and why wheels are round, and all sorts of things....

'There's one little boy in my class who is absolutely vicious. The first week I had him he hit me in the mouth and made by teeth bleed and I thought I would have to ditch him to another school where there are specialists. But I happened to hit on a good things with him. I brought eggs into the class and he watched them hatch and has been absolutely dedicated to them. He's the first to arrive in school now – he's always there to feed the chicks and to clean them out; and that boy, handling those chicks at two days old, displayed a gentleness which I thought was quite beyond him. This has taken me two and a half terms, and I taught him very little; until suddenly within three weeks I'd been able to teach him academically – he's willing to do things for me ...

'He organises other children, which is difficult for him to do because other children didn't like his aggressiveness and would have nothing to do with him; but now he leads a team of three that deals with the gritting and the water and all the rest of it, so he's having social contact with other children at a level where they accept it from him. You can have a conversation with him now without having to talk to him about what he's doing wrong; you can talk to him about things he's doing right ... you are building. It's incredible, but straightaway academically he has done two reading books just like that ... We just happened to have found the right answer with him'.

We went through the transcripts spotting and underlining what seemed to be each teacher's pre-occupations. All were concerned to some extent with managing a class, all to some extent with making the most of the children's own experience and interests. The number of each type of pre-occupation varied. We counted them up for each teacher and I got a colleague to double check. How many mentions of the need to *elicit*, create circumstances in which a child could draw on their own ideas and experience? How many mentions of the need to *instil* and instruct?

The two scores, *elicits* and *instils*, put together represented what I called the teacher's pre-occupation ratio. Giles, our youngest son was then in his Primary school, and in his spare time helping me to sort out all this information. He came back one afternoon saying *I reckon my teacher is about 7:8.*

My job was to issue a pack to each teacher on the day before a trial lesson was arranged. I took the packs to all sorts of schools –comfortable suburban, inner city fraught, out in the eastern fenlands, up in the Scottish Highlands. Next day I went back to be a fly-on-the-wall in the classroom and watch what happened.

The rather underhand trick was that there were two versions of the pack, though none of the teachers involved knew this.

The versions related to those pre-occupation ratios. One pack, which I call the *instil* version had work cards telling each group exactly what to do about the problem/opportunity the materials presented them. Everything quite specific just as an *instil* teacher might be instructing them. The other kind of pack was an *elicit* version which left each group's decision-making wide open.

I gave some mainly *instil* teachers an *elicit* pack, and some mainly *elicit* teachers an *instil* pack. All the others got what they were used to. All any teacher was asked to do was to look over the materials, and next day to introduce them to their class.

After that first double period? Well each teacher is free to drop the scheme, or go on with it, in the light of the response by the class.

Out of the 188 experienced teachers and the 16 second-year student teachers involved, two dropped the scheme after the first lesson: one because she was poorly, the other because he didn't like it. The rest went on. And on. And on. – Weeks, months, a term or more, a few for over a year.

Why?

I went the rounds again, at intervals, always as a listener never as a guide, to hear from the horse's mouth how each class (and their teacher) were getting on. Everyone (bar those two) was finding that the use of the pack was motivating the class a shade more, a bit longer, sometimes a lot longer, than usual.

Some of the *elicit* teachers landed with an *instil* pack said that the materials provided were very useful, but that to make the most of them he or she had encouraged the children to *strike out a bit on their own.*

If they had been issued with an *elicit* pack they said they were getting just the kind of response they liked to have, with maybe a shade stronger motivation because the materials were colourful and the subject intriguing.

Instil teachers getting an *instil* pack found it pretty much up their street, and the response usually faded out after a week or two, and then it was time to stop. But when an *instil* teacher got an *elicit* pack the first reaction was bafflement. Six weeks after one Junior teacher had tried out her pack, I visited her and asked what happened. She said, '*I knew as soon as I opened the pack that it was much too advanced for my children'*. So that was that? '*No, it's still going on. They were coming for more in their lunch hour. I should have been very unpopular if I hadn't let them keep going.'*

In my first interview with Mr. N. he emphasised the need for order and discipline.

> *'I reckon to slipper children for wilful disobedience perhaps half a dozen times in a couple of terms. ... I believe in discipline and children like it ... they need to know where they are. They need guidance from somebody else, some older person, what they can do and what they can't do. They need rules and regulations ...* '

He had not expected the children's responses to the different assignments in the *Living Space* pack.

> *'I was rather surprised. I thought there would be a great deal of 'Oh, I don't like this. I don't want to do this', but strangely enough there wasn't. They got on with it. ... To have the class thoroughly interested when the keenness is there. It is very satisfying.'*

Nearly a term later all the children are still going strong.

> *'A lot of them have done work at night, they've gone round the estates and asked various people their views [about changing the neighbourhood] and they've really enjoyed it. As for the model, they still haven't finished it and I don't think they ever will, they keep looking at it and changing things and they've really thought about this very deeply. I'm really amazed... Things happened that I hadn't expected. What struck me was the force with which children thought about things. The children who are not as academic, the less academic ones, these are the ones who surprised me with their ideas, their thoughts. The response was very good. They wanted to go on.'*

Mrs. W., the deputy Head of a Comprehensive school said she was accustomed to teaching by talking, all the way up from the Third and Fourth forms to the Sixth Formers.

> *'The lessons I give are still chalk and talk ... I know that the aim of education should be to produce a happy, thinking child, and I don't think my lessons necessarily do this. [With her Sixth Formers] we are really working towards the A level exam and my lessons are really lectures. I have to try to pour culture into them.'*

She chose to try out the *Living Space* pack with her Lower Sixth. Some of her colleagues were

> *'absolutely horrified: 'you will have a revolution on your hands – they won't do it'. Actually they were very happy doing it ... In minutes they got the idea and began to be very interested ... Since the Fourth Year these children have sat in the classroom and taken notes. This was quite new to them, and to me. ... They're just too excited for words ... It brought me up with a jolt. They were working things out for themselves, perhaps not always logically, but they were questioning themselves in the group. ... It's not just me that needs to be altered, I think it's the system as well ... I know I can do something about it in the school, because in the hierarchical system it does depend on the people at the top ... It has just made me stop and think, it really has.'*

It took about four years to complete the enquiry, getting each teacher's reactions stage by stage. What they had to say was a revelation all round. The so-called *elicit* teachers confirmed their own hunches about the latent capacities of their children, who sometimes surprised them with the *passengers* coming into their own collectively alongside the academically bright, egging each other on. There was something in the *buzz* created within each group as it got to grips with the materials and explored the possibilities.

As for the *instil* teachers who were confronted with *elicit* materials, their initial bafflement soon faded, as the children took over. I noticed, when I watched what happened in the introductory lessons, that the teacher in charge seemed almost at a loss, once the materials had been handed over and the children had got underway. The teacher would wander over to me where I was fly-on-the-wall, and maybe comment on the weather or some such, whilst the children continued, *self-propelled*.

Sometimes a particular group would be pointed out to me. One of the assignments (already mentioned in Chapter 16) offered a bag of wooden houses (like those in a Monopoly game) with a green desk-sized map. It was marked with a river, a bridge, a cluster of trees and the outlines of a village in the northwest corner. The teacher said,

'That's an interesting group over there with the green layout. The big girl, nice friendly kid, but not really likely to get anywhere much. She's a passenger, low achiever. The little lad, he's quite different. Always puts his hand up in a class discussion and usually writes a full page. The little girl, she's not a passenger, she's not even on the train. Never says anything, to me, or to anyone else for that matter.'

I watched them empty the bag of houses on to the layout and begin to arrange them. At first each worked separately, on the nearest part of the layout to them as they sat round their table. Then, imperceptibly they began to blend, muttering to each other as they explored possibilities. The big girl, working mainly around the bridge and the trees, had picked out one of the larger wooden buildings. She tried it out on one side of the bridge facing the trees, then upstream a bit, then on the other side with the trees behind it. Then she said quietly to the others, '*I think that's the best place for the old people's home.*' (Nothing in the pack mentioned old people, or a home for them; that was her idea).

She wanted to get them a nice background and an attractive view. The little boy who always wrote a full page disagreed. '*It's far too far from the shops.*'

At this point the little girl who never said anything to anybody, still busily arranging re-arranging the houses on her part of the new estate, said very quietly, '*My gran doesn't like living in an old people's home*'.

This matched a great many of the responses of the children, both Primary and Secondary, when they began to handle the situations the pack materials offered. They were looking all round the problem/opportunity, and trying out alternatives without sticking to the solution that came first to mind. And they were discovering problems and possibilities entirely on their own. That particular group ended up by siting the old people's home within the village, beside a smaller stream where there was a good view of the countryside, near to the shops, less isolated with more chances for a bit of gossip.

Later on, sometimes weeks later, teachers would see ways to relate the different groups' projects to other lessons; showing how everyone's ability to handle words and numbers suited their needs to sort out and solve the problems/opportunities they were encountering back on the ranch. The children found they needed English, Maths, Geography in order to get a grip on their *Living Space* assignments.

Over the weeks, months, or even longer, checking through the transcriptions of the interviews recorded, stage-by-stage, you could see that some of those pre-occupation ratios were changing. For most of the *elicit* teachers it all confirmed what they thought they already knew about their children's capacities to think things out for themselves, if the subject matter was really interesting. They also found something occasionally surprising. Children of different capacities, temperaments, outlooks, coming together in the same group were discovering something unexpected. They might begin by disagreeing, but trying things out, talking all the while, they were tempted to experiment with alternatives, comparing this way of laying things out with that, usually ending up with something not quite like anything anyone had first offered; but a satisfying conclusion nonetheless.

The *instil* teachers landed with an *elicit* pack were expressing their surprise, and before long their job satisfaction, at the hidden capacities the children themselves were revealing. For those teachers in particular the final interviews showed a shift in their preoccupation ratios, a measurable *attitude change* in themselves, and in the way they wanted to teach.

(A generation later some senior officers in the Department of Education and Skills came together from different parts of the country wanting to look at the *Living Space* materials, alongside some of the other materials, using the same approach, that we developed since those first two hundred teacher trials. They commissioned a smaller-scale trial of the same pack, with minor updates in some of the scenery. A new generation of 'run-of-the-mill' teachers tried them out and voiced the same reactions as their predecessors, sometimes even more emphatically. *'I was flabbergasted'* (enjoyably so), said one.)

In effect the children were teaching some of the teachers a lesson about their own capacities – given the chance to exercise them.

They were talking and doing; with the job in hand to keep them going in spite of initial disagreements. Just like Sunday washing-up in Hadley Wood, I thought. Only this time the doing part fitted all the different elements in the talking, hand in glove. *Hands on*, yes, that seemed to be part of it. But also, in keeping with the washing-up experience, *eyes down* on the job in hand. For the most part clustered round the subject matter, shoulder to shoulder like King Arthur's knights, yet not having to be face to face all the time.

The pack materials left little room for words, and that may be part of its attraction. What caught the eye were the thumbnail designs that gave clues to what the words stood for.

For the artwork we enlisted a postgraduate student in the Art School at Goldsmiths College, Jonathan Bean. He had come to the TV studio seeking space in which he could set up his End of Term display. The other students were content to use college corridors, Jonathan wanted space to set things out in glorious 3D. When the week's display was over and he was ready to move on I enlisted him, for what we thought at the time was just a holiday task, to illustrate the work cards we were preparing for the first *Living Space* trials.

Our collaboration has continued ever since, in what time he could spare from professional jobs elsewhere; first of all as a designer for Tyne and Tees Television and later Harlech Television. Later, beginning with the Jorvik reconstruction of Viking life in the North, he went on to design scenic locations which tempt people to taste, touch and actually smell what it's like to be in a place lived in by Vikings, or Victorian schoolchildren, or the home of George Washington and his family in Mount Vernon, USA, or the stamping grounds of nineteenth century sluts and villains in downtown Leeds or the Potteries.

For our purposes he evolved a set of *bean people* – little stick figures in silhouette which could represent blacks or whites, old or young, who could be all things to all people, wherever there were situations that needed such people to be up and doing. The backgrounds varied, palm trees, tower blocks, rondavels, slum terraces, upper classes houses and gardens. The *bean people*, merely by their attitudes and gestures, could look bored, angry, curious, quarrelsome, attracted, involved. They could be seen as doers, or celebrating what they did, and maybe surprising themselves in the process. Alongside all this activity there is usually someone doing nothing in particular, full of joie de vivre, and probably flying a kite.

The figures are mostly no larger than a postage stamp, but they help to get things across and allow people to identify with what the *bean people* are up to as well as what they are up against. You can seldom identify *leaders* in Jonathan's thumbnail drawings, unless they happen to be self-conscious platform speakers from whom everyone is turning away. But they help to generate a kind of fellow-feeling, in particular the notion that you don't have to be special in order to be up and doing.

Back in the 70's, the scale of the *Living Space* experiment helped to attract attention, not only from the people in education. One bright spark, Mike Burbidge, a senior officer in what was then the Department of the Environment, heard what had been going on and asked me to talk over what this might imply. He could see that at the start different teachers saw their clients, the children in their classes, in different ways. Some appeared to underrate some children's capacity to get up and go, to use their own initiative, responding to an interesting challenge. As for the children in the Primary schools, and the teenagers all the way up to sixth-formers, there were those that their teachers thought well of because they often put their hands up and asked the right questions, and always wrote a full page. There were others who had to be pushed, and even then some hardly budged.

Mike's working life was spent in responding to the problems of deprived housing estates where, it seemed, most of the residents had given up hope in the professionals, and in themselves; and where the professionals tended to think little of most residents' capacities, and felt themselves underrated and misunderstood.

There was a great gulf between Us, the residents, burdened with poor housing, bad transport, insufficient childcare, lack of amenities – and Them, charitable support workers, local government officials, politicians, who were expected to solve everything, but seemed to do nothing but talk.

Might there be something in all that schools stuff which could be salvaged and adapted to help bridge the communication gap between Us and Them? Allow the professionals to get a better understanding of the capacities of the people they were trying to serve? Coax the residents to *take a hand* in getting things done? Spell out exactly what's needed from outside to back them up?

The children involved in the *Living Space* trials spanned an age range from 9 to 16 plus, and an ability range from 135 IQ to below 70. What seemed to be common to everyone (besides their firsthand experience of living in a neighbourhood, or at worst a *housing area*) was the yen to get their hands on the materials and try out ways of making the most of them.

OK. What might there be in common between the grownups and the kids? Not just the places they were living in. Also perhaps a half-hidden preference for things to *do*, and maybe experiment with; not just to talk, or maybe moan, about?

The upshot was another neighbourhood-based project. Pack materials adapted to suit grownups and their own pre-occupations. Their concern about derelict, rubbish-strewn land, disused or under-used premises, a shortfall in support services, all summed up in the notion that *the talkers always win* whilst nothing much else gets properly done.

We set to and produced packs designed to help residents to consider ways and means to improve situations like their own. Imaginary, but realistic. What the academics might call *simulations.* But something more than the illustrations many academics are used to. We set out to convey what was involved without the need for words (or only a word or two at most).

We had a *Building Design* pack about an imaginary building, derelict – how could it be adapted? What uses could people make of the spaces available? There was a *Now Soon Later* chart with moveable cards to work out priorities. There were practical information cards in a *Fact Bank* which people could pick out and apply to problems and opportunities that might be worth tackling. A *Budget* chart allowed people to sort out how to use different kinds of 'Monopoly money' – restricted, unrestricted, available now or later. And to cap all – the *Open Space* pack with a dummy neighbourhood layout, presenting problems and opportunities waiting to be grappled with (*hands on*, of course!).

Our *Education for Neighbourhood Change* base in the Nottingham University's School of Education was conveniently in touch with many deprived neighbourhoods, nearby and further away to the north and south. There were good relations with schools and they might be the thin end of the wedge in getting the adults interested and, before long, involved in the neighbourhood decision-making materials.

I went the rounds offering the new packs to residents' groups who sometimes included professional support workers. The idea was to *simulate* problems and opportunities which were relevant to the real neighbourhoods. People taking a little time off for a locally run 'training workshop' could try themselves out, tackling those familiar problems and opportunities in an imaginary way.

The trials went on for another year or two and got an encouraging response across the board. The news got round, and attracted interest further afield. I took one of the 'Open Space' simulation packs to residents on the Dalmarnock estate in Glasgow. (Much like Govan, the place where George McLeod had his stamping ground and got a rewarding mix between out of work residents and the professionals who dealt with them.) The residents' try-out of the pack materials was favourable. But, they said, *Very interesting. But where's the place it's all about?* I said it could be anywhere. *Not good enough at all, at all. We want it to be Dalmarnock –* ***for real.***

Chapter Eighteeen

STREET CRED

Over the weekend we remade the neighbourhood estate model and turned it into a rough and ready version of Dalmarnock (warts included). The residents rearranged the houses and the roads and re-painted everything to match their rubbish areas, minimal gardens and next to no play spaces. Then they bundled the model (in one metre square sections) under their arms, and took them around where they could be laid out again to attract attention. (Later on, this process became more and more popular with other residents' groups, invading pubs, clubs, laundrettes, the public baths – when people were relaxing after a swim – and the Primary school foyers where parents were waiting to collect their kids.)

The Dalmarnock layout proved an eye-catcher. Not just a flat map, but in Glorious 3D (and realistically dingy Colour). People would cluster round to identify their homes and streets and rubbish areas. They got asked to check whether the makers of the layout had got things right. *Is your house or block of flats where it should be? Have we shown enough rubbish on the derelict spaces?*

Showing the layout around was just the beginning: an attention-grabber coaxing people to get involved (with no whisper about getting committed!) in moving around the layout, pointing out to each other the things that someone *(not me of course!)* ought to be doing to make things better.

Interest and curiosity aroused, people might come along to a social event with, incidentally, the 3D model becoming the centre of attention. Date and place fixed for the grand get-together (refreshments to be provided). Invitation list? Well the main thing is to let all the residents know about it via posters, leaflets and perhaps the media. And the grapevine – that's Us.

Anyone else besides residents? How about some of those Council people who keep letting us down?

Fierce discussion.

Former BBC colleagues of mine had recently been going the rounds with a recording car to cover some big public meetings elsewhere in Glasgow. There had been a lot of shouting, and some bloody noses. Residents were showing their anger with the powers-that-be who weren't being up to much, they reckoned. So what would happen to our meeting in Dalmarnock if we invited some of that shower?

In the end there was a compromise. Individual invitations were sent to about fifteen people, to come and see the *Planning for Real* project take shape. A good turnout, including two or three District Planners, the Police Superintendent, the local Councillor, the secretary of the Citizens' Advice Bureau, one or two from the Housing Department.

So far, so good. Layout that everyone can recognise is (roughly) Dalmarnock. Plus – and this is the important part – a range of coloured cards each about the size of a large postage stamp, each signifying something to be installed, changed, or eradicated. So we had sets of these option cards – in yellow, for all sorts of sports areas, in red for public transport facilities, accident areas, car parks. Another selection had all sorts and sizes of greenery. And so on, including a supply of blanks, labelled *My Idea* on which anyone can put a suggestion of their own which isn't already included in the kit.

On the day there was a full house. Curious and cautiously enthusiastic residents plus the fifteen professionals they had invited. And the media? Including the BBC, now showing considerable interest in a possible alternative to those bloody-nose encounters? They turned up, but were kept outside until the residents and their guests had done all they wanted, with the help of the option cards, to the layout. Plus time, in the right kind of conversational buzz, to have second, even third thoughts here and there, adjusting option cards from one place to another, maybe removing a surplus which merely showed that a lot of people wanted the same thing in roughly the same place. (I once counted sixteen adventure playgrounds on one Planning for Real model, eventually down to two, at either end of another city's layout.)

After everyone had done all they wanted, the BBC was allowed in to find out what they made of it all. Their answers were broadcast soon afterwards in a Tonight programme with the presenter's comment:

'A scheme which at a stroke of almost childlike brilliance puts reality into the lazy jargon of community participation.'

Community participation? Is that just Us, the residents? What about Them, the professionals? Where do they come in? As outsiders? Or inside, pegging level with the rest of us?

Word was getting around, first in the UK, soon abroad, that *Planning for Real* could be a change from – or maybe an alternative to – the talking shops.

In Rotterdam an energetic and influential development worker, Leo Herweg, set up an international gathering of professionals to consider the pros and cons of neighbourhood planning: residents' concerns, statutory requirements – the lot. It was to last a week and as a curtain-raiser Leo asked me to bring along a *Planning for Real* pack, with the 3D layout roughly matching the area surrounding our meeting place. The idea was to feature the model as part of the first morning's introductory session. People got to grips and the session went off with a bang. At the lunch break I was ready to dismantle the neighbourhood model, but someone suggested that it should be left on display. What happened throughout the rest of the week was that it continued to figure. *Plenary discussions* were broken off to test provisional conclusions, hands on. We all continued to work on the model sorting out problems and possibilities as they might apply to any neighbourhood.

So it could work for professionals and planners, on their own; and soon they were spreading the word to other parts of Europe.

Back in the UK, the Town and Country Planning Association was becoming very interested. For the most part they saw things as professionals wanting to do better, and maybe get a more sympathetic response from the people they did it for. Five key members pooled their experience and between us we produced a guide '*Us Plus Them*', as part of a *Neighbourhood Resource Pack* which spelt out some of the do's and don'ts of neighbourhood planning, quoting the relevant sections of the law, along the lines of the cards already provided in the *Fact Bank.*

To back it up and with some well placed endorsement from Mike Burbidge and others, I went round the country in search of communities with track records in taking the initiative and getting things done in their own way.

Just as with the teachers interviewed in the *Living Space* scheme this had to be a listening job with no intrusive comment from me. In this way, I put together a new series of one-page case histories, '*How We Did It*'. They ranged from a Tenants' Association in the 70's, 150 strong in Gibshill on Clydeside, to a handful of youngsters footloose and jobless in the 80's squatting in a derelict house in west Hull.

In Gibshill the 'goodies' attending a very traditional two-nights-a-week youth club, were being stoned by young 'baddies'. The police used to sweep by aggressively in panda cars. The area was reckoned about the worst in Scotland for mugging, burglaries, damage to vehicles and general vandalism. Then a revived Tenants' Association took over. They got hold of a portable hut, put it up and equipped it themselves inside three months, prevented the Council from appointing outside staff in favour of a seven-nights-a-week service run by a T.A. member – an ex-bus driver in his 50's with asthma and a bad heart, helped by a dozen T.A. members and twenty 16-17 year-old youngsters, catering for well over 400 children from 12-year-olds upwards. The door money each youngster paid made the whole enterprise self-supporting. The following year's Police Report showed that offences committed by young people had been 'HALVED'.

In Hull there were a magnificent seven of six jobless young men and one girl, calling themselves *Giroscope* because they were all receiving their benefits by giro, who managed to raise the money to buy the derelict house they squatted in. They renovated it completely, and over the years renovated 21 more houses, renting them out to several hundred others like themselves, providing housing at acceptable rates, short-term and long-term. They went on to adapt a set of old dilapidated workshops and make them available for small local businesses, each with an apprenticeship attached.

We followed up with a TCPA book '*Counterweight : The Neighbourhood Option*' drawing on the findings of a bunch of TCPA working parties, teasing out the do's and don'ts of joint action between Us and Them. As usual it included brief accounts of local groups' achievements.

Readers could take inspiration from each result, without necessarily learning *how* it was done. There was one community group which seemed to me to deserve a fuller treatment. Weller Street in Toxteth, Liverpool, was one of a bunch of run-down, neglected streets with Dickensian names, Copperfield, Nickleby – (not Micawber, that might be too near the bone in representing inability to plan ahead).

There had been Council talk of demolishing run-down areas and resettling people elsewhere not necessarily together on the same site.

Weller Street residents begged to differ, saying so to my tape-recorder in spades. They wanted to stay together somehow, on a site of their own choosing. Maybe as some kind of co-operative.

We decided to put what they had to say on some forty separate A5 cards, each to be considered as, so to speak, eyewitness statements, unadorned, so that other groups could pass around the evidence and judge it independently, reaching their own conclusions on the lessons Weller Street people were learning for themselves:

Here's a sample for you to consider.

Kate Kelly – '*Well, to me the co-op is a community that wants to stay together, don't want to be split up, stay together and try and help one another, that to me is what a co-op is.*'

Philip Hughes – '*If you don't know it by now, we're very unimpressionable. We don't easily get impressed by people. We've always said, 'Cards on the table'. Our people would rather have a man that bopped them on the nose than a shit hole who stabs them in the back.*'

Steve Cossack – '*There was a group of seven people on the working party, meeting four nights out of every week for six weeks. We had three sessions with the solicitors and another couple of sessions with the people from the Co-operative Development Society. At the end of the day we went back for a public meeting and said, 'As far as we can see, yes, it's a good idea, we would say, Go!' It was a straight hard talk. We explained what a house co-operative was and that was the start of the Weller Street Housing Co-op. I was stuck at the front of this meeting and I said, 'What are we going to call it?' Then this voice from the back, which turned out to be Billy Floyd, the milkman, says simply, 'You can call it Sussex effing Gardens for all I think. Get on with it!' The whole place erupted, everyone cracking off.*'

Kitty Hague – '*Then they started explaining about housing co-operatives how they work and it was all mumbo-jumbo to us, half of us didn't understand a word. So they called another meeting the following week. It was explained that we'd have a working party to go out and find out all about co-operatives, and come back to everyone and explain. It took weeks of these meetings before it sunk in with us that we could do it … I think there was only one or two who really stayed in and Billy Floyd was one of them. Being known – he was the milkman – he followed up every single house in this area and he's got the gift of the gab and he got round us to come and have a go. You can't lose out on it. Billy used to say, 'We'll do this, we'll do it, it's going to take a long time, but we'll do it.' That was Billy.*'

Steve Cossack – '*We said, 'Would anybody like to come on the Committee?' A few people sort of put their hand up. So we said, 'Has anybody any objections?' They said, 'No'. People started putting forward people who they knew, who they trusted. For instance Billy Floyd didn't particularly want to come on the Committee, but everyone said, 'Billy, Billy, Billy, Billy' so Billy came … There were seven of us in the group to begin with. Basically it just came together from talking to people in the street. It was always a pretty tight street, little terraced houses, you know, you can't fail to miss the people in your street. The lynchpin really was Kitty – Kitty Kelly, and she goes round, she talks to all the women and she was saying, 'Come on to the meeting and let's see what we can do.' We put notices up in the community centre and local offices, and the corner shop. When you look back the notice was very crude. 'ARE YOU FED UP WITH THESE SLUMS – COME AND DO SOMETHING ABOUT IT!' … It was funny really, it was anger that motivated people – they were all angry, and hence you got a good turnout.'*

Kate Kelly – '*We sang, got them all singing, another women brought her spoons and played the spoons. Then that coffee afternoon started off quite sedate, cup of coffee, biscuits, paid 15p then anyone wanting another cup, 10p more. Next time we bought a bingo board, 10p per game. Then everyone brings a couple of cakes, cheese and crackers, sandwiches, you know, quite nice and we have a little chat and then again bingo … By and by members are bringing presents and putting them in as prizes. All the money goes into the fund. Also having a good laugh about old times and what have you, and soon there's more and more people coming to the meetings because they know they're going to have a good laugh.*'

Billy Floyd – '*We had a procession of outside people who came to public meetings and tried to tell everybody how you went about forming the co-op … It was obvious it was boring a lot of people and a lot of them weren't going to understand. That's when we split up into working parties, and each little group attacked an individual task … All kinds of skills have got to be developed inside each group. That's what outsiders supporting should be aiming at, not imposing their will on the group, supplying them with crutches all the time by saying, 'We've got someone who can do that for you.' You've got to ferret out the qualities and skills from within the group and develop them individually. Otherwise the danger is that they will become dependent upon professionals … We had to go and research every tiny detail of information we needed. How you go about buying a piece of land, where the money comes from, the politics of it, how the political parties work in the town, what their strengths and weaknesses are … so when you do finally take them on, head to head, you are really tooled up with all the information you need and they're quite surprised.*'

Bill Halsall (the architect they chose) – '*There were a lot of visits to other sites and people extracting what they liked about different housing estates that we visited. It was very much starting from basics and looking at house plans and explaining exactly how to read a drawing and, you know, the pros and cons about whether you have the kitchen or the front door at the back. … But it was very much a two-way system. I call it communication, we were talking round a table to get a consensus.*

'*We used a working model for site planning and we've had a larger-scale model of the courtyards, and we've had the school kids build models of the houses. So we have a range of 3D models for people to look at, and they get conversant with the plans. Provided the plan has a clear drawing which shows a sink unit looking like a sink unit, they're quite happy to talk over plans and people aren't frightened of it. So it really wasn't that daunting a process to go on to planning the kitchens.*'

Philip Hughes – '*Everything fell into line … The women who went round interviewed the women in the families. Women can't kid each other. So people were honest about their needs.'*

Billy Floyd – '*We were greedy for information. We wanted to learn things. The politics was a lot of fun. Just seeing those guys at work in this Council was an eye-opener. Such clowns. Grossly outdated, the way they talked.*'

Peter Tyrell – '*We'd send a letter out to an official and we'd wait for a reply and after about a month we would go down to the office and we'd sit in his office and saying 'Hey pal, we sent a letter here and we're still waiting for a reply.*'

Philip Hughes – '*One of the main tactics is to make the bureaucrats think it was their idea. 'Great idea of yours' we'd say, 'We'll do that'.*'

Billy Floyd – '*The city officials said, 'The landscaping you want is very high standard, you know, all these shrubs and bushes and different plants ... there's no way we can maintain it.' So we said, 'We'll draw up an agreement so that you maintain the hard surface areas, brush and clean them, and we'll look after the plants.' And (at first) he said, 'No, no, totally unworkable.' But thought he had a solution to it all, 'Look you don't want shrubs or plants, you'd be better off with something that's easy to maintain and clean. We've got some really nice coloured tarmac. You can have it green or red.*'

Steve Cossack – '*I must give the impression that we hate professionals but we don't, we don't; but what we do dislike is that they've got this myth, this aura about them, you know – 'we are professionals'. We're trying to break that down. We've had to re-educate the professionals as it were, we've had to say to them 'Don't say excrement when shit will do' and give people credit for having some intelligence. We have proved people are capable of doing things, and keeping it plain, keep it plain. ... We wrote our management agreement ourselves. It's a legal binding document, so we gave it to a solicitor to look over first. And he said, 'Do you know what, I've been practicing for ten years' he said, 'and I've never seen an agreement drawn up as plainly and as simply and as comprehensively as this'.*

Peter Tyrell – '*When you first phone up and ask for Mr. Jones, after two or three calls it's probably you'll be asking for Fred. In the end we were on first name terms. It helped more than anything else when Mr. became Joe and Madam became Maggie. You could never had got that except by going into the offices and sitting there. We'd never have got it just by official letters, we only got that by taking the action we did ... We invited the professionals to our socials. They were coming attending our functions, our dances and everything else. They've been brought up and probably brainwashed to believe we were savages but once they came amongst us they were surprised and they were only too pleased to come up here. They were getting involved as much as us. Each time they come to one of our socials people would say 'Oh there's Charlie from the DoE' or ' There's Tommy from the Housing Authority'. It's no longer Mr. and Madam. They've got the same rapport with them as we have. It works both ways. It's made the professionals believe in the co-op because they can actually see the people who were making these decisions and they found that they were just normal, they weren't anything to be frightened of. You could heckle them, you could hold a conversation with them. They met ordinary members and the majority of the members said, 'Well who's that fellow there?' – 'Well he's so-and-so from this Corporation or from London'. At firsts they'd shy away but they go used to seeing them on the same level. They've got the same rapport with them as we have. They are as pleased as us that it's come out this way because surely every official doesn't just want to remain a faceless bureaucrat.'*

Bill Halsall – '*Summing it up, I think the success of Weller Streets is largely due to their being willing and keen to do it for themselves, and to do it right and to start from first principle and get all the necessary information and make mistakes if necessary but make their own mistakes. They were always receptive to real information, open to lots of ideas but not to anybody's opinion which was foisted on them. They were highly suspicious of anybody who came in as a professional and said, 'This is the way you should do it' ... That was the way it was, they wanted to do it for themselves their own way, and be receptive to ideas and information but not to be led by the nose. They would never be led by the nose.'*

Mr. Cowman, Head Teacher, Toxteth Primary School – *The Weller Street Housing Co-operative makes me feel very humble. I hope that doesn't too sound too stilted a way to put it. Over the years, I am lost in admiration for the approach which they make towards the everyday problems of life. They've had to live with uncertainty, for years on end. ... The impression I had was that this initially loosely comprised group did in fact turn out to be a highly disciplined group. Involvement was total involvement. As an organisation they set strict guidelines and adhered to them. Nobody else imposed them. They set them for themselves. It's the purpose behind all this that comes across to me. It's not a bit of rabble-rousing or a five-minute wonder. It's not gimmicky or showy or just for the moment. It's something that they wanted to see through from first to last.'*

Bill Halsall – '*OK. Weller Street is 61 units, which is a small neighbourhood really. It's quite a self-contained community down there, but if you can do it for 61 units, then why not do it for 120? Or why not broaden the process and, you know, begin to plan part of the cities by such a participation process. I am confident you could do that without losing that involvement in detail, if you went about it in the right way.'*

61 households with a mind of their own. A collective mind, but based on the hard graft of fact-finding and patiently teasing out a working relationship not just between themselves, but between Us and Them. You might even say that they had it in themselves to teach the professionals a thing or two (just as those children's *Living Space* decision-making capacities proved an eye-opener to some of their teachers).

Half the battle was to show how people went about the job of holding everyone together, and making the most of what professionals had to offer. We backed this up with a 'ladder' of 20 cards to hang on the wall that showed the 72 steps you might need to take, filling in 10 forms on the way up, in order to buy and improve a property for a co-operative group, or to build new.

I continued with this double-barrelled approach to innovation, reporting what people were learning from their own experience; and how the materials we were producing could help to streamline the decision-making of groups just setting out for themselves.

Half the battle was to translate what Weller Streets' people called the professionals' *mumbo jumbo* into *Plain English.* We put on record the story of Chrissie Maher whose view of professionals' outputs was that most of it sounded rubbish. (She actually started out by alerting the local councillor to the need for better rubbish collection by dumping a dustbin load on his doorstep twice running.) With other residents in Tuebrook, Liverpool, she began to make common sense versions of the rules and regulations the Council and the Government handed out. She managed to win over both politicians and professionals, mounting the Plain English Campaign with a miniature demonstration in Trafalgar Square. The Thatcher Government of the day instructed official departments to simplify what they issued to the general public. Official publications are the better for it, although the politicians themselves have introduced a different form of camouflage in the diversionary rhetoric known as 'spin'.

Our concern was to break information down into easily digestible sections, cleansed of administrative jargon. The ladder helped and the simplifying process was reinforced via the information cards in the *Fact Bank.* You had to get the gist of a particular subject within about 150 words on an A6 card. That had to be enough to indicate to a newcomer whether it was worthwhile going further, and to back this up as they read the linking cards that took them, step by step, further into the subject, ending up with a cross reference to other little families of cards which might have a bearing. There was one section devoted entirely to examples of groups like *Giroscope* that had got results (and were willing to be contacted to give advice). Alongside there were cards listing the different kinds of official, in local and central government, what use they might be to fledgling community groups. We quoted the correct reference number, and the relevant paragraph in it. (Much as we did long ago in the *Blitzgoers' Guide,* and later on when in Sicily we circulated the *protocol numbers* on refugee rights provided by His Excellency Tito Zaniboni).

The point of putting information on separate cards was not only that that broke the information up into digestible items, it also allowed a group with a number of overlapping interests to put the box of cards on the table they sat round, picking and choosing cards, passing them around, sorting out what was most worth considering, sooner or later.

Two useful conclusions: if you are all clustered round the cards spread out on the table, everyone's eye lines converge on the subject matter. Not an eyeball-to-eyeball confrontation, instead a convergence on the materials laid out, everyone chatting together out of the sides of their mouths. Plus: you can all sort and re-sort, seeing how different items might link together to form a practicable proposition.

We went on to work out priorities. Umpteen cards denoting problems to be considered, opportunities to follow up, activities worth joining in – all to be arranged and re-arranged on a chart labelled Now Soon Later. If anyone disagrees with an item's placing, all they have to do, unobtrusively if they prefer, is to turn that particular card face-down. (It says *Disagree* on the back.) Everything that stays face-up is what we all agree on (which is reassuring.) Then we can reconsider the *Disagrees* one by one, fitting them in to the general consensus.

Now Soon Later charts were a way of thinking about priorities without fuss. Different groups interpreted *soon* and *later* according to their own senses of time. What mattered was being able to see that there were some cards that could be got on with right away, one or two that we ought to think about and then act on soon, with the remainder seen as a lot less urgent, but still worth considering one of these days.

At the top of each NSL chart there was an optional addition which allowed a group to re-sort the cards which they had spaced vertically, arranging each stage horizontally according to whether WE COULD DO THIS ON OUR OWN / WE COULD DO IT WITH A LITTLE MONEY / WE COULD DO IT WITH SOME MONEY AND A LITTLE ADVICE / WE COULD DO IT WITH THE COUNCIL/OR AN OUTSIDE AGENCY / WE CAN'T DO IT – BUT WE KNOW WHAT NEEDS TO BE DONE AND WHERE AND HOW AND WHEN AND WHO SHOULD DO IT.

Spacing everything out like this (try it for yourself!) helps people to think and sort things out step by step, and gradually get a birds-eye view of everything and everyone likely to be involved.

Alongside the Now Soon Later chart there were other decision-making materials laid out for everyone to see and handle instead of just talking. I used the family round table as a template, cut out sheets of packing paper and marked them in concentric rings to form a Target. Everyone could get around it and select whatever mattered to anyone from a range of option cards paper-clipped to the outer edge. They covered every possibility that anyone had in mind to explore and there were also blanks labelled *My Idea* for afterthoughts once things got underway. All that anyone had to do was to detach a card which seemed worth considering and push it one ring further in from the Target's outer rim. As many cards as you think fit, preferably putting your name on the back of each one that you push forward. Anyone else seeing your card in the first ring and thinking it a good idea has a quick look at the back to see whose idea it is, and (unless the person named is a put-off) adds their own name on the back and pushes the card one ring further in.

In a few minutes, we found, dozens of people are on the move, round the table, shoulder to shoulder, looking down on the Target and the cards, briskly adding names and moving further in any card which they think is worth pursuing together – that's where the names on the back come in. Little clusters of people are forming, each group concerned to make the most of a particular opportunity or to tackle a particular problem. No one makes promises yet, but they are getting hooked. Not yet to take action, but to consider together what action needs to be taken.

Next step? Over to the Now Soon Later sheet to decide who's going to do it, and when.

Oh, and by the way, what about the option card that someone signed on the back and placed one ring in on the Target? And nobody else has taken it up. What seemed my bright suggestion has, at least for the moment, flopped. But no one else knows that it was mine. Because no one has got round to looking at the back and seeing my name there. So putting an idea forward, even if it's a bit far out, can be done anonymously, and if it doesn't catch on, no one is embarrassed.

Thinking things out in this way was helped along by the opportunities to seize on the evidence in detail before jumping to conclusions.

The evidence might partly be the whereabouts of problems or opportunities: where the rubbish was collecting, or where there might be the makings of the space for five-a-side or a toddlers' playgroup. It might suggest HOW to set out a problem – get out to a traffic danger area, list the times when the HGV traffic is at its worst, note the places where a pedestrian crossing ought to be provided. A group could go on to sort out WHO among them, or among their good contacts, was best placed to tell the media, or to lobby the Council, or to contact schools about the deployment of their lollipop ladies.

The 3D models – a Planning for Real neighbourhood model, or a Building

Design model of a place that might have scope for additional or alternative uses – allowed everyone to experiment. The option cards showed what people thought might be needed, but they could take in each other's ideas, and maybe expert advice from outside as well, as they shifted things around to settle eventually on the best place for this or that.

Having key words to think about, a few at a time, offered the same shared opportunities to sort things out. What do we need to *Buy*, or *Hire*, or *Borrow*, or even (very popular word abroad as well as here at home) *Scrounge.* And *Who* will be needed? *One* of us? *Several* of us? *Outside* helpers? *Government* officials? Oh yes, and where's the money coming from? Membership *fees*? A *whip round*? An interested *charity*? A Council *grant*?

And When? – Now Soon or Later!

This quarter, next quarter, next year?

Spelling things out together like this, we have found, can bridge some of the gulfs that otherwise tend to divide. If you can *show* each other where things could go – on a 3D model or on a chart laid out with everyone gathered round – there's an unexpected bonus. You're rubbing shoulders, looking down at the things you are concerned about rather than confronting each other face to face. So it's that 'washing-up situation' all over again.

In the early days making this kind of simplification could be a challenge to the professionals which sometimes put them off. There was an inbuilt tradition in many Councils concerned with showing everyone that they knew what's what. In the foyer of the Council offices there might be an architect's model of a planned new development, all done beautifully in 3D with a big Perspex dome protecting it and a little notice, 'PLEASE DO NOT TOUCH'.

We were into touching, not just looking at something, shifting things around to see where they might be better placed. The Chief Executive of one Council, hearing what we were up to with a homemade neighbourhood model in one 'difficult' area, issued a warning to all departmental staff that they should have nothing to do with the project. The *Planning for Real* model was proving an attraction, not only to the people living in the place, but also to some of the professional planners at the receiving end of the, Chief Executive's ruling – which they had quietly ignored. We were videoing the proceedings at the time in order to see how the process worked but were approached by anxious officials asking us to edit them out, in case the boss got to know.

The following year the people in the neighbourhood next door embarked on *Planning for Real*, and this time they could welcome the officials openly.

The first project had attracted such good publicity; so now the Chief Executive was all smiles, and anxious to share any credit that might be going round.

Elsewhere the planning people joined in from the start. On Moss Side, Manchester, they consulted with the residents who were making the 3D layout, and showed them where it might be useful to indicate changes in the neighbourhood that were in preparation. '*This is what's going to happen there (which you might find quite useful) so you don't need to bother about that particular innovation; but elsewhere there are places where things are up for grabs, and maybe we should sort out together the best ways to make the most of them, and what sort of resources we could call in.*'

In Birkenhead the *Planning for Real* notion was promoted by one young innovative city planner who got residents interested in making their own model, and coaxed colleagues into turning up alongside residents when the time came to explore possibilities together. They took the model round to seven different locations within a mile long strip of the city where problems and the opportunities were concentrated. Within thirteen months the detailed proposals worked out together had been taken through the relevant Council committees and put into effect on the site (alongside several smaller innovations that residents were tackling entirely on their own). A year later the Chief Executive rang me up to propose a sequel – the conversion of everything in and around a former college campus (now re-established elsewhere). All sorts of people could be involved, youngsters on an enterprise training scheme, volunteers from the residents, technical experts already employed by the Council. A combined operation. And the reason for his enthusiasm? Like the Weller Street people and their opposite numbers in the Council, he had found that Us and Them were not just on better speaking terms, but were *using their first names to each other*. Talking tough if need be, but talking sense, in words that everyone understood.

The Town and Country Planning Association was organising working parties bringing all sorts together to consider 'urban renewal', and the possibilities for another Garden City. Whilst the Birkenhead scheme was still underway I found myself sitting next to the Chief Planner of the Telford Development Corporation. Chatting in between times about what we were up to, he said that there was a patch of derelict land on the edge of Telford town that nobody knew quite how to deal with. There had been miniature mining shafts, now exhausted, deposits of rubble absorbed beneath the couch grass. Nowhere much that you could call level ground. So what could you do with all that if it became available?

The answer seemed to be a self-built village. The idea attracted an intriguing selection of potential Do-It-Ourselfers, some local, some further afield. We got the word around via local clubs, churches and the media. People turned up at weekends asking about the *housing plan*, and wishing to know who was on *the committee*. I sat on a broken-down wall and explained that there was no plan, and that no doubt there would be a committee one of these days. Meanwhile, how about casing the joint, wandering over those desolate, uneven, 22_ acres; rubbing shoulders (so to speak) with fellow wanderers, swapping ideas about what we could make of it, individually and between us?

We made a model of the derelict site and set it up beneath a makeshift shelter. Weekend after weekend it attracted those who began to feel committed. The *Planning* process for them was going to be *For Real*. One couple, Dave Cooksey, an unemployed bricklayer and Brenda his wife who was looking after their small herd of goats on a site a mile away from home, had very little to say compared with some of the others. But early on, when everyone was working out how the whole village might look, and considering the road round which the houses could spring up, Brenda took a spare lace from Dave's football boots and laid it out. *That's where the road could be?* Minor adjustments, then general consent.

Agreeing the plan was one thing. Mobilising the resources to put it into effect was taking time. While negotiations were still proceeding, Brenda and Dave decided to take the initiative. They moved out of their rented council house, bought a second hand caravan, gathered their goats from the distant patch where they had been allowed to graze and in the teeth of a freezing winter moved into their allotted space on the Lightmoor site.

Everyone else had got used to marking time. Now action spoke louder than words. Both sides – the prospective residents and the officers of the Development Corporation got the message.

(Soon after the whole project had been completed, and the house builders had set up home, the Chairman of the Development Corporation confided to me, '*Letting them have a go was just to satisfy our Planning Officer. We never expected the project to succeed.*')

It took a year or two to dig the sewage trenches, lay out the garden spaces, build the houses (swapping skills where necessary). But if you visit that home-spun village, called Lightmoor, that's where the Dave's football lace road is now. Along it went the Prince of Wales and other dignitaries after the Lightmoor village scheme had won the top award from the Times/Royal Institute of British Architects. (A few years later Giroscope got one too.

Earlier on the Birkenhead scheme had won through to the second award and all three in their turn qualified for a princely handshake.) So the *hands on* approach was gaining credibility.

Halfway through drafting this chapter I went back to Lightmoor for the two-day celebration of its twentieth anniversary. The patch of ground round which those self-built homes were planned is no longer derelict. There are trees that have grown up all around and for our celebrations there were little marquees set up by the families who live there now. Brenda and Dave Cooksey are there no longer. They died recently, but there is now a simple wooden bench, to commemorate the step they took in that freezing mid-winter, whilst everyone else concerned – authorities, supporters, prospective homebuilders, were still talking things over and over, thereby showing what it was all about – turning the talk into action.

The bench was on view for the first time, stylish without ornamentation. No speechifying, just a mention that it was there to be admired, and used. That mention was the nearest we got to formal speeches. The rest of the time over two days was spent in making music – a full-blown choir, a thirty-person volunteer drumming session put together during the morning and previous afternoon, impromptu choruses conducted by a nine-year old, amateur attempts by old and young at stilt-walking –stilts of course, nicely decorated – sack races, Diablo – the lot.

I stayed with Miri who was born in a kibbutz soon after the State of Israel began to take shape, moved here with her family, and found the Lightmoor project a home from home. She still revisits the kibbutz where she grew up, and shares the feelings of belonging there (as well as here). Like those Jewish volunteers who sang their songs of longing to us in the evening after we had practised our refugee relief skills together way back in 1943, she still wants to resolve conflict by compromise and collaboration instead of kill and counter-kill.

Including, if you like, the spirits of Brenda and Dave, three-quarters of the original Lightmoor 'settlers' are still there. The children I remember putting spare bricks together to make miniature houses whilst their elders built for real, are now all grown up, with one pair expecting to deliver the first grand-child in a week or two.

What do they all believe in? There are no formal affiliations. Political parties, religious denominations, academic ties do not figure, any more than people's preferences for the food they eat or the clothes they wear. There are arguments, occasionally, about the best way to *do* this or that or where to put whatever needs doing, for the general benefit. But that is run-of-the-mill, give-and-take which elsewhere would be labelled *community development*.

Development hasn't always been so positive over the last twenty years. Here and there the gaps between Us and Them have widened. In Brixton during the 70s and 80s the most unpopular elements were the police, accused of aggressive discrimination particularly against young people, especially when they were black. So there was plenty of anger to fuel people's initiative. They took it in the century's biggest UK riot, lasting three days, injuring 300 people, burning and bulldozing property to an estimated value of £7.5 million. The government of the day set up an enquiry and chose a mildly conservative senior judge to preside. Lord Scarman turned out to be an innovator himself. He was not content with assessing what happened and who behaved as they did. He went to the roots of the rioting, *the reason why*. His Report showed up the poverty and the discrimination which people, particularly young people, particularly young blacks, were no longer content to put up with.

He understood them, and they understood him, as a defender and a friend, greeting him afterwards in the streets whenever he made a visit. There's been nothing quite like his Report, before or since.

Filling in the Picture

There is more about Mini Studio experiments in *The Practice of ETV* and *The Use of ETV*, both published by Hutchinson in 1970. *Teachers Talking* (Allen Lane, the Penguin Press 1973) reported the teachers' reactions in depth before and during the *Living Space* trials. The application of Planning for Real was described in *Counterweight : The Neighbourhood Option*, published by the Town and Country Planning Association in 1984. These and other experiments are put in context with neighbourhood initiatives in many parts of the world, past and present, in *People Power* (Penguin, 1979) *The Power in Our Hands : Neighbourhood-based, World-shaking*, published by Jon Carpenter, 1997.

Chapter Nineteen

US AND THEM

Scarman woke people up, here and there, to the difference between the outsiders' view of Brixton people, and the reality: their justified anger and frustration, and also their fellow feeling, their self-respect in the face of police and media type-casting. And stemming from that, their recognition that it was time to take a hand in putting things right.

An eye-opener to all concerned? Maybe a bridge?

Meanwhile, in a small way, we were into bridge-building, trying out the materials and the techniques to construct working relationships which would translate the talk into action.

Planning for Real was being taken up by all sorts of groups, mainly on the initiative of local authorities, or influential support agencies; once in a while the first steps were being taken by residents themselves.

These initiatives were surprising some of the professionals, and confirming for others their belief that Us plus Them could be a winning combination.

The TCPA was the body most closely concerned with professionals involved in *community development*. Just what did that really mean? Was it best done *top down* or *bottom up*? Between us we decided to set up a new body, the Neighbourhood Initiatives Foundation, with representatives from the TCPA and the Housing Association's Charitable Trust on the Board. By this time Lord Scarman was showing interest, and he agreed to become our Patron. He and I wrote an article for *The Guardian* in which we said,

> *'Residents were spelling out to us the dangers and the opportunities as they saw and felt them, living day to day and hand to mouth … Across the length and breadth of the country, in comfortable communities as well as in stress areas, the gut reaction is: 'They never take notice of us. They've got their own plans' … Authorities are entangled by the complex working procedures imposed on them. The intention is to secure accountability, the effect is to confuse. … People need to take a hand not just have a say: words have to be the passport to action.'*

We ended with a sort of slogan: '*People will safeguard what they have helped to create.*'

At the foot of our article we quoted what one local resident had to say about life on her own estate, up north, roughly spanning the years since the Brixton riots of 1981.

> *'I would say it was ten or maybe fifteen years ago that it started to deteriorate. The docks and the factories were closing down. I started seeing the rot set in amongst the kids. It happened gradually. They were good kids and they used to go on the street and play football, but then they were beginning to do odd things. I couldn't put my finger on it and I thought 'What is happening?' Then the mentally ill were getting shoved out of the hospitals, the cuts started in the Social Security, and this is when I really saw the place go downhill. People were using any means to be able to live, to get their daily bread. There was nothing for children. And then it started. At one time you could leave your door open, people wouldn't venture to go in and steal. But now whether your door's open or shut, they need money to survive, and it's the same with the children. The shoplifting, the aggression, the anger.*
>
> *'I have never seen anything like it.'*

The place Nancy Peters was talking about was the Meadow Well housing estate on North Tyneside. I went there as the result of a commission by the then Department of the Environment (Mike Burbidge and co.) to visit twenty of the most deprived housing estates in England, pick out the one with the worst problems, and then see what if anything could be done about it with the help of *Planning for Real*.

I made my number with the Local Authority people but got a rather cool reception. Venturing on to the estate itself, there was one part, five streets with about 220 households, which reckoned to be up against the biggest problems. People there asked what I was up to but when I explained, roughly, what had been happening elsewhere, a handful of residents decided there was no harm in trying something out.

The something we chose was a skills enquiry. Six of the seven people in the handful agreed to go door knocking to find out who was good at what – in case anyone might have anything to offer which would come in useful in changing things for the better, one of these days. The group decided to visit around 50 households – in the end it turned out to be 46, with the 47th householder slamming the door and three others never at home.

The visits proved to be a shot in the arm for everyone concerned. The skills enquiry form had Jonathan Bean's thumbnail pictures to represent every kind of skill we could think of, and spaces you could tick to show whether you reckoned to be a Beginner, or Experienced. There was more room at the end of the form to add skills that we hadn't thought of.

The enquiries were unlike the formal interrogations that some people had endured before from officials or academic researchers, or sales people. The idea was to sit side-by-side, filling in the form together, having a general chat. The conversations ranged widely – about interests and activities enjoyed, local problems, and sometimes opportunities, that hindered or helped people to make the most of what they had to offer. No one had to make promises or to tell anything more about their lives than they chose to mention. But instead of a quick flip through a form lasting ten minutes or so, the visitors reported that they were staying for half an hour, an hour or more, having a really good natter about everyday life, in particular life on Meadow Well.

The result was a sea change in the way people looked at possibilities and problems: in particular the idea that (perhaps with the help of some of the other tools in the kit) they might DO something. So there was a miniature *Planning for Real* operation that drew in one or two junior officials from the Council who were interested in pooling ideas with tenants about garden fences as an alternative to hedges. Hedges allowed 'baddies' to hide behind them and prey on the rest of us. Residents from most of the households joined in, round the little layout, and to their surprise, most of the fencing they showed on the layout was quite soon installed by the Council – *for real*.

Meanwhile other people, who had not been visited, were coming along asking to have their own skills listed (along of course with a bit more chat). And elsewhere on the estate the word was getting around. People were proposing that they too should be involved.

There was a badly designed building used as a Youth Centre, with part-time staff having to concentrate on a few undemanding activities two or three evenings a week. Young people, attenders and non-attenders alike, were dissatisfied, but cottoned on to the idea of re-planning the building and everything that could go on in it – themselves.

They built their cardboard model/replica, big enough to span a snooker table. They hawked it around, attracting others like themselves to join in seeing how to make the most of the spaces on offer. (Plenty of option cut-outs available, with some blanks for new ideas.)

Elsewhere on the estate there were more small-scale *Planning for Real* trials, with residents setting up the cut-out houses, marking the roads, the derelict areas, and whatever was left for greenery.

What began as many small-scale exercises began to coalesce, just like the pieces in a jigsaw puzzle. Residents got together, with minimal help from me, to put forward a comprehensive Plan to the Council: *A New Heart for Meadow Well.* Not just fences to forestall thieves, but better uses of derelict space, and a more imaginative plan that the teenagers themselves drew up to revolutionise the use of the Youth Centre.

The proposals were set out with advice from a Newcastle architects' group, typed up, garnished with suggested layouts, and put forward for consideration by a succession of Council sub-committees.

We all waited.

I remembered the cartoon that Sam Marriage had shown me as we lay in the railway wagon en route for Tunis. Sam had preserved it from the Forces' newspaper popular with Monty's Eighth Army in the Western Desert. It pictured a slightly harassed Administrative Officer seated at his desk. The desk was empty apart from what would normally be the In tray and the Out tray. These were each piled with papers, and were respectively labelled MALESH and BARDIN.

These two Arabic words, known and used throughout the Eighth Army stood, roughly, for LATER ON and BY AND BY.

Clearly the Meadow Well residents' proposals had landed up, in someone's Council office, on one of those trays.

Five months passed without any positive response. Then a police chase ending in the deaths of two joyriders provided the spark. Young people had taken the lead in working out how the old Youth Centre could be transformed. Now they decided to burn it down, together with several other buildings nearby.

The 'Meadow Well Riots' got everyone paying attention. I was now welcomed by the Leader of the Council and colleagues who were all of a sudden looking favourably at possibilities to implement residents' practical proposals. Things began to happen. A new Centre was designed, with another cardboard model to which some of the teenagers contributed sitting alongside the Council's architect. A vacant building was snapped up to become a youth centre with a difference, where adults were allowed to join in at the invitation of the youngsters. Another under-used Council building became a base, for a time, for small-scale enterprises, applying some of the skills the residents' surveys were revealing.

It was at this point that *The Guardian* published our article about 'Neighbours in Crisis – and Opportunity'. From then on Lord Scarman's patronage of the Neighbourhood Initiatives Foundation helped to highlight the examples that other groups of residents and local government officers were setting. Results varied: some local authorities made use of NIF to mount 'consultations', using *Planning for Real* to publicise sessions at which everyone could put down their notions for improvements on the 3D layout; then the officials bowed out with congratulations to all concerned, and the promise that – *in due course* – residents' proposals would be *duly considered*. This left a flavour of MALESH and BARDIN, but at least there was something tangible which resolute residents could seize on and agitate for.

In other places residents and Council officers found they could join forces, just as had been happening in Birkenhead, to share out the work in hand.

The word was getting around, abroad as well as at home. Over in Boston USA the Massachusetts Institute of Technology had a reputation for trying out new ideas. There were two members of MIT particularly interested in innovation. I was invited to meet them and their students and show them what we had been up to. They tried out the pack materials in a kind of dummy run and on the strength of this decided it might be the answer to a problem that the Institute was up against. It owned land elsewhere in Boston and was in trouble with the residents living on it. Could *Planning for Real* be any use in this *Us versus Them* situation? And how about involving the Planning students themselves in a process that might teach them a thing or two. The 'project' became part of the students' studies. The students themselves proved to be door-openers. People found them the reverse of 'academic'. Up for a bit of a lark as well as down-to-earth in helping residents to make the most of a *real Planning for Real* exercise. The school also got involved, with children re-designing their own playground, and allowed to plant shrubs and even a tree or two, where they thought best. Relationships between the academic landlords and the local tenants steadily improved.

On the strength of this I was invited to work in Poland with an MIT team combining forces with the Warsaw Planning Faculty to tackle a similar *Us versus Them* problem in Lublin. Six Polish students were teamed with six American students, all at the service of planners and residents on a huge housing estate – eight tower blocks, 50,000 residents, mostly cramped up in two-room flatlets. Our hosts were members of the Housing Association council, an august body that had so far held itself apart from the residents. There were two or three Councillors who wanted to change the situation, and what they had heard from MIT about the problem/opportunity in Boston made them think that something on the lines of *Planning for Real* would be worth attempting. The idea was to begin with people in one tower block, and

BEWARE

- Ego trippers
- Official 'consultation', Mission Statements, when they become (unintentionally??) camouflage for inaction/delay.
- Committee and focus group meetings where jargon, excess paperwork and fluent talkers are deterrents to participation and commitment by everyone else.
- Preoccupation with putting down – e.g. teenage misbehaviour – at the expense of building up scope for potential delinquents to try out their own ideas, get a kick, have fun in tackling a neighbourhood opportunity.
- 'Leadership' at the expense of 'teamwork'.
- Institutional exclusion according to race, faith, status, age or gender.
- Double talk:

  extraordinary rendition aka kidnapping and torture;
  movement framework options aka choosing bus stops;
  testing and future-proofing long-term aspirations – whew!
  I'm leaving that to you to translate!
- What else?

maybe entice some of the professionals to come along to see what it was all about. I kept a diary.

July 19th, 1994. Although the flats look bleak, the grassed areas around are not litter-strewn. Some graffiti on the concrete walls, but not much vandal damage. The children running about on the estate, now on holiday, seemed both to the Americans and to me less stressed, more secure, with longer attention spans and an easier relationship with adults than we are used to back home.

There is a Plan for the whole of the estate, made by the authorities in Lublin in association with the Warsaw Polytechnic – especially concerned with the open space flanking the tower blocks. … The residents appear not to have thought of this open space as in anyway theirs, or of themselves having any input in deciding its future. …

The Polish students complain that their professors (back in Warsaw) have not shown much interest or given any serious support to them.

July 22nd. Dr. Dylewski, Director of the Lublin Planning Research Institute, has also been elected a member of the Co-operative Council and of the Lublin City Council. And he's a local resident. He says the most important thing is to get more responsibility handed over to the estate. … 'At present each estate council can only advise … we need to make estates much more self-sufficient … estate councils are more akin to residents' interests than to the interests of the authorities. … This illustrates the nationwide problem … maybe this [Planning for Real] project could become a model not just for Poland but for the whole of Eastern Europe.'

He had worked in England on Thamesmead where he thought there were similar problems of tower blocks. As he explained, on my tape-recorder:

'The important difference between the Lublin estates and the UK is the feeling of community. In Poland this is still at a very low level. There is little understanding of people's rights and of the possibility that they could make any kind of impact. People's chances to make suggestions to the authorities have been very limited indeed. When I was in the UK people at least felt that they could say 'No!' But people here have lived like slaves without feeling that they have any possibility even of saying No. They have lacked the ability to express their wishes.

'The majority of the representatives were elected for the estate in 1990, which was

a time of major political changes, and they were elected on the basis that they were against the previous communist regime.

'So the general feeling is of being anti-authorities, without having anything very positive instead – rejection, not creation. People were combative, but very few are able to create. Now that the struggle is over and communism has disappeared they're looking for a new enemy – perhaps Solidarity itself.

'The weakest point about the community now is this lack of a creative approach. There are some people who stayed creative throughout the period of the community regime. But their creativity was a private matter. They were friends with each other. They met in each other's houses, looked after each other, got each other out of trouble during the curfew.

'Even during the communist regime the authorities asked people for their views, but without really listening. They had their projects already worked out and they used consultation simply to get confirmation. People mostly regarded this as a waste of time. People still think this. They say of the authorities ***'They will do whatever they want'.'***

(I said the very same phrase has often been heard back in the UK.) Later on we were joined by Mr. Olchesky, the Chief Architect of the District. He chimed in,

'We were required by law to communicate our proposals and seek suggestions. But scarcely anyone answered. They didn't believe that anyone would take notice. Maybe they would say 'We told you in the past and still nothing has happened, or that you will only listen to us at the time when you are seeking election.' He said he had heard 'from the professors in MIT that in Boston they had a serious problem in bridging the communication between the University and the local community about local community development on University territory'. The professors had reported that the techniques had helped to bridge the gap between MIT and local people. … 'It is important that we convince especially younger people that talk will lead to results'.

He came back with three sympathetic professionals from his own office to attend the preliminary Planning for Real meeting with residents from tower block number Six. Next day he was back again telling us that his three officers had shown great enthusiasm and wished to be allowed in [for the next stage].

July 23rd. [The children had enthusiastically helped to build the Planning for Real model.]

Residents arrived more or less on time ... Whilst waiting for the officials to come there was a general discussion about their likely reaction. It was thought that they would either try to run the meeting, or else stay absolutely silent until the end and then make their own comments.

They arrived twenty minutes late because it turned out they'd gone to the wrong office. Meanwhile it was agreed that we should get on with the first stages of the scheme, using the Now Soon Later chart. By the time the three officials arrived we were all busy and one after the other they joined in, perhaps to the surprise of the rest. They became more and more involved, contributing to the general group discussion and having individual conversations with residents and among themselves.

July 23rd evening. A further meeting of the residents, with a member of the official Administration invited to join them, plus a rather drunk policeman who was eventually tactfully sidetracked as the rest of the meeting adjourned to the kitchen of the Maderna café where the discussion continued with the help of chocolate biscuits and cakes and ice-cream. The Administration officials rapidly became involved with the residents in a friendly discussion. This continued for more than an hour and then the members returned to the room where the model was in use, mingling with others and continuing to discuss possibilities together.

The students, Poles and Americans, continued enthusiastic. (With one American exception *who thinks the emphasis should be on working out how best to make the most of* ***market forces*** *in the development of the vacant area; and* ***residents' involvement*** *might be* ***a distraction***.)

The evening meeting [with the model] was led by the students. The model was displayed with an extra section showing the area of vacant land. Besides residents from the estates so far involved there was the President of Estate Two and the President of the whole of the area, plus the President of the City Council ... Everybody clustered round, including the Presidents, all busily putting option cards on the model with many conversations going on simultaneously. There was continued enthusiastic re-sorting of the cards with apparent excitement and enjoyment all round.

Afterwards Dr. Dylewski said 'I was astonished that so many people came. I didn't expect so many or so many different age groups. ... This was not just the attraction of the fact that the people running it were students from the USA. I was amazed at the involvement of the residents ... much more than I expected ... A very important contribution has been made by your method which awoke the hopes – something new, exciting and challenging for us. But we are not mature enough yet ... we need MIT's help. This method should be used all the time. At first I was unsure whether the method would work. Perhaps it might work for a short time and then stop. Now I think it is unstoppable.'

But he was wrong. Not about the enthusiasm generated, but because of the reaction of the professors in Warsaw. They were not prepared for their students to return after this summer break.

Dr. D was right in thinking that the students, American and Polish, were the key to success. From the academics' point of view the project was as much for them as for the residents. And the funding depended on that collaboration.

So gradually the momentum they had helped to generate faded away.

In Germany, about this time, the academics were already on our side. There had been a funding crisis in the University with the prospect that some academics' *tenure* would suffer. They thought there were alternative economies that would do better, formed their own co-operative and managed to hold on. Some had also picked up on the possibilities that we were exploring for collaboration between academics and residents. I was invited to help run a workshop in Berlin to introduce and adapt the materials we had been evolving. The problem/opportunity, we found, centred on another kind of Us versus Them – the Ossies and Wessies – mutually suspicious residents of East and West Berlin as it used to be until the Fall of the Berlin Wall in 1989. Much later on, the gap was between local residents and the incoming Turkish 'guest workers' in Kreutzberg.

Year on year the Berliners have been hosting fresh workshops, with residents from other parts of Germany – Stuttgart, Leipzig, Cologne, Hamburg, attending and then starting up on their own. We discovered all sorts of built-in differences that obscured the concerns and aspirations that people had in common. As usual it was *doing* that redeemed the talking. There are now German versions of most of the materials we have been developing in the UK. Early on one of the first Berlin *Planning for Reals* won the top award out of 700 entries from the Community Enterprise scheme set up by the German Bundestag. We all seem to be seeing things in much the same way, eye to eye, hands on.

Next stop Jamaica 1995 where the problems loomed very large. In the capital, Kingston, there were six neighbouring 'downtown' districts affiliated to rival political parties whose behaviour to each other was the reverse of neighbourly. There was a derelict football field separating Jones Town and

Trench Town but football was no longer playable for fear of snipers from one side or the other. The tombstones in the May Pen cemetery that lay between Trench Town and Tivoli Gardens provided occasional cover for others pursuing feuds whose origins were sometimes half forgotten.

The UK Department for International Development representative had seen what we were trying to do elsewhere and arranged for a repeat performance, as part of a visiting DfID consultancy team in Jones Town. Poverty and violence here were at their worst, street garbage breeding disease, drains and sewers blocked for over a year, police and support services reluctant to intervene.

There were familiar divisions between Us and Them – residents versus officialdom, young versus old, rival drug cartels. But there was one shining example to give us all hope, even before we started work. Rodney Street residents had endured a gun battle between rival gang leaders at either end of the street. This was too much for some of the younger residents. They got together and took over a derelict patch at one end of the street, cleared space for a mini farm, planted shrubs, flowers and a few saplings beside it, built their own hut for convivial breaks between the work in hand, and put up a mural, facing the rest of the street with their slogan:

TOGETHERNESS

The young 'Rodney Raiders' and a handful of their elders agreed to try out *Planning for Real* and a rough and ready *skills enquiry*. People responded and joined in for an environmental clean-up – in spite of pot shots from gunmen next door when they got too close to the No Man's Land that separated Jones Town from the rest.

They set up their own *forum*, put up street signs to help outside services find their way to trouble spots, got help from the Government's Kingston Restoration Company to help them install basic sanitation lacking in 141 out of 175 *yards* where people had their homes. Two more mini-farms like the one in Rodney Street took shape.

Then the residents next door – in Olympic Gardens, Denham Town and Trench Town got involved. An earlier attempt to bring them together had failed because gunmen had warned off visiting representatives from Olympic Gardens. Now a fresh attempt succeeded. They began a scheme to clean up and beautify the cemetery (incidentally thinning out cover for visiting gunmen). Denham Town teamed up with the Restoration Company to refurbish a derelict school. Trench Town (Bob Marley's old stamping ground) got going on a *Planning for Real* neighbourhood layout to outdo all the others.

Around 30, young and old, made the model, about 20 feet square, with every detail double-checked. It was set up in the community centre next door to that derelict football field I mentioned earlier.

There was a good turnout for the main 'hands on' session, but I counted only 18 present of the 30 who had helped to make the model. I learned that the remaining 12 had spread out in the surrounding streets to deter hostile gunmen.

Things gradually improved. People crossed the old frontiers to attend each other's markets. The new forums they set up endured without further intimidation. The authorities appointed '*a young and action-oriented project manager*', Richard Billings, starting out in Jones Town and gradually extending to nine more mini-townships, armed with *Planning for Real* materials adapted by a local artist to create a *Community Action Kit* – model cut-outs, skills survey, Problem and Action cut-outs – the lot. He told me that *'Planning for Real has given communities greater confidence in their own abilities, and has defused tensions between rival areas'*.

A year later his boss at government headquarters wrote me to say '*The community support has been overwhelming.*'

Meanwhile, in 1996, other Caribbean countries – the Grenadines – got involved. I was invited back, first to a gathering in St. Vincent. A Government Minister talked to us all about the gulf between '*the ivories*' (the politicians and administrators living in their own ivory towers) and people on the ground. The Local Government Commissioner backed her up: '*Bureaucracy frustrates the communities again and again. They put forward relevant schemes, and then wait three months or more for funds to be delivered.*'

But Samuel Carette, the Commissioner, did not stop there. He arranged for another *Planning for Real* back home in Dominica. Here there was already, deep down, a tradition of self-help. Citizens were expected to do something for the community once a year on National Day. But anything more was frustrated by what I have called the MARLESH-BARDIN approach of the administration. Samuel Carette, administrator himself, now reckoned that the best way, perhaps the only way to wake up officialdom was to set an example from the bottom up. This time it was the Building Design model that figured. In three separate housing areas people put together their own cardboard models – one of an existing building needing a face-lift, the other two of buildings to be started from scratch. I saw them begin, all hands-on. Three months later I returned to see that the new building in Sinekou was already half-completed – everything done by eleven skilled full-time workers paid from local funds for three days in the week, giving the other two days free; helped on by volunteers giving a day or two here and there, for love not money.

Elsewhere mini-projects were being set up – an arrowroot mill, a bakery, a self-service market, a housing repairs scheme, a tourist site – all to be staffed and sorted on the strength of their own local skills surveys.

I went home reflecting on what seemed to me a sort of Universal Truth – all sorts and conditions of people have it in them to do things, and get a kick out of doing them together – once they discover how to make the first move themselves, without waiting for *the ivories* to join in.

There was another international conference, with our work on display, attracting two visiting South Africans, one white, Nico Ferriera, and one black, Max July. Between them they had taken the lead in setting up the Stutterheim Foundation, to link up and celebrate community development schemes that bridged the old Apartheid divide. They arranged for me to come out, bringing the hands-on materials, see what was being achieved, and how the toolkit might be put to work in the training schemes they were developing for *grassroots* workers.

Max took me to see what was already happening. On the way, down dusty laterite roads, we passed a village where he mentioned, rather casually, his family had lived before they were forced out and *resettled* under the Apartheid regime. Later on we stopped briefly beside a modest memorial stone where there had been an armed confrontation between the old Us and the old Them. But that, he explained, was Then, not Now. The *armed struggle* was, hopefully, over for keeps. Now the key problem was to bridge the gap, not primarily between blacks and whites, but between different language groups, and between those who could read and write, and those who were *letter blind.*

Our materials were adapted with visuals redesigned by a local artist, and the training schemes took them over.

The feedback from local users was encouraging:

> *'It's what we've been waiting for all these years. Everybody took part, the less people are talking, the more they are* ***doing.****'*

> *'They were all in it together, working together. It improved their confidence in themselves. It catches their eyes even if the person is illiterate.'*

Back home the Neighbourhood Initiatives Foundation we had set up was disseminating *Planning for Real* packs in the UK and setting up mini training schemes for freelance fieldworkers and for some local Councils wanting to get schemes going under their own steam.

I had been working on another book *The Power in our Hands : Neighbourhood-Based, World-Shaking*, to bring together the evidence, world-wide, and back through time, that people everywhere had it in them to *make change*. Lord Scarman gave his verdict in a Foreword, and convened a meeting in the House of Commons for the launch. More interest, more trials at home and overseas, and in particular another invitation from the Department for International Development.

This time it was to go to Kenya, as a solo effort, or rather a duet between two of us, both steeped in the same assumptions about *people power*. Norman Chipakupaku is a Zambian, a one-time member of the Kenneth Kaunda's Cabinet, who has developed his own scheme to foster small-scale co-operatives. He set up Trade Africa Plus 2000 to make the most of what were sometimes unrecognised resources: including a plant ignored by the grown-ups in many African villages, used by the kids as a substitute football, whilst on other continents it makes big money for local enterprises.

He is back and forward between African states and the UK, particularly Scotland. He has a Scottish wife and family, and is closely linked with Community Business (Scotland) International two of whose members joined with us in the *Hands On Consortium*, to cope with the expanding interest overseas.

Norman and I were commissioned to visit, and revisit Western Kenya, the area bordering Lake Victoria. Our first visit was whilst President Arap Moi was still directing how the nation should behave and who amongst his friends and allies should get the spoils. His people at ground level, after years of exploitation, had got used to lying low and saying nuffin much. They were longing to be rid of Them but had lost faith in Us, ourselves. But there was an election a month or two away, though its outcome, given the Presidential power system, was not very promising.

Our first contact was with a voluntary agency without many resources to do things, but with a good range of local contacts, in the villages, the market and Kisumu City. We were recommended to a dozen or more villages and went the rounds to meet people on their own ground, be acquainted, arouse interest. In this way we recruited some fifteen volunteers willing to make the journey by bicycle or truck and take part in a *hands on workshop*. Some spared time from farming their plots, others were support workers each serving a cluster of villages. They all knew exactly what life was like at the sharp end: few jobs, Aids spreading, poor morale. Between us we tried out, in dummy runs, the various decision-making strategies in the packs. This took three days by which time everyone was committed, the materials themselves had been given minor revisions to make them acceptable back home in the villages, and over the weekend a local artist refigured some of the artwork (not that it was much needed, because Jonathan Bean's stick figures have a universal impact), concentrating on the backgrounds that needed a palm tree here or there.

From then on everything was in their hands.

Everyone was still dubious about the future, inclined to think that Arap Moi would go on as usual, aware that in each village most people had little hope of anything changing for the better. But thanks to the commitment of the workshop people, the do-it-ourselves idea began to catch on. Norman and I went back to the villages to be entertained with increased enthusiasm, and informed about the mini-projects that were beginning to take shape.

We went home and waited for the outcome of the Presidential elections. To many people's surprise, Arap Moi lost out, together with some of those who had been exploiting their offices to make *plenty money*. The two of us returned and were taken round once again to learn what people had already achieved, just in the four months since our previous visit. We had taken pains in our September workshop to explain how the different tools in the Power Toolkit could be used, but were careful not to suggest what kind of projects they could be used for. '*Here's the kit. It's important to know the difference between a screwdriver, a chisel and a monkey wrench. But what you decide to make with them – that's entirely up to you.*'

Now, in February we returned and were taken to see the new projects that were suddenly springing up: feeding schemes and education services for Aids orphans, a seed bank, a health service using herbal medicine, small-scale crafts schemes to tempt tourists, and, proudest of all, a new bridge. (Remember the one the young Igbos built and celebrated all in a day, back in Nigeria?) The new bridge spanned a stream which in flood had drowned two women. It was made using logs from trees contributed by different villagers in the community. Nails and rope were purchased with the money contributed through a *merry-go-round* (a local whip round).

Norman had paid special attention to the fishermen in the villages bordering the Lake. They were now on the way to setting up their own co-operative which would attempt to bypass the middlemen who bought cheap and sold dear. In Kisumu City there was the market, the biggest in East Africa, buzzing with small enterprises, some of which now began to recast themselves as co-operatives. A Credit Union was set up and in turn developed a network which linked up with small-scale enterprises in far away villages, helping them to tailor their products to market opportunities.

There were now several Voluntary Agencies interested, beside the one that had given us our village contacts. We handed over the culturally-adapted masters of the pack materials, now assembled as the *Africa Action Pack*. Each agency began to reproduce packs and hand them around to its own contacts. Bishop Francis Abiero decided to disseminate packs to workers throughout his diocese as part of an Economic Enterprises scheme. He told us:

'The pack is very important. It tells [each of us] 'I am not useless. I have something that I can provide ... a skill that could be used for the community'. The facilities are there. If we want to build, we have the land. Even if the World Bank gives us money, the stones we need are at home here, the soil is here, the water is here, the technicians are here ... The cost of construction will be lower by using the local facilities that we have.'

Some schools got interested. One Headteacher gate-crashed on a meeting of the village fieldworkers. He had already got parents to make bricks for a new classroom, they were piled high taking up most of the room he used as an office. He reckoned that parents and teachers could do the building work between them with some help from the students themselves. We showed him the *Living Space* pack that we had brought along with us, 'just in case'. He took it, and linked up with other schools to try it out. Four years later he still stays in touch.

Norman and I reported back to the Department for International Development. We decided to let the users of the packs speak for us.

What they said chimes in with people's responses in Poland, Germany, Holland, Belgium, Italy, Bosnia, the Caribbean, South Africa, the USA - and back here in the UK.

The various *hands on* materials have caught on over the years in all sorts of places. Usually the starting point is some kind of a workshop where the packs are to be tried out. The person who brings them is often me. Someone else has heard about them, or seen them in action and arranges for me to meet them and their mates on their home ground. When I turn up I usually find chairs arranged for everyone to sit in rows and a speaker's table with maybe a flipchart or an overhead projector screen close beside. People expect a *talk* and afterwards perhaps a *demonstration*. So sometimes I give them a kind of send-up – Introductory Remarks followed by reference to an imaginary Chief Assistant to the Assistant Chief on my right, Alderman Mrs. Bagwash on my left, and over by the door *our good friend who has prepared the leaflets and brochures that we hope you will take with you when you leave.*

That charade goes on for about five minutes, with perhaps the inclusion of an imaginary contribution from the audience by someone struggling with notes to get a proposal across which no one else fully understands.

'That's more than enough talk to be going on with.' So we re-arrange the chairs, round tables on which various parts of the toolkit are laid out for people to cluster round and begin to use. Explaining what this involves takes another couple of minutes, and off they go. Meanwhile I sit well out of their way, and before long I quietly move out of the room for a cup of coffee or whatever – without anyone noticing. By and by, coming back they hadn't realised I had been away and it takes some effort to distract them from what they're busily doing.

The payoff is that I can point out that I'm now *redundant*. No need for an external leader. Each group has become *self-propelled*.

Afterwards, back home on their own stamping grounds, they find the same applies. And of course this is what the packs are designed to do. But what matters most is not the packs themselves but what they reveal about people's ability to stop being bystanders and to move on to the pitch.

What does that say about the rest of us? What are the danger/opportunities facing us here and right Now – Soon – Later? Where are we coming from? Where are we heading?

And just how relevant are the responses of those Kenyans?

In my final chapters I'm offering my own conclusions.

Meanwhile, what are yours? Take a passing look at what they said to me.

PAUSE FOR REFLECTION : FEEDBACK

Here's what those Kenyan village workers made of it.

1. "Many groups from 1973 [onwards] had collapsed but [now] here we have seen groups [in which] we have created awareness, understanding and now they are revived. In PfR what we learned really is changing the attitude and at the same time how to help the community understand how to use [their own] activities. ... We [also] went to schools teaching how to prioritise things, Now Soon Later. ... There is achievement, the literacy centre class has been initiated through PfR. We have also started an old age group making activities for them. We have also talked to youth to change their attitudes to drug abuse and many other things. We are happy with our programme [because] youths [themselves] have volunteered to do this and talk to other youths ... even some who have been collapsed have come back through PfR ...the community is really changing because even the school teachers are now asking how to go and train more about PfR ... In a short period we have done this. For a longer period we are going to do more because we have seen many groups that have collapsed and we are going to revive them to do something for themselves rather than waiting for [an outside] donor. We want more packs [because] that is one way of seeing things, learning practical, that we can now see and change. ... We will use them with new groups who are coming to us and they can also go and teach others."

2. "The pack materials are so important, so simplified, self-explanatory, empowering the people to make their own decisions and I think it is the basis of sustainability ... the toolkit is so simple not much [outside] help is needed ... even those who don't know how to read and write see the pictures [the option cards and the 3D cut-outs] and they quickly understand so they need minimal [outside] help to get the tools going ... the beauty of the toolkit is that it enables each individual to participate and take part in decision making and prioritise his or her needs, which we have not been able to achieve before but that is surely going to be possible now. The opportunity is there because even those who cannot read and write can participate in prioritising problems and move ahead."

3. "The ancient method we were using we were just [talking] and not reaching a point. Now they have a point and when starting to do a thing they have to complete it and they know the right time to do it, the right people to do it, the right place to do it and we are very happy about it … The materials attracted the attention of the community at large and now we have gone far and gone to activities and we have seen that with less Big Mouth we can work as a community without waiting for somebody to come and help us."

4. "The [local] groups are revived, even those that were stalling … dropping out, giving up. But [now they are] motivated and working on our income generating activities … to take care of Aids orphans. … We are able now to take care of the sick ones, because we now prioritise our problems and we visit them and do what we could do on our own without asking for help from the NGOs or from government. … We also counsel the sick ones so that they don't just lie in their beds waiting for death. Now because of PfR these people that are sick are looking at life positively … able to do things on their own which previously they were not doing … they feel better, part of the community and they can also contribute towards the development of the community."

5. "When I got back to the community I visited all the groups that I belong to but [after introducing PfR] they changed … They lacked knowledge of management and were squandering money but [after PfR] they had that knowledge, the group revived and people are working in collaboration … how to prioritise our problems and the activities that we can do to generate income. They were handling [the materials] with a lot of interest … they made our work very easy."

6. "We have started making handicrafts such as baskets, and then we divide the money among the group so they maintain their families and their children can also now [afford the money] to go to school."

7. "[Previously] we were reluctant [but with] PfR we changed our minds and we started training [local people] to think about using locally available material that could make them self-reliant. … [As a literacy teacher] I was happy with PfR because it changed my life. Now I am serious in everything I am doing."

8. "I foresee that PfR ... is going to change the life of people in our community and in Kenya as a whole because in the very short period that we have taught it to people we have seen a great change in their lives and in the way they conduct their activities in groups ... In fact there were skilled people in our community, but we just ignored them. After PfR we went for those people and they are now out helping ... we have engineers in the community, we have teachers in the community, we have counsellors. We are now going to use these people, the skilled people, to come and help. Now even building a house we have people who can do something, make use of their skills in the community."

9. "Q. How have young people been responding?

A. I have six children, who have been coming together to work together, and leave off drinking. They're working in a garden making some vegetables. So these youths are changing their attitude. .... They sell the vegetables they have planted, get the money and they all get shares. ... The youth leader has volunteered to organise the youths [unpaid].

Q. Who decides what the group should do?

A. The people are sitting down together to plan how to make use of Soon, Later and Now ... to prioritise things ... divide the duties, and distribute the work ... They are saying that now they are thinking it is possible in future to make their lives to be a bit self-reliant ... [I myself] am thinking to do something not as a person who is just there but [using] the little skills I have to help others. ... The youths themselves are thinking that they really can do something."

10. [Headmaster of Maseno School, recorded in that room of his, half filled with home-made bricks.]
"It has really made us have a sense of unity between the parents, teachers and the pupils ... The parents are the ones who are organising and planning for the future ... Formerly the parents did not really come as a group to do whatever was needed. They used to think that the school was for the teachers and not theirs. They didn't really believe the school belongs to them. But since we introduced PfR they have that sense of belonging."

11. "The problem [has been] that most of the people think too big and would like to start big projects instead of starting small projects that are village-based and will boost the economy of the villagers ... We have refreshed

our minds [with the PfR method] on approaching solutions – so that instead of talking much we talk a little and apply more action. We have really gathered a lot and we are hoping that the future is going to be very bright. It is going to be very great."

12. "I think these materials are very good in the way that they involve people to think of their needs, look around them, … at what resources are available … it's the most wonderful way of involving people in planning and in implementation."

13. "We are happy because we know we are not going to fail. We are heading somewhere and we know where we are heading.

Q. What are your next steps?

A. Everybody has his own land, even the orphans. We can do something on our own but not everything ... we are planting maize, beans, groundnuts and soon we are going to plant sunflower for a cash crop … we will need a grinder to grind the seeds for the oil. Then we shall start poultry farming … we are a women's group [mainly] and the women really started this. If we can get this poultry farming we shall be managing it ourselves, buying clothes for the orphans, even paying their school fees. We shall be encouraging ourselves, our business will be uplifting."

14. "[The materials] reflected whatever was happening in the community, even in our homes, that was the attraction. … They really touched people and that is why many people are interested and started to practise what was on the cards. ... There is a change and there will be development as we continue practising what we have learned. [Already] we have started doing a lot of work from what we gained [through PfR]."

15. "The community at large has now identified the problems we are having about the orphans in the area and we came out with a solution that we must start our own centre for the orphans."

16. "Things have started to be very effective, the community members have been mobilised and many have formed more groups … and they really enjoyed that style of [doing things] ... they identified their problems faster with less time and less energy."

17. "I have learned a lot about teamwork with members of the communist themselves, not [people] far away from the community."

18. "Things have worked effectively since we identified the problems in the area ... we started a nursery school [for the orphans] we brought them together and are catering for their food and medication and many other things ... the community are providing the food and maybe a little contribution of money and we buy flour with the money. ... The tools were very useful because even the illiterate could identify the problems. Using the toolkit needed no learning academically. ... Sharing out [the work] was very easy. We could share the work within [our] team and then [between the team and] the community."

19. "[We found out what] skills were available, some trained teachers who could teach our young children, some who were skilled in pottery, rope-making, knitting. It works like this: I was taught how to make it and now I can sell it ... Even those who [were] idle they can have something to do within the community and assist the orphans and raise their living standards. [People found] out that they had skills like pottery, basket making, carving and that they could do these things in a group and exchange ideas.

Q. And people who were skilled could help beginners?
A. Yes."

20. "I mobilised the groups in the community and started teaching them to use the toolkit. They were very interested, at first they thought it was a joke and then afterwards it was something they really wanted. It made them know their problems and ... they were surprised to see they have some opportunities they did not know before. ... And they have skills, especially some old men who are good at some things that they had forgotten about. .... After identifying all their problems they decided they can start something by themselves without aid and they started taking care of orphans at home and teaching the orphans and contributing food and clothes to the needy orphans. ... It did not really take long and [others] have taken notice and are joining in in large numbers. ... The next step if we can get fertilisers is to improve our land. We are going to dig so as to get food for malnourished babies and the orphans and the old grandparents."

21. "People enjoyed the cards they were using with their hands, that attracts them. People worked very well in October, but in November and December there was political fear ... but after the election we came out very quickly and quickly attracted [more people]."

22. "The materials are easy to work with, they attract people to join in, the pictures attract them.

Q. Do they think it is just a joke, just a game?
A. It is serious, that is why the project is coming up."

23. "Q. What difference has building the bridge made?
A. In previous years [at flood time] mothers had to carry the children across the river to go to school. In this location we have 1200 households, but school centres, market centres, hospitals are on the other side of the river. Two women drowned, one an expectant mother, and our animals grazing along the riverbank also drowned. So we went to the community elder and we talked to the chief and [then] we mobilised the community. ... even the skills of we ourselves, the youth. ... and we built the bridge."

24. "One log was cut just here [beside the bridge. The others] were brought from the hills. ... All were donated by different people. ... The youths and the community at large brought them, using donkeys, cows and the efforts of human beings to bring them here. It was a very tough job."

25. "The impression I have of people doing things here is that they want action rather than talking. They also want something to be seen."

Chapter Twenty

BACKWARD GLANCE

I said at the beginning of this book that like almost every other piece of writing, there's a problem. What we mean, and feel, and intend can only partly be conveyed by words alone. Words themselves can sometimes obscure, mislead. Yet somehow we need to size ourselves up as human beings in order to figure out how to cope with what lies ahead of us on a planet which is physically changing as you read this sentence.

The French have a phrase for thinking ahead – *reculer pour mieux sauter* – taking a step back in order to leap further. So bear with me if we take a brief look at where we've come from because that could shed light on where we might be heading.

What do we take for granted? Our origins? And (more French!) what moves us, our *raison d'être.*

Some fifty miles east of Kisumu, Kenya, not far from the villages where people were trying out and adapting our toolkits, a much more interesting discovery had been made: the remains of a teenager born some 14 million years ago who at first seemed to be more man than ape. Not long afterwards, in the valley of Lake Turkana, Kamaju Kimeu, one of Dr. Louis Leakey's team discovered what was left of a boy, who had been alive and kicking some one and a half million years ago. A youngster between nine and twelve with massive 'nutcracker' jaws, found lying alongside the chipped stones he fashioned as tools to scrape and crack the bones of any animal he was lucky enough to kill. He had a small brain, not probably big enough to consider how to interact with others, or to plan ahead.

That's about all we learnt during the last century about our remotest forebears. We know a lot more about the Neanderthalers 125,000 years back. Just five feet high with brain pans slightly bigger than most of ours, using stone axes and bone tipped wooden spears, working together to round up the game, moving on as the game moved and the seasons changed.

You could say that so-called primitive man (and woman) came of age when they found how to make and use fire. It cooked their food, lit the caves and shelters they lived in, and many generations later enabled them to refine other elements, combine copper and tin to make bronze, melt the ore hidden in the rocks and turn it into gold.

Meanwhile as the climate alters, sea levels drop, oceans freeze and people move further south, teaching themselves to make and carry fire with them in clay pots, building rafts to hunt on water as well as on land. Then as the ice age ends, they are overtaken by more knowledgeable newcomers, Cro-Magnons named after the place in northern France where their bones were found. People who have learned more by doing more together.

On for another 15,000 years to the limestone caves in southern France and northern Spain and what was then the lush green Sahara; the first rock paintings, done in red and yellow ochre, white chalk, black manganese, identifying the animals they wished to hunt down.

Then, 10,000 years from our own day, the first great cities within the land of Sumer, (called Shinar by the Bible writers); dominated by Ur; a city with walls seventy-five feet thick, two and a half miles long with a tower at the centre 250 ft by 140, three stories high, crowned by a temple palace from which to study the stars and serve the moon god. (Rather more impressive than the cardboard and plasticine affair that figured on the sand tray my father contrived to introduce Abraham and his family to us seven-year-olds).

The Sumerians traded amongst themselves and with other cities beginning to form in the northwestern Indies and in Persia – exchanging copper and later on bronze for limestone, basalt, timber, lapis lazuli and cornelian. They found how to make a potter's wheel, a spinning wheel, later on a cartwheel, solid timber bound with a bronze tyre.

And they learned how to put themselves on record, hieroglyphics set in clay, to keep accounts, celebrate achievements.

Meanwhile there were groups of shepherds and hunters moving northwards from Spain and Portugal across the lowlands of France, settling sometimes as farmers, then as later generations, moving on again. Eventually settling in the rich southern plains of Britain, and still later overtaken in their turn by newcomers from northern Europe, the Rhineland, Russia: makers of bronze weapons and tools, decorated pottery. They could plan ahead, fashioning eighty great Sarsen stones, fifty tons each, rough cut in the quarries of Prescelly and on Marlborough Downs, hauling them by sledge and raft to Salisbury Plain, setting them out in a pattern as the '*Stonehenge computer*'.

Enabling their astronomers to take the sightings from which they predicted eclipses of the sun and moon, the times and dates of moonrise, sunrise, moonset for three hundred years ahead.

The evidence we have in the things they left behind them is mainly what they did between them, unaided by anything more than previous experience; and what they set out to **show** to succeeding generations, the standing stones, the cave drawings, the ornaments on their pottery.

What they thought about is something else entirely. We can only guess. It's in the last two or three thousand years that we can share with our ancestors what they wrote about the world they lived in, and perhaps the other world to which they might go. And deeper down, their feelings, emotions, hopes and fears, impressions and assessments of each other.

Caveman, spaceman, deep-shelter-man – we have one thing in common – adaptability. Not just accepting things as they are. Not just the instinct of self-preservation, but the curiosity and the willpower to grapple with events, to find out about them, transform ourselves and our surroundings to make the best of what's on offer. This capacity is not limited to a few leaders or a particular period in history. It is part of everyone's make up, like the power of speech or the love of beauty. Without it we should be human cattle, bred to be fleeced or slaughtered.

Over at least the last million years most of us were born, grew up, and died within a close family circle. If any adventurous youngster went pioneering he either made his pile and came back home again, or else stayed on with his mates as a *settler* in a new land, staking his claim, founding a family. Within the new family circle everyone settled down as closely as before. Parents, grandparents, aunts, uncles, cousins and second cousins, you lived among neighbours and kinsmen who knew you only too well.

Alongside there is sometimes a self-discovery. Calamities thrust us back on our own resources and we re-discover the human qualities of ingenuity, perseverance, the worth of good company and the zest of overcoming odds together. When all over the world people have been confronted by war's horrors and rigours, there is sometimes an eye-opener. Here and there, in the streets and cellars of London, Liverpool, Chungking, Tokyo, Dresden, Berlin and Baghdad, ordinary people have been re-discovering their kinship with their neighbours, and their capacity to outface their fears and come to grips with the chaos around them.

Ever since the First World War, the pattern has been changing. Europeans were the first to be uprooted and very soon after, the *native troops* they commandeered in the countries they claimed to *Protect*. Conscription detached the young men from their hometowns and villages, and kept them footloose long enough to get used to new surroundings. Those that returned no longer took family ties for granted. What war had re-shuffled, the peace-time years dealt out in new patterns.

Anyone born and bred within a neighbourhood, surrounded by candid, inquisitive friends and acquaintances – and then pitchforked among strangers, needs no convincing that their way of life has changed abruptly. We may be still in touch with our relations somewhere else, visit each other sometimes, swap cards at the New Year. Or as newcomers, taking refuge in another country from the poverty and persecution back home, we may for a time be *disoriented*. Either way we are no longer within the old charmed circle of *our street* or *our village* or *our alley*. There is no one who knows us well enough or cares about us sufficiently, to tell us what he thinks of us. There is scarcely anyone within immediate reach whom we know well enough to depend on.

Our lives now are shadowed by the fear of death and destruction. Our true expectation of life veers between the 70-odd years that an insurance doctor estimates, and the fifteen minutes grace provided (to those in the know) by Early Warning Systems of Nuclear 'defence'. It is a perfectly practical possibility that manmade satellites could be the last and almost the only repository of mankind's skill and knowledge, circling forever round a dead planet.

Too often this prospect overwhelms us. We say, '*Whatever will be, will be*' and think of something else. Or we luxuriate in horrors forever telling over the accounts of Auschwitz and Hiroshima, steeping ourselves in the guilt of each new murder case, as if knowing the worst so far were a charm to fend off worse to come.

Of course this may only be a temporary phase; in time the world may settle down, childhood friends will once again survive as old and trusted neighbours. But, looking around us now – is this likely to happen soon? In our lifetimes even?

However infinitesimal this interruption may seem in the lifespan of the human race, the fact that matters to us is that it has occurred now, within our own lifespans and marks us out in contrast to all our ancestors since men and women first walked on the Earth. We are not only taller, healthier, better-informed, more systematically curious, better equipped and more resourceful than mankind has ever been before. We have enmeshed ourselves in bigger and more complex organisations, and armed them with the means of more complete destruction of body and mind. Being at the mercy of our own creations, we feel ourselves never more isolated, ineffective, and alone.

And this is where we come back to the match between words and action.

As a seven-year-old, the big picture on my bedroom wall showed a man in a flowing robe standing on the beach, with a little girl just behind him bracing her feet against his heels, clutching a loose fold of his upper robe, leaning backwards to swing for joy. In front of him there was a rather wizened man, someone used to posing awkward questions which might catch people out, a lawyer perhaps, challenging this Jesus to tell him '*What shall I do to inherit eternal life?*' And the answer he got has been handed down ever since – *Love your God with all your heart and soul and your neighbour as yourself.* So the cross-examination continues: *Who is my neighbour?* And the questioner, plus a few bystanders by now, gets told the story of the Good Samaritan.

It's a very unsettling story. The man fallen among thieves and left half-dead in the ditch is seen by a couple of respectable passers-by, the sort of god-fearing people that questioning lawyer would be mingling with every day of his life – a priest, and by and by a Levite, one of a rather exclusive tribe dedicated to the care of the tabernacle which holds the words of the prophets. And they pass by on the other side, leaving the man in the ditch. Then along comes the sort of person whom such respectable citizens would rather not have dealings with. An ethnic outsider from neighbouring Samaria, where they don't do their worship in the proper way, and they probably talk different. And he is in trade, not academically respectable at all. But he stops and cares for the wayside casualty, mounts him on his donkey, takes him to the nearest pub, leaves a bit of money for them to look after him until he recovers and goes on his way, probably without having the ghost of an idea of whom to thank.

The big picture up on the wall implied the difference between two sorts of people: Jesus (and the little girl swinging on his coat-tails) and the man who questions him, maybe at first to show him up, and then really wanting an answer to the follow-up question, an answer that maybe he found too hard to swallow.

The sticking point, and what stuck in the mind of the little crowd of onlookers, one of whom passed on the story to others, was the awkward fact that the good man in the story was a Samaritan, one of Them, not one of Us.

What people remembered more often than not, about this carpenter's son, Jesus, was the things he did, the stories he told about people who also were doing things – the farmer scattering seed on his patch of land, the shepherd searching for a missing lamb. And when his followers were at loggerheads with each other about what to make in words of what he was showing them, how he lifted a child from among the crowd and set her or him down in their midst and said, '*This is what it is all about*'. They remembered that, when they saw Jesus beside the daughter of the ruler of the local synagogue. The little girl seemed dead but Jesus said, '*It's all right, she's just asleep*'. And he said to her – and people remembered the very words he used, in the Aramaic language in which he spoke: *Talitha cumi!* Which being interpreted by the writers of the New Testament, and a few centuries later those who translated it as the English Revised Version – '*Little damsel, I say unto thee, arise.*' But my guess is that it was something much more down to earth, as if he was saying to the child, '*Ups-a-daisy*!' Lifting her up, patting her shoulders, giving her a hug.

So those eyewitness accounts are passed on, re-told, and a generation or so afterwards, set down for everyone to read. Mostly what's remembered is the way this Jesus *showed* what he meant, getting down on his knees to wash his followers' feet, entering Jerusalem not in a royal chariot, but on the back of a donkey, passing around the bread and the wine for everyone to take part, even Judas. Then, what happened to him, being mobbed by the crowds, arrested, arraigned, taunted, crucified. Afterwards how he showed himself alive, after all, and left his followers to take on the work.

And then, what followed.

Back in the 1920s there was a play which attracted a lot of comment. It ran and ran and years later it was the first play I attended at about the age of ten. It wasn't exactly history, nor was it about modern manners and romantic encounters. E. Temple Thurston, the playwright, came across the legend of *The Wandering Jew* and turned it into a box-office sell-out, partly because he got in the title role Matheson Lang, a brilliant barnstorming actor-manager, who happened also to be the half brother of Cosmo Lang, the Archbishop of Canterbury.

The legend is about Matteos, a jeering bystander at the crucifixion. From the cross Jesus responds and tells him that he must live on '*until I come again*'.

The play takes this Jew on his wanderings through time. But he is not the kind of time tourist that H.G. Wells featured in *The Time Machine*, or the little green man from Mars who crops up whenever a tired scriptwriter wants a change from human beings.

The Wandering Jew is contemporary with every time through which he goes. He is not just a looker-on. He feels.

The play only hints at what he saw and did. We are left to fill in the picture of his life before that encounter on Calvary.

So how did that imaginary man think and feel in the real world?

He could have been a regular attender at his local synagogue with occasional visits to marvel at the splendours of the Temple, wander about its precincts, eavesdrop on the learned doctors of the law discussing the nuances of the sacred texts, listen to the beautiful singing, feel a sense of belonging with all the others sharing the same experience – Jerusalem people, and visitors from the provinces and from foreign parts, some of them of different races, newly converted to the Jewish faith.

And in the midst of all this there is an outbreak of violence, in comes this ex-carpenter, Jesus, from a village in the back of beyond, with a ragtaggle band: fishermen, an ex tax-gatherer, with women hangers-on including a known prostitute. And this man who everybody has heard about because of the way he scorns the most learned interpreters and upholders of religion, who is said to be doing all sorts of marvels, is violently overturning the tables of the respectable tradesmen and financial consultants in the forecourt, blaspheming within the precincts of the Temple, calling it den of robbers.

Days later, the Wanderer is amongst other orthodox well-brought up Jews, crowding to hear an official statement from the chief of the local Roman government, embodying Roman firmness which tolerates, and to an extent upholds locally established religion. This fellow Jesus has been arraigned for some kind of treason apparently asserting his kingship of a regime above and beyond Roman or Jewish statehood. Pontius Pilate showing his clemency and respect for popular feeling offers a choice between two convicted criminals – Barabbas, a run of the mill highwayman, whose exploits may attract a sneaking feeling of admiration – paraded alongside this oddball unsettler of a society which isn't all that stable, and needs above all things calm and conformity.

Like nearly everyone else the future Wanderer shouts the collective verdict, 'Crucify him!' And having taken part so far he goes along afterwards to watch the execution.

Seeing this man on the cross, he jeers along with the others, '*If you're the Son of God, why doesn't He save you*?' and spits his derision for good measure. And he gets the response that makes this Jew the Wanderer. Later he hears Jesus praying to the God of Israel to forgive the people who put him there. That's probably the turning point.

The Wanderer is still a man in two minds. Everything he has been brought up to accept and revere is suddenly exposed to this new experience.

Something which can't be buried. There are more and more people claiming to be adherents of the dead Jesus, some of them asserting that he is not dead. One of these followers goes too far in claiming this, blaspheming, as the elders in the local establishment see it, sentenced to death at the hands of god-fearing local people, themselves taking part in the stoning. There are other onlookers there to see justice done, including a fellow from Tarsus, who already has a reputation for spotting and rounding up other such blasphemers and dissidents on behalf of the authorities. Some of those doing the stoning drop their coats at his feet.

The Wanderer goes away still in a tumult of conflicting thoughts. As time goes on he hears more about the way these unbelievers are asserting their blasphemous beliefs. He could be one of the crowd listening to the debate amongst those who still regard themselves as orthodox members of the Jewish faith, and who believe Jesus was the very person whom the prophets foresaw as the deliverer of the nation of Israel. Amongst them is that ex-tentmaker from Tarsus who by some mystical experience when he was travelling on the road to Damascus, has been suddenly won over, and is now going much further than some of those who were in at the beginning.

It was the stories of those Samaritans that got people arguing: the Samaritan rescuer of the man in the ditch, and the Samaritan woman at the well joking about being one of the dogs beneath the table who snapped up the leavings of the orthodox Jews. Samaritans were not really *kosher*, they couldn't be properly regarded as members of the chosen people who had been so patiently awaiting the arrival of their messiah.

But Paul, the Johnny-come-lately, the newly converted tentmaker from Tarsus was jumping to the conclusion that not only Samaritans but everyone else in the known world could be seen as people choosing to take in the teachings and follow the example of Jesus, and set about the service of all humanity.

He has the gift of the gab, and the itch to travel the known world, describing his conversion on the Damascus road, testifying to what he says God has revealed to him in the person of Jesus. He comes back to Jerusalem and fraternises with some of the former followers of Jesus who have in their turn been preaching to other orthodox Jews, recruiting converts to the new, Christian, version of the Jewish faith. Still respecting all the rules and rituals of Judaism, including the rite of circumcision, and the requirement that you only eat your meals with others of the Jewish faith.

Paul, circumcised like every other Jewish baby son, knocking about the Middle East with all sorts of other faiths, enjoying their hospitality, eating and talking with them in their homes and in their public meetings, as he preaches the Christian gospel – back in Jerusalem he is the odd man out. The old hands and some of their local converts are friendly, but on one crucial issue, reserved. At a public meeting both sides expose the difference between those who stood by the old tradition, and believed that theirs was the nation chosen to do God's work, and the others, some of them newcomers like Paul, claiming that their mission was to all men, (and even, within limitations, women). And Paul goes further than that – not as a resident priest but as a missionary crossing frontiers, confronting those in other climes, brought up in other faiths, exchanging ideas and experience, drawing on combined resources to do the work, beginning to see what Jesus stood for as the fulfilment of mankind's universal longings. Leaving James and the other stalwart traditionalists to get on with the work within their own intellectual boundaries.

What did the Wanderer make of all that?

Did he follow in Paul's footsteps? More likely he stayed back in Jerusalem for the time being with people he had been brought up to know best; as a practising Jew, and perhaps now a practising Christian Jew.

So he was still there, a generation on, when the Romans had had enough of Jewish civil disobedience, and taught everyone a lesson by moving in to destroy the Temple, kill some thousands of suspect resisters, and make many thousands more homeless refugees, displaced persons, fellow wanderers, seeking asylum wherever their talents and ingenuity could gain them entry.

In that upheaval, the break-up of a nation, the *diaspora*, we lose sight of the Wanderer, making himself at home here and there for the time being, but always eventually on the move. Always the odd man out.

Your imagination might trace his footsteps over the centuries. People were not quite sure about him, but clearly he was a man of experience, and might come in useful.

On his travels perhaps he comes across a man in his late forties who began life looking after the sheep on his father's farm, married the widow of a rich merchant, travelled with the caravans along the Red Sea coast of Arabia, talked with other Arabs who were beginning to question idol worship, learning something of what other peoples, especially the Jews, believe. He has been able to take time out from everyday living to think about the world and its maker. He is dissatisfied with the worship of many gods, and begins to tell other people what he believes is the one true God. He says it over again and again, not being literate himself, so as to fix it in everyone's memory; and people listen. They go on listening, and over the months and the years he tells them what he is discovering. He acknowledges that all this reflects and confirms the thoughts and the teaching of predecessors, like Jesus the Jew who was executed long ago, and Gautama Buddha who was a fellow seeker long before him. The way that they lived and taught is in tune, says Mohammed, with what I have learned and am telling you here and now.

Still later the Wanderer may have been in Paris among crowds of people, particularly young student people, listening to Peter Abelard, a Christian scholar still in his 30s, who has something special to say about the ways in which anyone, everyone, can discover what life (and death) are all about.

'By doubting we learn to enquire, by enquiring we perceive the truth.'

So there is something solid to go on. Recognition that we begin as doubters, clueless almost, or as you might put it, with an open mind. But this is the starting point on a journey we all make.

Abelard's challenge unsettles some of his peers who reckon that everything one needs to know and is required to believe, is already established. So there is no excuse for doubt. Besides, the young scholar is getting his patron's daughter, Heloise, in trouble. So he's waylaid and castrated. But the love affair continues and becomes an assertion of what matters beyond the flesh. He goes on teaching and his words remain at the back of other scholars' minds ever since.

The Wanderer moves on and lands up, perhaps, far to the east at the court of Kublai Khan. This is the emperor who has inherited the half world that Genghis Khan had conquered. But now, relatively speaking, a man of peace, interested in anyone with good advice to pass on. So he surrounds himself with interesting people, Islamists, Buddhists perhaps, certainly Jews and among them, let's imagine, that time traveller.

A couple of Italians turn up, being almost the first Europeans to travel up the Silk Road, to do a little business, and tell some travellers' tales. They certainly interest Kublai. He's heard indirectly about the lands from which they came, loosely summed up as Christendom, and he wants to know more about the people who have fashioned it. In particular, the teachers of the Christian faith. So he hands a golden tablet to the Polo brothers, which allows them to travel unscathed through all the lands that are now at relative peace. They are empowered to gather one hundred Christian teachers who will be honoured at the Khan's court, and can freely tell about their faith.

The Polos travel home peacefully with the Khan's safe-conduct but when they cross the final frontier they find their own people at odds with each other, rivals for the papacy, killings and counter-killings, intrigues, statements and counter-statements. It takes another three years before the Khan's invitation is seriously considered, and then all the Christian teachers than can be spared are just two.

And they drop out on the return journey, for fear of trouble ahead.

But the Polo brothers, this time with a seventeen-year-old nephew called Marco, still remember the goodwill of the Khan. Even though they come empty-handed, they press on, in Marco's words, '*through the snows and the rains and the furious winds*' across the Gobi Desert, until they reached Cambaluc (which nowadays we call Beijing) and there the Khan proved his greatness by welcoming them back in spite of the dusty answer to his invitation. They stayed around, Marco got a job traversing the Khan's dominions and reporting back. In between times there was a little, unsuccessful revolt by a faction led by the Khan's uncle, turned Christian, Nayan. When the revolt was over, wrote Marco,

> *'The different kinds of people present, Saracens, Idolaters and Jews, and many other people who do not believe in God, mocked the cross that Nayan had borne on his standard. And they said to the Christians who had been present, 'See how the cross of your God has aided Nayan'.'*

Perhaps the Wanderer was among those Jews, but maybe not among the mockers. He would have heard the Khan's rebuke (which Marco Polo recorded):

> *'Calling many Christians who were there he comforted them, saying, 'If the cross of your God had not aided Nayan there was good reason for it ... Nayan was a disloyal traitor ... and the cross of your God has done very well in not helping him contrary to justice. For, in that it is a good thing, it cannot do but what is good'.'*

So in the Jew's wanderings, something like that saying could have stayed in his mind. It's not in Temple Thurston's play, which brings the wanderings short at the time of the Inquisition, when the Jew is brought before the court accused of being some sort of unbeliever. Nobody is quite clear about the precise heresy. But he's different, and asserts an identity which challenges the orthodox.

The big moment in the play is when he stands in the courtroom, facing the Inquisitors in their robes, with their books and papers laid out before them. Behind them a great bejewelled crucifix. And, hard pressed, resigned to the verdict he knows they will deliver, he dares to talk back:

'There is the sign, the cross! It was not a cross like that he carried up the hill to Calvary. Rough beams of sycamore that never knew the temper of the plane. … Roughly hewn the day before and on one arm whereon they nailed his hand a little twig clung to the mother tree. … That was the only jewel on the cross and they who mocked with words and spat on him – that was such mockery as yours whose hollow worship in a painted shrine is more unreal than the spittle on your lips!'

That's the climax of the play and it ends soon after when the Jew's wanderings finish at the stake.

The legend of the Wandering Jew is imaginary. The Inquisitors, and the jewelled crucifix, and for that matter the original cross (one among thousands with which the Roman occupying force lined the roads to teach Jewish and other dissidents a lesson) – they're all *real.*

Suppose his wanderings continue for half a millennium more into an age that in some ways anticipates our own: that wigged and powdered eighteenth century as the history books convey it.

Mattheus, the Jew, like other immigrant asylum seekers, is sometimes up against discontented, jobless, local people who are on the margins of the development that is taking place in the New World.

Over several centuries, the European powers have been slugging it out to grab and cultivate whatever raw materials are on offer (or, rather, what the peoples in the New World are required to yield) – sugar, coffee, tea, tobacco, precious metals – plus *raw humans* to pick and pack them for the home consumer. Private enterprise in imperial England (with Scotland, Wales and Ireland in tow) is coming out on top, determining the terms of trade (USA twenty-first century fashion).

Back home, what are called the *common people* are making the best they can of what for them is a bad bargain. Life goes on with a grudging acceptance of things as they are, leaving *the lower classes* apathetic, uncommitted. People are accustomed to accepting what their *betters* – the rector, the squire, the Established Church, and far distant, the various Members of Parliament who are for the most part *placemen* (no women!) dependent on the patronage of the aristocracy and big business – take for granted. Including the notion that the God they believe in thoroughly approves of the way things are.

A verse (now omitted) from the hymn *All Things Bright and Beautiful* sums it up.

The rich man in his castle,
The poor man at his gate,
He made them, high or lowly,
And ordered their estate.

But disorder is on the way. Respectable people, getting the best of all things bright and beautiful, are doubtful, even hostile. It seems there is a kind of infection abroad. The Bishop of Gloucester condemns

'a wild and pernicious enthusiasm which aroused the passions of weak, credulous or distempered people.'

Enthusiasm?

Something that possesses people? Or that most of us discover we already possess within ourselves when we begin to tinker with a problem and then try to turn it into an opportunity.

Three men, each of them starting out without the benefits of money or political influence, became what some scientists might call the *catalysts* of change, the leaven in the lump, the enemies of apathy.

The next chapter begins with their stories, as a kind of foretaste of our own.

Chapter Twenty-One

FORERUNNERS

Enthusiasm? What's that to do with us?

The man whose enthusiasm aroused the ire of the Bishop of Gloucester was John Wesley (remember the film we tried to make about him, Chapter Four). Some people talk about our own times as the Age of Apathy, at least in the western world. They might have said the same about the society in which Wesley lived. He grew up in a modest parsonage in Epworth where later his father was buried. He preached on his father's tombstone outside church premises because he had fallen out with the established Church of England and they would not allow him to preach from inside.

As an Oxford divinity student he had belonged to an inward looking group sharing their problems, studying the scriptures and earning the nickname from the other students of *the Holy Club.*

Until his thirties Wesley was still a troubled man, wrestling with his feelings and his beliefs; arguing with himself even as he followed the conventional pattern as a clergyman. But one evening, in a meeting place in Aldersgate Street, listening to someone giving readings from Martin Luther – '*at about a quarter before nine I felt my heart strangely warmed'*. Until then his understanding of the Gospels had been, so to speak, detached. Now he became *possessed.* From now on he had to convey those feelings to everyone who would listen.

He rode up and down the country preaching to people wherever they happened to be – in the market, in the fields, (and in my great-great-great-grandfather's barn). As what was called a field preacher, he attracted huge crowds wherever he went. They came because he spoke to them heart to heart, in words shorn of ecclesiastical flummery. He had the knack, he reckoned God-given, to say what people needed to hear, in words they understood.

The end product wasn't just a one-off emotional release. People saw themselves and each other differently. They stuck together, but still within the Church of England so far as Wesley was concerned. In each neighbourhood where he and later on his colleagues had preached, the groups that came together became known as *society classes*. They met to pool their new experiences, study the scriptures, tackle problems, opportunities, help each other out. Gradually they were getting a fresh understanding of their role in the world and in their own communities – caring for the downtrodden, people in jail, the poverty-stricken, the dying.

That was as far as Wesley himself saw their role. But in the years after his death some of those *society classes* nourished people who decided it was time to stand up to the powers-that-be, in industry and in politics. They were the mainstays of the earliest trades unions, and the Chartists campaigning for the right to vote for a parliament of their own choosing.

They went about this systematically, seeing what they were up against, and how to overcome obstacles in the way. Very *methodical*, they were, and that's how they got their nickname. And this gradually yielded something that the rather conservative John Wesley would have disapproved, almost imperceptibly they became part of a movement. People suddenly saw themselves in a new light, on a level with everyone else (the occasional aristocrat like the Countess of Huntingdon, included) – and committed to action.

Onlookers, at the turn of the century, called such people *Tom Paine Methodists*.

Tom Paine began his working life apprenticed to his Quaker father's small business making stays to keep working women's figures in shape. As a teenager he broke away to go as a deckhand on a privateer, preying on merchant ships in the war with France. Coming home with his modest share of the prize money, he knocked about in the coffee houses and bookshops, married and was widowed, married again and separated, got and lost a government job as an excise man on the watch for smuggled rum. Meanwhile, although not much of a church-goer, he kept in touch with some of his father's Quaker colleagues, preached once in a while for the Methodists, began writing for local newspapers. His work attracted the notice of Benjamin Franklin, the representative of the thirteen American colonies still under British control. Franklin helped him to emigrate to America, for a newspaper job in Philadelphia. Not just a newspaperman, soon a pamphleteer on behalf of the other American settlers with a chip on their shoulders about the behaviour of the British Government.

The settlers in the American colonies, like most such people, were inclined to be rather more independent minded than the stay-at-homes. They were used to meeting and talking together on their own ground; sometimes in places where they worshipped, more often in coffee houses where they talked and joked and griped about everything uppermost in their minds, with the helpful lubrication of locally produced coffee and rum.

They were at that time much concerned about the arrogance and bumbling self-delusion of His Majesty King George III, the man they supposed to be in charge of the government back home. He was taking their tax money and spending it on the war with France, and on Whitehall officials and other *placemen*; with nothing left over to spend on developing the colonies as they deserved.

The coffee house gatherings were a natural for everyone with opinions to ventilate. Tom Paine's ideas echoed what everyone else was thinking, and put the key issues into sharp focus. He struck home with a pamphlet, circulated in sections which eventually became a book. With a turn of phrase that quickened the imagination, sometimes made people laugh, he flagged up the general concerns, and made them specific about rights, responsibilities, popular control.

Like Wesley he had the words to speak to everyday people in their own tongue. What began as a pamphlet developed into *Common Sense*, a book which sold 100,000 copies in its first year. A local historian said it was

> *'written on a stile, manner and language that has produced the most astounding effects, read by every American and recommended as replete with truth.'*

The Americans, over several generations, had made their own living in their own ways; and, they reckoned, developed their own resources on a scale that matched, and maybe outmatched anything that people back in England and Scotland could achieve. It was time to make a change.

Common Sense was read aloud in the coffee houses as well as handed around and studied at home. It was the talk of every town in the thirteen colonies, and the inspiration of more and more people who wanted to put things right. Among them was Thomas Jefferson who welcomed Tom Paine as a friend, discussing with him the notions that were finally set out in the Declaration of Independence. This became the magnet round which the colonial people's ideas – and King George's Occupation Forces took shape.

The War of Independence had began uncertainly, as local people found out how to act together in what became in part a guerrilla war. Everywhere the English soldiers went there were Americans peeping over the hedges, lurking behind the doors, and then quietly nipping off to villages next door so that they could be prepared for action. None of this required much talk. When the Generals leading the resistance wanted to muster support they were able to use the same kind of network. Everyone was in the know and could get together without fuss to sort out who would do what, and where and when.

The war aims of the resistance were primarily to achieve white independence. Black slavery – about half a million throughout the thirteen colonies, came lower on the list. Leaders such as George Washington and Jefferson had slaves of their own. Jefferson himself had misgivings, reinforced by what his friend Tom Paine had to say:

'Christians are taught to account all men their neighbours .... Man-stealing is ranked with enormous crimes. Is the barbarous enslavement of our impotent neighbours, and treating them like wild beasts subdued by force, reconcilable with all these divine precepts? ... If they could carry off and enslave some thousands of us, would we think it just?'

It was another set of upstarts from the ranks who made the running, back home in England. They met in the rooms of a London printer, attracted by another piece of revolutionary writing, a prize-winning essay on slavery written by a twenty-five-year-old Cambridge divinity student, Thomas Clarkson. He had researched his paper, reinforced it with first hand accounts from those who had seen the evils of slavery in the 'castles' on the African coasts where newly captured men, women and children were imprisoned whilst they waited for the ships that would take them to be marketed on the plantations which free enterprise had established in the New World.

The group included Phillips the printer, and up to a dozen others including a former Igbo slave Olaudah Equiano, who had managed to earn money on the side and buy his freedom. He could talk from first hand experience of the whole process of capture, imprisonment and transportation like cattle, to the market.

In the early days the group had no friends in high places to back them up. But here and there, scattered across both countries, almost unknown to the general public, there were groups with unconventional ideas. The Quakers rejected all the paraphernalia of church going. Their meetings for worship were mostly silent, and the words they used to each other, inside and outside the meetinghouse, were simple and direct, purged of all the conventional politeness. They didn't go in for dressing up for particular occasions and they kept their hats on where others were only too ready to doff theirs to their elders and betters.

Untrammelled by the conventions, they had reached their own conclusions about the right way to behave, not just to each other, but to their neighbours; not just at home but also abroad. They called themselves the Society of Friends. Their friendship extended worldwide. Over the seas in Philadelphia the local Quakers were the first to go public and challenge slavery head-on. (The nickname Quakers came from what people said was their humble, self-reproaching, *quaking* response to God.) Now, first in London, and then elsewhere in England, they put together a petition to parliament. Soon after they joined the group with Clarkson and the others, setting out to reach people everywhere and make them see what slavery involved.

Much like the Americans, there was great scope for interaction at street level; in the coffee houses, the Quaker meetinghouses, and sometimes the marketplace. The role of local printers like Phillips was crucial. There were many small-scale newsletters and gazettes, often edited by the printer himself, always on the lookout for interesting copy. Early on the group circulated a kind of diagram, poster-size, based on first hand information from, amongst others, John Newton who had himself captained slave ships until, in his later years, quite suddenly, he *saw* what he had been doing.

The picture on the poster showed the hold of a slave ship, with 482 bodies laid in chains, side by side, tight packed as living merchandise. It gained a circulation of 7,000. Later, on leaflets and with the help of the Wedgwood firm on pottery, there was a logo – a slave, manacled, on his knees, with the caption *'Am I not a man and a brother?'*

With just enough backing from his family to keep him going, young Thomas Clarkson followed Wesley's example, walking and riding from one end of the country to the other to bring the evidence home to people wherever they gathered. Not usually in the fields, preaching as Wesley did, but making contact with every kind of local club and society and the local news editors. In this way neighbourhood groups took shape, and helped to distribute the posters and arouse other people's concern. They could also handle some of the items that Clarkson brought with him. He was giving the newsmen what they needed – *actuality* – specimen manacles, leg irons, thumbscrews, that reinforced the vivid first hand accounts of the *stealing* of whole families from their homes, the prison conditions in the holding centres on the coast, the living cargo lying in their own blood and faeces in the slave ships, the Caribbean markets where families were split apart and sold, one or two at a time, to the plantation masters.

It was what nowadays would be called a *documentary* approach. Hard facts, without the need for spin. Eyewitness, first hand, detail by detail.

Seeing is believing.

Slavery, like private profit and hereditary rule, was part of the local economy, not just in America but in every society which people set up for themselves. Over the centuries, Greeks, Romans, Angles and Saxons, Franks and

Scandinavians, Arabs, Indians, Persians and Chinese, took slavery for granted.

In eighteenth century England well brought up people were convinced that all this made sense, along with the rights of often quite benevolent gentry to make the most of the lands their well armed ancestors had seized from the peasants who used to farm it. They happily agreed that the takings from the slave plantations could be usefully invested in the new industries that were beginning to transform the country.

In England there were comparatively few slaves bought and sold. What most people knew about them was first that they made money for everyone concerned in the trade, and second that those who were to be seen in England were sometimes novelties, fancy attachments to the well-to-do, usually got up in elegant costumes to match. Elsewhere, in workaday garb, they were household servants much like any others, with the advantage that they did not have to be paid.

Now, thanks to Clarkson's ginger groups, some people were having second thoughts.

The opposition to all this was very well established. People, if they thought about it, felt they knew that without the profits from slavery, the country's economy could not survive. It was later estimated that the annual turnover from slavery was roughly 40% of *the economy*, £2.25 billion in modern terms. The money made by the slave trade was embedded in everyone's livelihood. The sugar in your tea, the *funds* from *business* in the West Indies plantations helped to keep the county gentry and their needy dependents going. They had to be accepted, much as the arms trade (aka the *defence industry*) fuels our economy today. Like our own arms dealers, the slave dealers reckoned to be thoroughly respectable, and they paid dividends to all sorts of people, remote from slave dealings, or the slaves themselves, as insulated as ordinary investors and manufacturers are today from the receiving end of landmines, long-range artillery, rocket launchers and cluster bombs.

Clarkson and co. were challenging such assumptions. They won through eventually with the help of one well-placed, beautifully spoken Member of Parliament, William Wilberforce, at the time the only MP ready to believe that the trade could be stopped without disaster to people's livelihoods. He had become convinced of the evils of slavery and determined to defeat the slavers. At his first attempt, however, he was only able to win over a handful of MPs. Others were preoccupied with more pressing matters, and a good many had shares in the trade.

So the first target of the group's supporters was simply the Abolition of the trade itself, the marketing process. It took nearly half a century before there was enough influential, top-level, support to complete the process with Emancipation, the compulsory release of all slaves, throughout what was by that time Her Majesty Queen Victoria's dominions.

Emancipation was achieved at a price. Business interests inside and outside parliament ensured that the slave owners were duly compensated, market price, cash down. But it did not, after all, break the banks. Instead it reinforced people's confidence in their ability to initiate changes from the bottom up. It marked a shift in the balance of power.

In the same century some others with a scientific bent were getting freer rein to consider every kind of natural – rather than supernatural – phenomena. A key question in scientific minds was to figure out what makes things burn. They reckoned there must be something within any material that was *flammable* and this made the difference between *non-living matter*, and matter that, so to speak, contained a soul. In 1708 Georg Stahl put forward a theory that caught on throughout Europe. He found that when metals such as magnesium burned they gained weight. He reckoned the weight increase was air entering the metal to fill the space left after something vital had escaped.

Was this something magical, stolen from the gods? But, with flint and steel it becomes manmade. What's the process by which the vital spark comes into being? Does it come from nothing? '*No*', said Herr Stahl and his colleague Johann Becher. There's another element beside the basic elements which we already know about. You can't see it, or feel it, as yet. But it must be there to make fire happen. That crucial element we shall call *Phlogiston* – the invisible *something* that comes or goes when something else ignites.

This is what those leading scientists reckoned to be true. Even though they were not able to identify and isolate it. As a Working Assumption it got by, for the time being, just as a thousand years or so earlier thinking people could see for themselves that the sun went round the earth. Phlogiston was the accepted label explaining something that was otherwise beyond words.

But later on, in the light of much further thought, the whole idea was, shall we say, exploded. After all, there was no such thing as Phlogiston. Back to the drawing board.

So far as the scientific thinkers were concerned, the existence of Phlogiston was now a False Assumption. But that didn't explain the way fire happens. Fire that helps to create or destroy, is still a fact of life.

So what do we make *now* of the forces within us and outside us that shape our lives?

Chapter Twenty-two

OVER TO YOU?

As a race we are nearly a foot taller than our mediaeval ancestors. The suits of armour that were custom-built for Saracens and Crusaders are a tight fit for the average lad about to enter Secondary school. To look a knight in the visor, you have to prop him up on a museum pedestal.

Of course we know more than our ancestors. Their lives, their legends, their interpretations, their discoveries are part of our inheritance. Besides this we have grown out of some of the limitations on independent thought that used to be imposed by awe of the monarch and the priest or fear of the devil. Man's persevering curiosity marked him out from the birds and beasts and fishes many million years ago. His (and her) progress ever since has re-traced the restless drive of an enquiring mind. And, equally crucial, an inclination to size things up and try things out.

Plenty of *concerns*, to use the Quakers' word. Plenty of frustrations, and a tendency to become bloody-minded about the misbehaviour, the apparent obtuseness of the powers-that-be.

It's not difficult to set up a Hit List, targeting what needs to be changed, somehow. (Here's one, **see page 282**, for you to scrutinise, and maybe enlarge.) We are more aware than those eighteenth-century people of what's gone wrong, the media keeps showing it up. But it may be that we have less belief in our own abilities to put things right.

What's the difference between *Then* (in Wesley's and Paine's and Clarkson's time) and *Now*? Has President George Bush any more grasp of the realities now than *mad King George* had then? Are today's arms dealers less vulnerable than the slave dealers were then? And we ourselves? Have we been dozing on the sidelines as most of those eighteenth century people were, until some *moving spirits* woke them up?

So how is it that *ordinary people **take** the lead*? It's usually a mixture of words and action, in which people puzzle things out together, not always very systematically, and gradually home in on what to do: Now – Soon – Later. If you remember that was the way Weller Street people on Merseyside reacted

Hit List

- Schools short of the resources to do much more than pump information into youngsters and then extract it for examination purposes. Bullying and truancy increasing. Teenagers ganging up to make their mark.
- Traffic, fouling the streets and costing the earth.
- Drugs as a stimulus to doing nothing much.
- Business cartels buying very cheap from the growers and the processors, packaging the results at prices that gradually put local shops out of business.
- Skyrocketing energy costs and food-carrying mileage by the supermarkets, whilst the globe begins to overheat.
- Have's getting fatter year by year; have nots starving to death.
- Overcrowded prisons, dangerously short of resources to care, understand and rehabilitate as well as punish. More and more re-offenders.
- New kinds of apartheid, separating by race, religion, nationality.

What else?

to the way town planners were proposing to reshuffle streets and put up tombstone tower blocks. Residents could see for themselves what that was likely to do to what they reckoned was **their** neighbourhood. Working out how to counter it created a kind of buzz. They had the advantage of living within reach of each other so that they could talk things over, and get around to other neighbourhoods to *see for themselves* what was worth applying to their own condition. It all took time but they managed to end up next-door neighbours in a new housing scheme they helped to design (with living greenery not a *choice between tarmac, green or red).*

In Birkenhead, local people with some help from enlightened local officials, were able to take a close look (on the 3D model they created) at the ways in which their own patch could be rescued. There too there was a buzz and it was enriched (as the head of the local administration pointed out to me later) by the way in which people who had formerly been Us and Them had begun to chat with each other. They went on to devise together an entirely new scheme, the conversion of a set of buildings with the work shared between Them and Us. And of course plenty of conversational buzz, on the job in hand.

We celebrated the same feisty relationship just recently at our twentieth year anniversary – on the site of the village we built together on Lightmoor.

In Kenya, even before President Arap Moi was toppled, when people in Kisumu Province got the chance to see and size up the problems and opportunities for themselves –

'we have refreshed our minds … so that instead of talking much, we talk a little and apply more action … it is going to be very great.

'We have discovered that we are sitting on gold, our own human resources.'

In South Africa, with the same eye-opening process –

'*Everybody took part, the less people are talking, the more they are doing*.'

In downtown Kingston, Jamaica, the pace was set by the youngsters who began to reclaim Rodney Street from the drug dealers and the snipers by creating a kind of rendezvous for everyone – garden, play space, homemade community hut, barbecue, surmounted by their slogan: TOGETHERNESS. That reinforced the fellow-feeling that the Planning for Real scheme had begun to reveal. The head of the government back-up service commented:

'The community support has been overwhelming.'

Fellow-feeling? Remember the story of the first Christmas on the Western Front in World War I? The squaddies on both sides, British and Germans, meeting in No Man's Land to swap rations, make jokes, play football together? They managed it just the once before the Generals put them back to work killing each other.

What is it that forces us apart?

Apartheid, under other names, has a long history. In South Africa it began partly because the Boers, who had got there first and taken over native African resources, found themselves threatened, even displaced by the British incomers, set to impose their own culture in return for the British lion's share of the diamonds, the gold, and other less glamorous resources. In the long run it was Boer values that underpinned the notion shared with most of the British settlers that the whites knew best, as well as having acquired the best of the resources available.

Mixed in with the urge to acquire there was also what both sides quite sincerely felt to be a mission to educate and *civilise* – always on the understanding that the economic order, and the incomers' share of the goodies – came first.

Being *separate* was a defence of some of those values, alongside the territory and the economy. The more threatened by the Africans themselves, the greater the need to follow the example worldwide of other invaders over the centuries, and pull up the drawbridge, strengthen the walls, proclaim to everyone that *we know best*.

Sooner or later this assertion gets a racial and/or a religious justification. We reckon to be special, suitably rewarded bearers of the White Man's Burden, inheritors of the right to rule. Echoes of the *Herrenvolk* as the Nazis put it, a master race challenged in turn by Jewish claims to be a Chosen People.

The racists have less evidence of superiority to go on nowadays though that doesn't diminish their pride in being exclusive. As for the religious interpreters, there is a division between those who reckon that everything is already rock-solid, written on stone, and others who respect the evidence that has been handed down, like any other historical records, as something to be amplified as time goes on, thought over, understood afresh.

This means going back to what was remembered at the time, and chronicled later, about particular people whom we now admire, and maybe venerate. Just as those eighteenth century scientists dreamt up the notion of Phlogiston to account for the phenomenon known as fire, the chroniclers were grappling with something real and fundamental. They may, just possibly, have got the definition wrong, even though we all can recognise the reality it describes.

That still leaves us with the separatists determined to maintain the barriers or put up new ones and to play down any talk about the things that are common to us all, what we all understand and value in ourselves, and in each other. The most important thing to share, right now, is experience.

This has to do not just with our feelings, but with our actions, how we behave. Deep down we recognise something we can share – what we know about each other at first hand.

At first hand? That's the problem/opportunity.

It is no longer so easy for the powers-that-be to get in the way. Appeals for help, rallying calls, attempts to bridge the gap between Us and Them – along with domestic chitter-chatter – are becoming more and more *accessible.* Not only conversations, also the pooling of information we can tap on the internet, just when we want it. And we can add to that resource whatever we choose to contribute. So there are networks that for the most part are within our reach. Even in countries like China which have tried to control the input from outside, people are finding ways to disguise their own communications, to develop a kind of playground slang that Teacher hasn't fully grasped.

So, after all, we are becoming capable of outflanking whoever tries to confine us. All sorts of people are finding that they can get in touch, across some of the frontiers; not only the boundaries that divide nations; also the unstated, unspoken barriers between different sorts of people living *within literally a stone's throw* of each other.

We have the means to communicate on a scale we never had before. Experience. How can we make the most of it? At first it's the *buzz*, the casual gossip about the weather, the local team, the flowers in the window box. People talking to each other – over the garden fence, in the bus queue, are likely to mention their concerns, the traffic dangers, the litter, the druggies, the shortcomings of the bus service.

And, maybe, the resources that might be within reach.

That's where communication begins to turn into commitment. There are possibilities, opportunities – rather shadowy at first – to get something done. Who's going to do it, that's another matter. But the closer the possibilities come to home the more likely that people like us could actually do something about them.

Beginning cautiously, with rather tentative brainstorming: survey the routes taken by the HGVs, and the traffic danger spots, combine forces to clear the litter from a derelict patch, and level it for a five-a-side or a toddlers' play area – get more scope for teenagers to make their mark, maybe a graffiti wall to decorate a boring building, or a funky fashion show? Club together to

RESOURCES WITHIN REACH

- Under-used premises – social centres, schools, shops, places of worship – that could be shared.
- Under-used facilities on offer (photocopier? PA system? library information services?) Scope for a recycling centre for discarded PCs, printers, laptops as newcomers, housebound and elderly start out and the experts upgrade.
- Under-used transport (with driver) occasionally available.
- Elderly with local knowledge, long memories and (sometimes) time on their hands.
- Bored teenagers, footloose, with local knowledge and a need to make their mark.
- Frustrated professionals trying to bridge communication gaps and become part of something better.
- Schools and their parents, and their students – wanting opportunities to share ideas about neighbourhood improvement.
- Local press short of 'local interest' copy.
- Local skills, expert information, useful contacts.
- Shared interests among e.g. children – involving community police as well, making videos, sports training, greening the neighbourhood.
- What else?

consider solar panels on the roofs, or gable end windmills? Maybe a credit union to spread the financial load? A shopping service for the housebound? Handrails for the disabled at home? Shared transport? A community vegetable garden? Some hard graft identifying the drug dealers and monitoring their pitches? The possibilities mount up. And they are there for the taking. All sorts of music-making (teenagers to the front) to celebrate whatever we manage to achieve.

Sometimes it's a dummy run, using some of our 3D materials to construct a situation, explore possibilities together. Here's how one Sheffield housewife describes it.

> *'We saw what we were doing. You could translate words into actions ... there was a definite affinity growing up, just as two people who live together can start off a sentence and you know the rest of it ... We got on to common ground quicker, because with words everybody's words are the same: but the imagination may be different ... In the mind everybody can be seeing a different thing and maybe stick out for it ... But where you've got this model to work on ... you looked at it and said, 'Let's try this'. So we tried it and if it was wrong, we changed it. 'All right, let's try it again another way' and this is where we came to a consensus. ... It was like speaking your thoughts ... You visualised each other's thoughts, you project your own thoughts into vision ... We got to a state in the end where we didn't need to speak.'*

And amongst all the planning, how about including a bench to sit out and pass the time of day together, sizing up not only what is being done, or not done, by Them – the authorities and the donor agencies – but what could, sooner or later, be done by Us. (With maybe a helping hand from Them, if we can make them see we mean business.)

You might say some of that is old hat. It's how people used to meet and chat, and meanwhile get weaving. Do they still? Yes, but not invariably in the old neighbourly across-the-garden-fence fashion. That still happens, but it is these days overtaken by a resource that lies literally in the palm of our hands.

I can just remember my grandfather (the Justice of the Peace and parliamentary wheeler and dealer on behalf of his engineering firm) making his first contact with his newly installed telephone. There was a mouthpiece on a bracket screwed to the wall near the front door, (where Father Christmas was alleged to enter). Hanging beside there was the earpiece, about the size of a Pepsi bottle. When Grandpa's telephone rang for the very first time he responded by putting his ear to the mouthpiece and trying to talk through the receiver. (I have a certain sympathy, getting used to an updated mobile.)

Mobiles are the thin end of the wedge. Five and six-year-olds are blithely into infotec, swapping jokes and chatter. Ninety percent of UK twelve year-olds have their own mobiles. World sales of mobiles should pass one billion by Christmas 2007. China, India and Bangladesh users are increasing by 13 million every year. A quarter of UK users are in their teens and early twenties. Nearly half the rest are under 34.

All of us are getting used to the idea, and most of us already own the gear. On the hop we can make additions to previous arrangements which we had forgotten about, without having to look for the nearest old-fashioned telephone kiosk. We talk or text our friends and relations to remind them of our existence, maybe share our frustrations, or our joys, give ourselves reassurance that they are still *there* (or will be as soon as they pick up their voicemails). If accidents befall us, on the motorway or halfway down the cliff face, we can call for help, and maybe give reassurance to those who thought the worst.

It's not just one-to-one. We are beginning to get used to the *blogosphere*. Networks grow from next to nothing, at first between friends and neighbours, before long across country, even across frontiers. In war-torn Lebanon a Canadian-Israeli blogger and journalist, Lisa Goldman, reported in the *Washington Post* that

> *'bloggers from both sides of the border ... had been providing live updates, commenting on one and another's blogs(and sometimes linking to posts by bloggers on the other side of the border) ... Will this turn out to be the first time that residents of 'enemy' countries engaged in an ongoing conversation while missiles were falling?'*

Conversations, off-setting the threats, the communiqués and the ensuing slaughter. But of course the trick is to get there first before the conviction-driven killers and the self-righteous counter-killers get the chance to take over.

So how far is that likely to get us? And where does it all lead?

Once people take a job *in hand*, however simple and short-term, it becomes easier to get acquainted. It's the doing more than the talking – you may be actually rubbing shoulders on the job – side-by-side, rather than face-to-face in a formal encounter.

This is not a matter of ironing out our differences, but pooling skills and experience, making the most of what's on offer; like the two toddlers in the French cartoon: little boy and little girl inspecting the fronts of each other's knickers and proclaiming '*Vive la différence!*'

STARTING POINTS

- A few of us (who like a gossip) visit other residents, individually, jot down their skills and interests and publish the list, in shops, clubs, schools, churches, synagogues, mosques, saying *'Look how many skills we have in this neighbourhood already! Come with your friends and families to a celebration party.'* (That's just the bait to bring people together and get them joining in)
- At the party (which might include contributions of food, music, artwork etc. already located) there are materials on hand for people to explore opportunities for easy and prompt action, such as –
- survey of traffic danger spots
- teenagers create a graffiti wall to decorate a boring building and/or set up a graffiti board beside their chosen street meeting place
- shopping service by local friends for the housebound
- multi-cultural fashion show
- community (veg) garden
- group monitoring hour by hour on the pitches of drug dealers
- shared transport for journeys to and from school
- exchange visits with other neighbourhood innovation schemes
- weekend clearance of derelict sites for 5-a-sides or children's play
- pilot scheme for solar/wind energy installation(s)
- credit union to share out costs and pursue opportunities
- 'Living Newspaper' on a bulletin board for people to post jokes, recipes, neighbourhood news items, gripes, offers to exchange skills and services
- developing blogs to reach across frontiers (between next-door neighbourhoods and/or other groups elsewhere in the country and/or overseas.
- What else?

Being different is not the same as being separate.

What we have in common is an inborn curiosity, not just about ourselves. What makes a baby tick? It is finding out about its surroundings from the word go. What's at the end of my arm? Fingers! What can I touch with them? Myself. An object that I can push or pull, a person who I can make respond. I can do things to them, notice what they do to me, gradually join in doing things together.

Anthea has taught children all her life and says it's all about self-preservation, and even then it doesn't always apply to everyone. We agree that there's a blend of feelings and motives that incline most of us to try things out; and enjoy it when we manage to try them out together. *There are always exceptions*, says Anthea. I say that feedback from the teachers in the Living Space schools revealed that even the children they had written off were coming out of their shells, joining in, keeping at it. Well, perhaps some teachers were carried away and there were exceptions. But even those might still be susceptible once we find the way past the barriers that maybe their home circumstances have helped to erect. So as a guideline, I claim, *on the whole* as my Headmaster used to say, and deep down, nearly all of us get a kick once in while from doing something together and sharing the job satisfaction.

That *fellow feeling* has helped our species to survive so far. It's a resource within nearly everyone. On it our future as a species may depend.

What do we have in common? Not beliefs but the feelings that make us what we are. What we share is our common sense, as Tom Paine put it; and certain common concerns that override the differences that the separatists choose to emphasise. Not the way our children should be dressed, but how they are responding to life around them, including us. Not our ceremonials but the joys and sorrows we have in common. Not the styling of our homes, but whether they allow us to be private or sociable, warm or cool, attractive to our families and friends.

All such limitations go on the back burner when *crisis* looms. Nowadays that's the in-word. It once meant a kind of judgement. Suddenly coming up against a situation which shows us up, stops us short, makes us think. It can work either way – making us despair, not just in the situation, but in our own abilities to cope with it. But more often it works the other way. We are forced back on ourselves, our own resources, and we sometimes find there are others in the same situation. And there's something in common.

Take a step back, two generations ago when people in Stepney were in the throes of the East London Blitz. Official communication disrupted by the bombs, local government almost out for the count. What happened?

Residents themselves took over, improvising shelter, organising emergency feeding and clothing, becoming amateur fire fighters, getting up shelter concert parties. Elsewhere, in the countryside, government had the sense to draw on the same fellow feelings, eroding some of the old class barriers, in home-to-home billeting for air raid evacuees, *dig for victory* allotment schemes, local transport pools.

It wasn't all heroic. There were spivs and go-getters here and there but they didn't count for much by comparison with the rest of us. And in the immediate aftermath of war, like the wild flowers that bloomed unexpectedly alongside the weeds and the rubbish in the bomb craters, there were street parties. And eventually that nationwide Festival of Britain, celebrating togetherness alongside the spivvery, smart practice and single-minded pursuit of the fast buck.

Overriding concerns. Take a second look at the Hit List. Most items are danger signs of what lies ahead; like those we recognised in the years before World War II. Then it took over, along with the Blitz, and we looked at things in a different way. We learned about each other from a shared experience.

If we chose.

You may have wondered, reading the previous chapter, at my offering the examples of those three raw beginners (John Wesley, Thomas Clarkson, Tom Paine) who found how to reach and involve everyday, run-of-the-mill people, outside the corridors of power. It seems to me that in the long run they made their mark not primarily as leaders (though John Wesley was on the bossy side in his later years), but because they were able to open people's eyes to what we all possess – *common sense* (as Tom Paine first put it), a common concern to make things better, a level footing as fellow members of the human species.

Little by little ordinary people come to recognise their own potential, what I have called the *power in our hands*. In the Americas it was the colonists' independent-mindedness which backed the boycott of King George's taxes, developed the intelligence network and sustained the citizen army which finally defeated the Occupying Force.

We can see the same process at work, people coming to conclusions that *Enough is Enough* – that anything – even an armed uprising – is better than things as they are.

Whether the new situation is an improvement on the old – that's another matter. The evidence so far is that, more often than not, what was meant to be a war of liberation, of independence, becomes a civil war in which innocent people are the main casualties. That seems to have been the case in Sri Lanka, the Congo, the Sudan, Biafra, and before long Iraq. There is a sort of No Man's Land in Cuba, Libya, Algiers, Egypt, Vietnam and perhaps Korea, where local people have counter-attacked an occupying force but at the cost of accepting the top-down regime they find themselves landed with.

In such places the key word at the start is *Resistance* – a concerted effort to get rid of oppression and mismanagement. But that is only half the battle.

Come back to practicalities. How do we set about what needs to be done next?

Halfway through drafting this chapter, I took delivery of a World War Two stirrup pump ordered on ebay and went with it to the little island of Erraid where family and friends come together for a summer break. Over the years, one of the casual do-it- ourselves projects has been digging out a fire pool close to the Croft, banking it up to hold back the seaweed that the high tides bring. Last year was the first time that we got the banks high enough so now we have a resource outside the Croft from which, with the help of the stirrup pump we can reach through doors and windows to fight the flames inside. All this is important because some years back the nearest fire brigade, based in Bunessan on the Ross of Mull, undertook a trial run – flat out going down the road to the shore, unloading their gear, boating across, setting up again and into action. All that took 45 minutes.

So we reckoned it would be just as well to rely on ourselves at least in the early stages of the firefight.

The great value of the stirrup pump is that if absolutely necessary it can be operated single-handed. You fill your bucket from the nearest stream or pool, take it within reach of the fire, stick the pump shaft in the water, with one foot steadying the outside stirrup, grasp the end of the hose – with the other hand vigorously pumping. Of course when the bucket's empty you have to back off and refill, so teamwork is best. One of you goes as close to the fire as possible, hosepipe in hand. Another stays with the bucket pumping hard. One or more supporters, armed with their own buckets, rush to and fro renewing the water supply in the pumper's bucket. (If this sounds like Gerrard Hoffnung's story about the bucket of bricks on the builder's pulley, don't worry. Fire fighting teamwork with the stirrup pump is usually on the level and no one has to do anything complicated for the teamwork to succeed.)

All good stirrup pumps are complete with an adjustable nozzle enabling you to choose between attacking the heart of the fire with a jet, or spraying the surroundings. This, you may remember, was the way we learned to fight big fires in the Blitz: a distinct improvement on my earlier effort using the baby's chamber pot to contain a small incendiary before it got out of hand.

The strategy recommended is not to waste time at first by aiming directly at the incendiary which will simply splutter more and scatter burning fragments. You use the spray to deal with the surroundings, what might catch fire, and the edges of the conflagration which could be tackled first. Then, gradually advancing, you switch over to the jet and deal, point-blank, with the source.

In between fire fights – which is most of the time – the stirrup pump comes in very useful when you want to spray the flowers and the vegetables that grow beyond the reach of a hosepipe linked to the kitchen tap.

Two complementary uses, so to speak, in peace and in war. Resistance; and renewal.

We are up against worldwide conflagrations: the incendiary activities of the racists and the one-track minds, backed up by those who benefit from arson.

So how should we go about the fire fighting? There are official bodies supposedly equipped to do the job, if and when they get round to it. But currently that takes a very long time, and meanwhile the fires spread. So in our own amateurish way what do we do first?

There's no point in sitting on our hands in the sidelines, commenting anxiously on the blaze.

We have to get to grips with it somehow, or else …

How? Consider those two ways of amateur fire fighting. One method is to aim direct at the fire's core and the religious, political and racial pyromaniacs who fuel the flames. Depose the dodgy politicians! Sack the tabloid editors! Sideline the religious fanatics … Challenge the ethnic loyalists to make the most of their heritage as fellow members of the human race.

Essential in the long run – and the sooner the better! And the process gains momentum through demonstrations, sit-ins, mass boycotts – making news that forces its way past the unofficial censors and the two-timers in the media.

Some onlookers avert their gaze, but for others it's an eye-opener. That's the way *Jubilee Debt Campaign*, *Making Poverty History, Trade Justice,* and *Protect the Human* begin to reach the uncommitted.[1] Those bystanders, on the edge of events, are beginning to feel the heat, like most of us. They may respond to a different kind of challenge, at least to begin with. Something do-able

---

1 See Contacts List 'Taking It Further' (p302) for these and other pacemakers.

that's within immediate reach, and yields job satisfaction. In the early stages getting the hang of it need not be too demanding.

The secret may be in finding common ground from which to operate. So the first step may be to convert the words of that old Greek philosopher: *Know thyself* becomes *Know each other.* That means making the most of the people we know, or hardly know. Not doing this as inquisitive busybodies but as neighbours with the same concerns, fellow enthusiasts for whatever grabs us.

Being in touch, literally. We have to get used to going a few steps out of our way in order to make everyday, neighbourly contact with people who are being brainwashed into thinking that loyalty to a particular lifestyle means staying apart from others whose lifestyles don't in all matters match ours. So for starters people on either side of the religious or the ethnic fence, who are not yet willing to be gagged or blindfolded, have to go a little bit out of their way to find opportunities for ordinary, everyday contact, in the shops, in the street, on the sports field. Conversation first, opening up opportunities to swap ideas about mutual concerns, children's play space, traffic dangers, eyesores, things which everyone can talk about without religious or racist reservations. Not just talking but beginning to **do** something together. Unless and until we develop this kind of *working relationship*, the Us and Them barriers will remain, and probably grow.

Recognising common concerns, making common cause at first on small matters, is halfway to overcoming the barriers. It's about getting the habit of having dealings with other kinds of people, and getting a kick out of making something work between us.

That may still leave us with that so far unanswered question.

We are aware, only too aware, of something within us that makes us tick, and affects the ways we respond to life around us. We can assess its effect on the way we think about ourselves, individually, what makes us proud, ashamed, anxious, exhilarated, affectionate.

The great interpreters of life and death have dreamed dreams and seen visions, and then tried to convey their understandings to the rest of us. Not just by words, but by example. There's a communication gap which can't be bridged by words alone. It's how each of us feels – about each other, about ourselves, that matters. How we respond – or fail to respond – to events and the world outside us. A medieval writer called this feeling, when we fall short, *The Ageynbite of Inwitte* – as we might put it, the remorse of conscience.

Our instinctive recognition of what's good or bad is our own *Inwitte.* Something like a spirit level: the tool George McLeod and his workmates on

THROUGH ROUTES

(aka critical paths)

- Contact people on their own ground (home, school foyer waiting for kids, market, bus queue, place of worship, etc.).
- Spread the word about the skills and interests that might be on offer.
- Catch people's eye with visuals worth looking at.
- Arouse curiosity about possibilities being revealed.
- Bring residents and professionals together informally.
- Swap experience and bright ideas.
- Involve everyone in identifying problems, opportunities, local resources within easy reach.
- Allow participation to take shape informally, at people's own pace.
- Allow groups to set up small schemes of their own choosing.
- Help groups to set their own priorities – now, soon, later and share out the jobs in hand.
- Access training opportunities – short courses, expert coaching – which are available free to those wanting to acquire the tricks of the bureaucratic trade (policy statements, Business Plans, funding applications.)
- Involve outsiders who could lend a hand to tap funding / offer expert information.
- Share the credit; celebrate success.
- Open up further possibilities to keep the momentum.
- What else?

Iona relied on to rebuild the Abbey walls and doorways fair and square. The sense of balance that every child on stilts possesses. There is something in us to rely on. God-given? Or the fruit of three million years of blind evolution? Judge for yourself. But it's there, like touch, or eyesight or hearing – to size up ourselves and those we deal with.

Other people, using their own judgement, may tell the rest of us what is *key* as they see it. They may be expert in dovetailing all sorts of customs and rituals to make an ornamental doorway to the good life: the kinds of food to eat, the sayings to repeat, the clothes to wear, the ordering of each day – but if that doesn't square with a working relationship with the rest of the human race, the door won't fit.

Working relationship? Anthea reckons that's an understatement. It should read *our belief in and our affection for* the rest of the human race. I am sticking to what is basic to all of us, the disillusioned as well as the bright-eyed altruists. It's a universal capacity, for good or ill.

What we do, to ourselves and to each other, and how we feel about it can't easily be expressed in formal print or on the air. In the process some of the reality vanishes. Poets, musicians, artists have better ways to arouse our sympathies – sorrow, pride, affection, the lot – when everyday words fail us. Remember Tom Paine and the Quakers? They told people like Tom Paine about what they called the *inner light*. A wordless resource, that they said was God-given, within everyone. A means of showing up the double talk of many politicians, penetrating the smokescreens of their PR people; of countering the one-eyed religious zealots who would put the rest of us in blinkers. Something straight to the heart, as Wesley discovered, something which *strangely moves us* to take our part as doers, not spectators.

We have what you might call a common bond that transcends words, and encompasses humanity. We learn from shared experience. From our very beginnings it has been our gut feelings, our perceptions that enable us to make common cause, across the barriers imposed by race and religious doctrine.

What could have become an almost endless bloodbath in South Africa between the upholders of apartheid and their opponents ended up relatively peacefully with the keynote of the new society sounded by Archbishop Desmond Tutu's *Truth and Reconciliation Commission*. The streets housed countless small-scale initiatives, alongside the scattered resistance fighters themselves, pooling resources in mini co-operatives, vigilantes to uphold law and order, street parties, sports activities, singsongs. People could see for themselves what they could achieve together, generating the staying power to outface and outlast the people who depended on apartheid – being separate – in order to divide and rule.

All over the world there are ordinary people, frustrated, but no longer content to put up with corruption, double-dealing, intolerance. So resistance is a key word. The danger is that that is as far as it goes and when the powers-that-be are overturned only the bitterness and the anger are left.

Whilst I was working in South Africa I met Gugile Nkwinti, one of the leaders of the campaign that ousted the old regime. He told me something that has stayed in my mind and I have often quoted since. He added a new word:

*'Our job now is to change from street resistance to street **regeneration**.'*

Street level is where, in the long run, it begins to count.

That's where, if anywhere, we begin to recover our nerve and our belief, our respect for each other. You can't do this just by words anymore than you learn to swim by doing press ups on the riverbank. The only relationship that works is a working relationship – in a family doing things for each other, with each other, roller-coasting the ups and downs. In a neighbourhood – but what is a neighbourhood these days? It's a place where our children, and sometimes their parents – come to school; where – perhaps – there's a community meeting place where people drop in to chat – could be a pub, a bus stop, a place of worship. Just to pass the time of day. And no more?

Well, there's always something to complain about, sometimes something to celebrate. And once in a while something to explore – follow up – look into – investigate together.

The incentive to go that far, more often than not, is some catastrophe, in our street, or beyond. It's that which drives us together and makes us a force worth reckoning with.

What kind of force?

Something like the Yellow River I told about in Chapter Ten. It begins in the foothills as tiny rivulets which don't amount to much. Then they flow together and gather momentum down the rocky mountainsides and on to the plain. From then on anything can happen. Some such rivers never get further than a muddy waste, a vast expanse of reeds and rushes which is not much use to anyone except the water fowl and the rats. But not so the Yellow River which gathers force within the dykes that people have built for it. From then on, depending on such people, it becomes a threat – devastating the countryside when the dykes were breached to halt the advancing Japanese, (or, lately, when the waters are choked with garbage) – or a universal bonus –

nourishing the fishermen, powering the turbines, speeding the travellers on their way.

People power isn't something to be condescending about, writing it off as if it stops short at the rivulet stage, with lots of people being nice to each other within each neighbourhood, and leaving it at that. The pressure of events is forcing us, all over the world, to canalise our pent-up feelings, for good or ill.

You can't do this by words alone. In the long run what we have to **do** together matters much more than what anyone has to say. Rescuing a desolate neighbourhood, perhaps with a working alliance between parents and teachers, making music, sports, videos to celebrate, exchanging skills and experience across barriers. Bypassing the rhetoric to set out the worldwide priorities for the survival of the human race.

Making Common Sense, as Tom Paine would put it.

And as it stands, beginning where we are, here and now. It's about our prospects for survival in a time the poet called *the Breaking of Nations*, when institutions become fossilised, and our material resources are squandered. Maybe we have to start again from scratch with the resources within us (as we did long ago in the Blitz), improvising temporary solutions until we can build something more permanent. In the process, having a laugh, outflanking disaster, recovering our nerve and our self-respect.

Anthea says I talk too much of Us and Them. If she is right it's because I've been preoccupied with the communication gaps, the power structures, the exclusiveness that tempt us to feel we matter more whilst we stay apart, above or beyond the rest.

Embedded in every association – religious, political, sporting, ethnic, bureaucratic – there are people, the great majority, who *belong*. The feel at home with each other, talk the same slang or jargon, go along with the same customs and traditions because they form a familiar pattern.

We've each of us our own view about who's best – but that tends to be who's best for us; and also, in a different way, who's best for the likes of Them. We are football supporters, not club fanatics.

Of course each one of us is unique. That's what makes our species such an interesting and powerful blend. But together we are something else.

The first chapters of Holmyard's Elementary Chemistry taught me the different between a mixture – each element retaining it own properties – and a compound when they react together to form something new, with maybe more powerful properties of its own.

We can have it both ways: keeping our identities as individuals; and asserting our fellow feelings in times of crisis or of celebration: making contact at street level and on the internet, comparing experience, getting wise to each other – infiltrating you might even say. Between us we can home in on opportunities for rewarding action, not just talk: tackling the Hit Lists, neighbourhoodwide, citywide, nationwide, worldwide (probably in that order), rebuilding our confidence in each other, brick by local brick.

It's the job in hand that brings us together – without a forced merger of faiths or loyalties; just as in pre-war Shadwell, East London, Jews, Anglo–Catholics, Communists, Presbyterians combined to confront and defeat Moseley's Fascist marchers; resist rapacious landlords; and, soon afterwards, make common cause against the Blitz.

The people I have worked with and written about are the evidence on which the case for our survival rests. No one special. Just men, women and youngsters (like the Rodney Raiders) who grab an opportunity to get something **done** together – not just talked about. Starting small, celebrating as we go, generating the momentum, the staying-power to outface and outlast the one-track minds that would divide us.

The yeast that makes the dough rise.

Over to you.

ENVOI

I set off in the late summer to finish the last chapter on the Isle of Erraid, which is the nearest thing to what I call a family home. Three hundred miles or so up through Scotland to the Oban ferry. Across the sea to the Isle of Mull, and then thirty-nine miles from east to west along the loveliest road I have travelled anywhere in the world.

What's so great about it that for me it outranks the roads that border Vesuvius and Etna, and the country lanes in Cornwall and Devon, or the Seventy Two Bends zigzagging up and over the mountain range I crossed in South West China?

The Mull road bounds up and down and from side to side like a lolloping puppy. Gentle twists and turns, wandering in the shade through the outskirts of the forest, then away through the glen where the waterfalls glint as the rivulets flow down the mountain sides; then a straight burst across open countryside, lush green with a hint of purple heather in the far distance; and suddenly the deep cobalt blue waters of the wide, silent loch, close beside.

It's a one-track road, only just wide enough to accommodate a lorry or the tourist bus en route to Iona. If you want to overtake, or pass by an approaching vehicle, there's no road space, and precious little room on the verge. So, even if you are on a motorbike, one of you has to give way, step aside in one of the occasional lay-bys the road-makers provided, and let the other pass, like a genteel pedestrian on a narrow pavement.

There's really no alterative, short of bulldozing the other vehicle on to the grass verge or maybe into the rock-lined ditch. So road rage gets you nowhere. (And in fact it's never occurred in the two hundred or more journeys I have made so far from East to West and back again.)

Why mention all this? Well there's a comparison I'd like to make, which you may have guessed already.

East and West we have different starting points – religious, racial, historic. Some start out later and lag behind. Other late-starters suddenly begin to accelerate, catch up and prepare to overtake.

And when you come up close? It's not much use shouting or hooting. It's either collision or some kind of 'mutual accommodation' as politicians and the media might like to put it. Of course it's not a One Way Street, or a continuous traffic flow. We move in fits and starts, travelling to and fro to deliver what we've got on board, or pick up what we need, at either end of the journey. We can see roughly where we need to be heading, and in the long run we're going to make it.

That's enough of a parable to be going on with. It's an assertion of the facts of everyday life, the lessons of history, the conditions for the survival of our species.

And of course it's a lot easier to assert than to apply, here and Now – Soon – Later.

But we've got to start somewhere.

Or maybe you've already begun to overtake ...

TAKING IT FURTHER

Contacts to make with useful organisations

ActionAid UK, Hamlyn House, Macdonald Road, Archway, London, N19 5PG, tel. 020 7561 7561, www.actionaid.org.uk email mail@actionaid.org Works in Africa, Asia and the Americas, listening to, learning from and working in partnership with over ten million of the world's poorest people.

Amnesty International UK, The Human Rights Action Centre , 17-25 New Inn Yard, London, EC2A 3EA, tel. 020 7033 1500, www.amnesty.org.uk email sct@amnesty.org.uk Campaigns for human rights worldwide; seeks release of prisoners of conscience; works for prompt and fair trials for all political prisoners; opposes death penalty, torture and other cruel or degrading treatment of prisoners.

Black Environment Network, 1st Floor, 60 High Street, Llanberis, Wales, LL55 4EU, tel. 01286 870715, www.ben-network.org.uk email ukoffice@ben-network.org.uk Promotes equality of opportunity within the ethnic communities in the preservation, protection and development of the environment; maintains a network of individuals and organisations working for change.

Campaign Against the Arms Trade, 11 Goodwin Street, Finsbury Park, London N4 3HQ, tel. 020 7281 0297, www.caat.org.uk email enquiries@caat.org.uk Works for the reduction and ultimate abolition of the international arms trade, together with progressive demilitarisation within arms-producing countries.

Campaign for Nuclear Disarmament, 162 Holloway Road, London N7 8DQ, tel. 020 7700 2393, www.cnduk.org email enquiries@cnduk.org CND campaigns non-violently to rid the world of nuclear weapons and other weapons of mass destruction and to create genuine security for future generations.

Church Action on Poverty, Central Buildings, Oldham Street, Manchester, M1 1JT, tel. 0161 236 9321, www.church-poverty.org.uk email info@church-poverty.org.uk Aims to help poor people to speak out on their own behalf via educational and campaigning work; has about 2000 individual groups members maintaining active links with all the main Christian denominations and other church-based and secular social justice networks.

Civic Trust, Essex Hall, 1-6 Essex Street , London WC2R 3HU, tel 020 7539 7900**,** www.civictrust.org.uk email info@civictrust.org.uk dedicated to bringing vitality, sustainability and high quality design to the built environment.

Community Matters, 12-20 Baron Street, London N1 9LL, tel. 020 7837 7887, www.communitymatters.org.uk
email: communitymatters@communitymatters.org.uk Supporting democratically elected community organisations and linking up with local authorities.

Credit Unions, Units 1.1 & 1.2, Howard House, Commercial Centre, Howard Street, North Shields, Tyne and Wear, NE30 1AR, tel. 0191 257 2219. The Federation provides advice and support for community groups wishing to set up credit unions, with emphasis on self-help and community development, especially in areas of economic disadvantage.

Family Welfare Association (formerly Family Service Units), 501-505 Kingsland Road, London, E8 4AU, tel. 020 7254 6251, www.fwa.org.uk email: fwa.headoffice@fwa.org.uk. Supports some of the poorest families in the country. Provides grants as well as social work to support people of all ages, working with them to help solve their own problems.

Friends of the Earth, 26-28 Underwood Street, London, NE1 7JQ, tel. 020 7490 0881. www.foe.co.uk Environmental pressure group campaigning on a wide range of issues including pollution, transport, energy, waste, habitats, forests and sustainable development.

Grameen Bank (Muhammad Yunus), Grameen Bank Bhavan, Mirpur-1, Dhaka-1261, Bangladesh, tel. [8802] 9005257-69. www.grameen-info.org Provides credit to the poorest of the poor in rural Bangladesh without any collateral. At Grameen Bank, credit is a cost effective weapon to fight poverty

Greenpeace, Canonbury Villas, Highbury, London N1 2PN. Tel. 020 7865 8100, www.greenpeace.org.uk email info@greenpeace.org Campaigns against abuse of the natural world through lobbying and non-violent direct action protests, which are back by scientific research.

Islamic Aid, 47 Theydon Street, London, E17 8EN, tel. 0845 130 8990, www.islamicaid.org.uk email: mail@islamicaid.org.uk Islamic Aid seeks to make immediate and lasting improvements to the lives of people affected by poverty, war and disaster.

Joseph Rowntree Foundation, The Homestead, 40 Water End, York, North Yorkshire, YO30 6WP, UK, tel. 01904 629241, www.jrf.org.uk email info@jrf.org.uk Seeks to better understand the causes of social difficulties and explore ways of overcoming them.

Jubilee Debt Campaign, The Grayston Centre, 28 Charles Square, London N1 6HT, tel: 020 7324 4722, www.jubileedebtcampaign.org.uk email info@jubileedebtcampaign.org.uk d Demanding an end to the scandal of poor countries paying money to the rich world and calling for 100% cancellation of unpayable and unfair poor country debts.

LETS Link UK, 12 Southcote Road, Tufnell Park London N19 5BJ, tel. 020 7607 7852. www.letslinkuk.net email admin@letslinkuk.net Local Exchange Trading Systems or Schemes – are local community-based mutual aid networks in which people exchange all kinds of goods and services with one another, without the need for money.

Lightmoor New Community (Contactable via Neighbourhood Initiatives Foundation – see below.) A self-built, self-managing village near Telford.

Make Poverty History, c/o BOND, Regent's Wharf, 8 All Saint's Street, London N1 9RL. www.makepovertyhistory.org Largest ever anti-poverty movement with organisations representing more than 150 million people in over 80 countries.

Médecins sans Frontières, (Doctors without Borders), 67-74 Saffron Hill, London, EC1N 8QX, tel. 020 7404 6600, www.msf.org email office-ldn@london.msf.org An independent international medical humanitarian organization that delivers emergency aid in more than 70 countries to people affected by armed conflict; epidemics; natural or man-made disasters; or exclusion from health care

Neighbourhood Initiatives Foundation, The Poplars, Lightmoor, Telford TF4 3QN, tel. 0870 7700339, www.nif.co.uk email info@nif.co.uk Helps to empower people to shape the future of their neighbourhoods using techniques like "Planning for Real" to encourage residents to participate in the identification of problems and the development of solutions; works with local authorities, housing associations, voluntary agencies and community groups.

New Economics Foundation, 3 Jonathan Street, London, SE11 5NH, tel. 020 7820 6300, www.neweconomics.org/gen email info@neweconomics.org Projects include social auditing, formulating alternative economic indicators, energy conservation, researching links between economics, trade and the environment.

Oxfam, John Smith Drive, Cowley, Oxford, OX4 2JY, tel. 0870 333 2700. www.oxfam.org.uk Works with poor people worldwide regardless of race or religious beliefs in their struggle against hunger, disease, exploitation and poverty, through relief, development, research and public education.

Practical Action (formerly the Intermediate Technology Development Group), The Schumacher Centre for Technology and Development, Bourton on Dunsmore, Rugby, CV23 9QZ, tel. 01926 634400. www.practicalaction.org.uk Email; practicalaction@practicalaction.org.uk Works with poor communities to help them choose and use technology to improve their lives for today and generations to come

Quaker Peace and Social Witness, Friends House, 173 -177 Euston Road, London, NW1 2BJ, tel. 020 7663 100, www.quaker.org.uk email pqse@quaker.org.uk QPSW works, worldwide, in partnership with local nonviolent and social justice groups to confront injustice and prejudice and to increase communication and understanding.

Scarman Trust, Kemp House, 152- 160 City Road, London, EC1V 2NP, tel. 020 7689 6366, www.thescarmantrust.org email info@thescarmantrust.org The Scarman Trust is a national charity committed to helping citizens bring about change in their community in the way that they want. The Trust funds and gives practical assistance to hundreds of remarkable people with a 'can do' attitude.

Soil Association, South Plaza, Marlborough Street, Bristol BS1 3NX, tel. 0117 314 5000, www.soilassociation.org.uk email info@soilassociation.org Promotes organic farming and gardening; awards a symbol for display on organic produce which adheres to certain standards; produces a range of publications; offers advice on organic practices.

Trade Justice Movement is a coalition of more than 70 member organisations campaigning together for trade justice - not free trade - with the rules weighted to benefit poor people and the environment. www.tradejusticemovement.org.uk

Undercurrents, Old Exchange, Pier Street, Swansea SA1 1RY, tel. 01792 455900, www.undercurrents.org email info@undercurrents.org Provides media support to campaigns through the use of video/DVD; activities include training, a news service and compilation/distribution of videos and DVDs; also runs and supports the Camcorder Action Network – a network of people around Britain willing to take video footage of campaigning actions.

Voluntary Service Overseas, 317 Putney Bridge Road, London, SE15 2PN, tel. 020 8780 7200, www.vso.org.uk email infoservices@vso.org.uk Links possible volunteers with opportunities in the developing world.

World Development Movement, 66 Offley Road, London, SW9 0LS, tel. 020 7820 4900, www.wdm.org.uk email wdm@wdm.org.uk Works in over 100 countries to conserve biodiversity, promote sustainable development and reduce pollution and waste consumption; runs programmes for policy reform and education as well as undertaking or supporting thousands of practical projects mostly working with local communities.

World Jewish Relief, 74/80 Camden Street, London, NW1 0EG, tel. 020 7691 1771, www.worldjewishrelief.org.uk email info@wjr.org.uk Dedicated to saving, renewing and sustaining Jewish life, WJR is the only charity providing a unified response to humanitarian crises worldwide on behalf of the UK Jewish community.

Currently operating in 13 countries across the globe, the organisation initiates creative relief programmes that benefit not only individuals in need but whole communities, treating both with the respect and dignity they deserve.

• • •

Plus –

what you and your mates may invent or adapt to suit the stage you've reached already. The journey is from where you are, here and now.

Bon voyage!